Still
Points North

THE DIAL PRESS NEW YORK

Still
Points North

ONE ALASKAN CHILDHOOD,
ONE GROWN-UP WORLD,
ONE LONG JOURNEY HOME

Leigh Newman

Published in the United States by The Dial Press, an imprint of
The Random House Publishing Group, a division of
Random House, Inc., New York.

Dial Press is a registered trademark of Random House, Inc., and
the colophon is a trademark of Random House, Inc.

Newman, Leigh.
Still Points North: one alaskan childhood, one grown-up world,
one long journey home/Leigh Newman. — 1st ed.
p. cm.
ISBN 978-1-4000-6924-8
eBook ISBN 978-0-679-60355-9
1. Newman, Leigh. 2. Alaska—Biography. I. Title.
CT275.N485A3 2013
979.8'05092—dc23
[B]
2012016525

Printed in the United States of America on acid-free paper

www.dialpress.com

2 4 6 8 9 7 5 3 1

First Edition

Book design by Karin Batten

To my family

Dear, my compass
still points north
to wooden houses
and blue eyes

fairy-tales where
flaxen-headed
younger sons
bring home the goose . . .

ELIZABETH BISHOP, *Untitled*

Contents

Author's Note

Everything in this book really happened (even the flooded tent, the rapid-filled canyon, and the king salmon). I have changed everyone's names, so if you see yours in here, you can feel confident that it's not you. I also changed some of the chronology in order to make for a more smoothly flowing story: My life did *not* fit into a tidy narrative, especially when it came to the ceaseless and undocumented stream of countries I visited, and the last scene with my father contains dialogue from several different conversations. Please also know that although certain bits of outdoor lore are presented here as advice—for example, the only way to survive a grizzly encounter is to run away very, very quickly—they may not, in fact, ensure your survival.

PART I

*Forget
Me Not*

CHAPTER I

The Great Alaskan

In the largest state in the Union, a state built on gold rushes and oil pipelines, ninety-pound king salmon and twenty-pound king crabs, a lot of things come prefaced by the phrase *Great Alaskan*. There's the Great Alaskan Salmon Bake and the Great Alaskan Lumberjack Show and the legendary 8.6 Great Alaskan Earthquake and, of course, a species of larger-than-life male citizen, who shall be referred to from here on out as the Great Alaskan Dad.

Some identifiers: The Great Alaskan Dad flies his plane on floats in the summer and on skis in the winter. He hunts for caribou, moose, wild sheep, wild goats, geese, and ducks, plus fishes for halibut, salmon, and trout. No matter where he goes, his outfit remains the same: falling-down hip boots, patched wool pants, drugstore sunglasses with Polaroid lenses for spotting fish underwater, and a Stearns life jacket with a red plastic tag that reads PULL-IN-THE-CASE-OF-AN-EMERGENCY, which has never been pulled, despite his frequent, always almost fatal emergencies. A buck knife—the blade stained with dried unidentified blood and slime—dangles from a lanyard somewhere on his person.

At one time or another, he has suffered from an unforgettable—for all involved—case of beaver fever, a violent lower-intestinal disease caused by drinking downstream from an active lodge. At one time or another, due to a plane crash or bad planning, he has had to live—for days, in the bush—off tasteless ancient pilot bread and a jar of powdered Tang.

The Great Alaskan Dad can sew on his own buttons, patch his own waders, repack his own shotgun shells, and repair his own outboard motor, even as the boat is filling with water in the middle of the ocean. The Great Alaskan Dad can land a Piper Cub on a 150-foot-long gravel bar, which is technically impossible according to all aviation authorities. He can outrun a grizzly bear by running very fast or at least faster than his hunting buddy (which, by the way, according to a Great Alaskan Dad, is the only way to survive a grizzly bear, so don't curl up, play dead, and make yourself into a human meatball like those dopey forest rangers advise) with a hundred pounds of freshly dressed moose on his back. He can make a fire out of wet green wood, in the middle of the winter, just as the blizzard starts, using his last match, which he strikes with his fingers nearly, but not totally, paralyzed by frostbite. He can—and will—also defend the veracity of the above three claims to the point of shooting saliva across the room, should any family member dare challenge the few overly extravagant or Jack Londonesque details therein.

In addition, although he might not bring this up around the campfire, the Great Alaskan Dad has invented a diaper out of alder leaves and garbage bags when all the Pampers that the Great Alaskan Mom packed happened to fall out of the raft. The Great Alaskan Dad has piloted a plane while his airsick Great Alaskan Child projectile-vomited inside the fur-lined hood of his parka. And he has—not mythically or romantically or hyperbolically in the least—

grabbed that same child's belt loop or leg right before that child fell into the raging stream or fell out of the flying plane or slipped off the boat or wandered off the cliff or tumbled down the crevasse of the glacier or ate the poisonous blue berries that were *not* blueberries or sauntered directly into the path of a black bear with two newborn cubs.

Where all this experience might not help him, though, is in the land of toothbrushes and crustless peanut-butter sandwiches, recommended daily vitamins and monsters under the bed. In short, the world of domestic survival, which is where my Great Alaskan Dad and I land the first summer after my parents' divorce.

It's June, the first week of salmon-fishing season. For the past six months, I've been away from Anchorage, Alaska, where I grew up, in order to relocate with my mother to Baltimore, Maryland, her childhood home. The first day I'm back up north, I find out that Dad has moved from our old house by the mountains into a new house across town. The house is big and sunny and filled with lots of wall-to-wall beige carpet—but no furniture.

It's eight o'clock at night. "Time for bed," Dad says. He rolls out two identical down bags—bags designed to keep you warm in temperatures up to forty below—on the beige carpet. I hop in mine, zip it up to my chin, and crumple up my jeans for a pillow. The sky through the windows is a blazing, sun-heated white. We have no blinds or curtains.

"Shut your eyes," he mumbles.

I shut my eyes. But I'm eight years old. I squirm. I hum. I kick Dad, whispering, "I can't sleep. Can you sleep?" over and over.

"Tell your brain it's nighttime. Your brain will believe anything, if you say it over and over."

"It's nighttime," I say, my voice echoing off the blank plaster. But my father's brain is better at believing than mine, it seems. He is asleep already, his mustache twitching mid-dream.

Two weeks later, we're duking it out in the upstairs bathroom.

Dad stands roaring in the doorway, trying to convince me to take a bath—or at least comb my hair. I crouch inside the shower stall, hiding, wearing only my flowered underwear and undershirt. I'm a tiny, runtish girl, with twiggy fingers and a dense rind of dirt on my elbows and knees. The shower is an enormous stretch of blue tile and glass, with three shower nozzles at three different heights: one for Papa Bear, one for Mama Bear, one for Baby Bear. The idea for this family-sized bathing arrangement came from my mother, who designed this new house not knowing that by the time it was built, she and I would have already moved Outside, as Alaskans call anywhere beyond the borders of the state, including Paris, Rome, Buenos Aires, Istanbul, and Hackensack, New Jersey.

Dad and I might not have spent last winter together, but I still know one thing: If you're going to run from my father, you really need to make sure that you have a long, unobstructed area ahead, if not a vista, because he's going to be right behind you—catching up.

Water drips from the broken faucet, pinging against the tiles. A Dad-shaped shadow drifts across the shower door. The glass has a premade cloud inside it, a crystallized puff of decorative steam. "Come on," he says. "Let's get realistic."

I curl up tighter.

"Either you're coming out. Or I'm coming in."

Dad counts to three. I listen dully. But there is nowhere for me to go except between the thin lines of grout. In he comes, tossing me over his shoulder and setting me down on my bottom on the bathroom counter. I scream. Dad's face goes ashen. He stands me up on the counter, off my thighs.

In the long mirror lining the wall above the double sinks, we both look at the edges of the rash on the backs of my legs, a rash I have been hiding since my arrival, never undressing in front of him, bandaging the boil-like welts myself—not entirely successfully. The crusted scabs have broken open and reinfected. A trail of thin, clear ooze leaks down my thighs.

Dad blinks. He steps back. There is no medical reason for my rash, the doctors have told my mother. I consider telling Dad this too, if only to stop his face from scrambling around for an expression. But if there isn't any medical reason, I'm pretty sure the rash is somehow my fault. The same goes for my weight loss. I'm a bad eater or I have a bad stomach or I don't try hard enough to keep the food inside. My teeth stick out; my ribs stick out; my head is a big wobbly ball on the top of my neck.

"Okay," Dad says. "We've had a rough spring. Nothing to worry about. Nothing some antibiotics and a little protein can't fix."

In his hand, however, he still has the comb, a black dime-store comb with rows of tiny, close teeth. It is the one hair instrument he owns. It belongs on the counter with his one bottle of shampoo, which he also uses as soap and shaving cream, and his one disposable razor. He lifts the comb toward me, slowly.

I throw my arms over my head. The comb is going to snag on my hair, or what's left of my hair, which is, by now, a matted, snarled pelt. I haven't gone near it, not even to wash it, since coming to Alaska. I've tried to, once. I've thought about it. But I'm still too scared of touching it or having anyone else touch it—a fear that my father also does not know about, not having seen me with lice a few months prior, nor at the beauty parlor where the stylist swooped up my waist-long blond hair and sawed it off by the base of the ponytail with her brisk, professional scissors. The result: a ragged blond tuft that caused little old ladies in restaurants all over Baltimore to redirect me to the boys' room.

Dad sets down the comb. He leans his fists on the counter, his arms muscling up. Is he mad? Am I in trouble? Dad loved my long hair. He used to make us matching mustaches from it, draping the long blond strands over my upper lip. Mom didn't tell him about the lice, probably. The two of them don't speak.

Dad leaves the bathroom, coming back a few minutes later with a kitchen fork and a pair of fish-gutting scissors—bent-bladed,

thick, heavy surgical scissors that he brings from the hospital to fil-
let salmon in the garage. He lines up this equipment on the counter
on a hand towel as if he's in the operating room. He is a very good
surgeon, grown-up strangers in town always tell me, pointing to
their knees and hips, showing me they can walk again, thanks to
him.

But I'm trembling already. I keep my eyes on the comb, just to
make sure he isn't about to use it. The comb is worse than the scissors. The comb will get stuck in the knots and tear out my hair by
the roots. Dad points to the counter. I lower myself into a crouch,
resting my chin on my knees. The bathroom smells of steam and
pee. In the distance, the windows of the house rattle as a floatplane
takes off on the lake outside.

"Leigh," my father says, which is already worrisome. My name
is Leigh, but only according to my birth certificate. Dad calls me
Leifer, or Pookey, or, sometimes, Pooks.

I hunch up a little tighter. He approaches with the fork. "What
I'm doing now," he explains in a calm, rational, professional voice,
a voice he uses with his patients at the office, "is loosening the knots,
in order to determine which we can untangle." He moves slowly. He
keeps his hands away from the comb. But I don't want this Doctor
Dad, this understanding, gentle surgeon who picks through my hair
with the wide teeth of the fork, teasing out the hairs strand by
strand. I want my dad, who should be telling me to stop the water-
works and suck it up, who three years from now, when we tip our
raft in a rapid-filled canyon and watch our gear float off downstream as we head directly for a boulder and I begin to scream hys-
terically, smacks me on the top of my skull with an oar and tells me,
"You're okay! Got it? Now paddle!"

I lean into the mirror. My father gives up on the fork and begins
scissoring through the little hair that I have left. Clumps brush
against the back of my neck and slide to the floor. My rash itches.
My legs shake. I dig my toes into the counter. Dad makes a hard,
strangled sound.

He is crying. I shut my eyes. I hunch forward, the air shivery and cold on my neck where the hair is gone. Not to hear him or his choky-sounding sobs, not to let him hear my own tears that keep slopping out, I do the thing that he always does when he's gutting fish or tying flies. I hum a floaty, no-tune song, blowing the air up through my teeth so it comes out as a whistle.

Two hours later, on the dock at the back of the house, Dad and I don't discuss what he did during the previous spring while I was gone. Nor do we discuss why my body is melting down. Nor do we discuss the new custody arrangement, which gives me only eleven more weeks this summer in Alaska, plus Christmas in December, meaning that, from this point forward, I'll be spending most of the year, for the rest of my life, in Baltimore. Instead we get the plane loaded and get out of there, away from the mirror, away from the bathroom and the house and the city of Anchorage, into the bush.

Our plane is a four-seat Cessna 185 on floats. Over Cook Inlet, Dad keeps us low, swooping over the cold gray expanses to point out surfacing beluga whales. I sit beside him, wearing my matching headset and holding my matching steering wheel. He pretends to fall asleep after a while. I take over the controls, the way I'm supposed to, checking and rechecking that our nose is level. "Dad?" I say over the crackle of radio static. "Dad?"

He saws off a phony snore, his eyes still shut. "You're fine. You're doing great."

"But—"

"Keep your eyes on the artificial horizon."

I stare at the two-dimensional plane in the gauge, its wings teetering over the line between the painted land and sky. No throwing up, I tell myself. Copilots don't throw up. Or get scared. Or let their planes crash into the ocean. Or look over to see if their father is really sleeping or just pretending to sleep. And he is pretending, right? He always pretends. It's like a fire drill, but in the sky.

"Eyes on the horizon, Leifer," Dad says, opening his eyes. "You're in control. You're one hundred percent capable!"

I take my hands off the steering wheel. And puke in his lap.

At last, we spot the deep, gray channel of Beluga River. Dad brings us down with a hard slapping landing. There are no romantic northern pine trees here, no sap-scented breezes. The air reeks of fish and gulls, the water flows by choked with mud and red, bloated dying salmon. Walls of alders line the riverbanks, clouds of mosquitoes hum in the branches. Grizzly tracks paw across the sand.

We dump our tackle boxes by a driftwood log. At this time, my dad isn't the master fly fisherman he will soon become—the fisherman-artist with his delicate rod, catching and releasing, throwing C-shaped casts over dappled creeks. It is 1980 in Alaska, a state with 3,000 rivers and 3 million lakes. The sporting mores are not quite as respectful, or picturesque. We set up our spin poles with giant shiny Pixies—slabs of silver metal gussied up with an appetizing glop of plastic salmon eggs. The hooks are yawning trebles, in effect mini anchors with three lethal barbed points.

As usual in the summer, the river is red with fish, throbbing with movement in shallows where the salmon fight for space to lay their eggs. With the sun broiling down on us and hours and hours to go before the 11 P.M. sunset, I prowl the bank in my boy-sized hip boots, the tops sloshing down off my thighs, the feet filled with freezing mud and water.

I cast upstream, and get my hook caught in a bush. I cast downstream, and get my hook caught in the weeds. I snag on a rock in the shallows. I hook my own jeans. Down the river, as always, Dad has a fish on. He fights it through the boulders, wading in up to his chest.

I swing my Pixie in the sun, studying the drops of water glistening off the line.

"Leifer!" Dad says, holding up a salmon. "Hook in the water."

I climb onto the plane float, sitting on a life jacket to protect my rash. Deep in the current, my lure bump-bump-bumps along the bottom. I daydream about a seagull that I train to sit on my shoulder like a parrot. My line jerks. My rod bends a little funny. And—bam—my line is sizzling through the river, zigzagging through the shallows. I jump off the float, already running, half letting the fish yank out more line, half pulling it back up the shore. Not to mention half listening to my dad as he shouts: "Watch your drag!" "Pump and reel!" "Watch your tip!" "Reel. Reel!" "Thatta girl!"

Fish-drunk and screaming, I inch the flopping salmon onto the beach, then run for our trusty wooden club. Only now do I see what I've hauled in. The fish is unmistakable—the swollen back, the hooked mouth, the mottled gangrene-colored skin. I've caught a humpy, the lowest species of salmon in the salmon family, a fish mocked statewide for its swamp-creature looks and lack of intelligence. Worse, my humpy is soft, lumpish, at the end of its natural life span.

I look up at Dad, waiting for him to laugh.

He rocks on his heels. "Now," he says. "That's a beauty!"

"But—"

"A keeper!" he says. "Throw her in the take-home pile." To prove his point, he steadies the fish for me, holding it firmly against the gravel. Slowly, I raise the club. The fish looks up at me with glittering, green, very alive eyes. Its gills heave. Its fins twitch. I shut my own eyes as I bring down the club hard, over and over—bits of blood and skin splashing up onto my cheeks, the skull creaking, giving way to mush. Still I don't stop, as if I'm listening for Dad to thunder at me, *That's enough.*

But he doesn't. Above us, seagulls wail, swooping down for scraps.

———

Hour after hour, for the rest of the day, we bring in humpy after humpy. Our tempo turns swift, methodical. We bash them on the head, bleed them by the throat, throw them in the waterlogged storage compartment in the floats. The more we catch, the more we have to catch, as if, in our minds, the next unnecessary salmon will justify the previous. Neither of us talks as the pile grows, the pebbles at our feet turning flecked with blood.

If Mom was here, we would have made a fire to keep her warm while she read her novel on a log. If Mom was here, she would have told us to knock it off—not because we'd caught enough fish, but because we were all too tired and hungry and it was time for a big hot plate of spaghetti.

The moon rises. The mosquitoes swarm. The sun lowers in the white sky. Still, we stay and stay, catching and clubbing and bagging, not going home as if we don't ever have to go home, until it is too dark and dangerous to stay any later, and we have to take off.

"Great job today!" my dad says, over the headset, as we fly over Fire Island. "You're a champ fisherman, you know that?"

"I think my last one was eight pounds!" I say. "Maybe."

"Sure it was. A state record, I bet. We'll have to look it up."

I smile. It isn't a real lie that we're telling each other. It's a fairy-tale lie, a fish-tale lie, the kind Great Old Alaskans tell each other about the five-hundred-pound halibut that once leapt into their rowboat and sank it before leaping back out and swimming off. Besides, I might really be a champ fisherman. One day. If I practice my casts and keep my rod tip up and live in Alaska for forever, just like Dad.

CHAPTER 2

Can't Lives on Won't Street

Back across the inlet, on the deck of the house, Dad and I have plenty of visceral truths to confront. In the form of: mealy, mushy, gray-tinged, barbecued humpy. A fine steam rises off the fish, smelling the way it will soon taste in our mouths—like a riverbank, after a school of dead fish washes up in the mud. We shake on salt, a lot of salt. We gulp our Frescas. We stare down at our plates. Then we look up at the sky, as though a rare trumpeter swan has just flown by.

Our new house is built on Campbell Lake, a man-made body of water that allows my father to land our plane in the backyard, a big luxury for people living on the edge of a carless, roadless wilderness. Except for the occasional, distant honks of traffic, it's hard to tell that we live in a city, or that a few miles north, the downtown is filled with oil-company towers and high-rise tourist hotels.

Campbell is a protected natural preserve. Behind the houses on the opposite shore, the foothills of the mammoth Chugach Mountains rise up, sheathed in fireweed purples and alder greens. Salmon roll across the surface of the water. Geese and ducks glide by, their babies paddling madly to keep up. As late as it is, almost midnight, our neighbors are mowing lawns and fussing with the tie-downs on their planes, trying to use every minute of light they have before the days shorten and darken for winter.

"Well," says Dad. But his voice wobbles.

"I'm starving!" I say, holding up my fork. "I'm double-starving."

"Me too."

And we dive in, eating the way we always do, tornadoing through our overfilled plates, rubbing our entire faces off with paper towels, horrifying my mother—if she'd been here—by spitting the thin, transparent bones directly onto the ground. In this case, there's an advantage to our wolverine etiquette. We eat too quickly to taste.

"Humpy's not so bad," I say.

"Tastes like wild hickory nuts," says Dad.

This is some kind of grown-up joke, I know. It comes from a Grape-Nuts ad from before I was born. But my dad doesn't have any grown-ups to joke with anymore. When he laughs, I laugh, too.

By July, we aren't living full-time in the bush. We can't. Dad has to work. He's an orthopedic surgeon; people in the hospital need him to fix their backs and hips. But it's not as if we live in our house, either. The rooms remain empty, save for a few decorative white throw pillows that Dad has tossed around the living room as if to evoke a couch. In the morning, he goes to the office and I go to a terrifying, loud place in the nearby woods full of kids and kickballs and crusty jars of paste, also known as day camp. As soon as it turns 3 P.M., we hop in the 185 and fly away as fast as we can get the plane loaded.

Ashamed of our humpy massacre—or perhaps too tempted to repeat it—we move from Beluga to an isolated stream we call the Secret Spot. As pristine as Alaska is (especially in the 1980s), fishing rivers are known. Even on what seems like a completely deserted stretch of bank, you'll find evidence of outdoorsmen past—a lure on a branch, a heap of blackened firewood.

At the Secret Spot, though, there is zero sign of humanity. Not even a loose tangle of line in the water. The stream looks almost tropical, overgrown with lush, jewel-green alders and small, wet patches of darker green moss. The water is slow and deep, the silence total, except for the occasional riffle or plash of jumping fish, all of which belong to a more respectable species of salmon: bright, meaty silvers.

We catch these salmon, however, with the same grim, ruthless determination, filling up thirty-gallon garbage bags that we cache in the shallows or the plane floats. At night, we pitch a tent, fry up tiny fresh rainbows on the propane stove, and play games of gin by the lantern.

One morning, I wake up just as the sun is rising. I have to go to the bathroom, a complicated process when it comes to girlhood and jeans and long underwear and regular underwear and unzipping half asleep. I undo the door to the tent and crawl out. And there— only a few feet ahead—sits a black bear. She's playing with an alder branch, rubbing her head against the trunk of the tree, making a *woof-woof-woof* sound. My father's arms reach out from the door of the tent and yank me back in, flat on my back. He puts his finger to his lips. Then he hauls his rifle out from underneath his sleeping bag.

He points the barrel at the door. I lie very still. No bear. No bear. *Woof-woof-woof.* The crackle of branches.

Time slows, then sludges as we wait for the bear to charge the tent and Dad to shoot it. Or for Dad to miss and for the bear to maul us. Or for the bear to skip us and scavenge for our salmon and wreck the plane, stranding us in a spot so secret that nobody back in civilization knows about it. Or for the bear to do what we hope it will do, which is what bears mostly do—go away.

We wait and wait, more *woof-woof-woof.* Dad keeps his gun

trained on the door. I curl beside him, watching the shadows of the leaves through the fabric, growing sluggish in the hot damp tent, knowing I should stay awake, but surrendering, finally, to an almost lazy feeling of safety—Dad is here, Dad will protect us. I fall asleep on his shoulder, never hearing when, hours later, the bear finally wanders off in the alders.

Soon enough Dad and I are forced to buy one piece of furniture—a freezer. We are a salmon machine by now, hauling in catches of reds, pinks, silvers, kings, whatever kind of salmon is running, plus anything else in our path: pike, trout, graylings. All the while never asking ourselves why we have to keep catching fish, long after we need any, long after two people could possibly eat them in any kind of reasonable time frame. And we have to eat them.

We are good, moral Alaskans, who use what they kill, fins to gills.

Every once in a while, though, the magnitude of our slaughter strikes us—or maybe just me. We never fished like this before Mom and I left Alaska. Somehow, on a flight back into town, I get it in my head that if Mom were still here, we would be able to eat all this fish. The problem is not that we are killing too many, but that we don't have enough people in our family to eat them. I don't say this to Dad, though. I don't want him to cry again.

Besides, when you are fishing and clubbing and gutting and filleting, there is no time to think about mother or families or people that are gone. Fishing is a lot of work. My job is to haul the garbage bags out of the floats and gut our most recent twelve or fifteen— we're careful not to count actual numbers—fish down at the dock. Unfortunately, I have never been that wild about gutting, save for the fact that the activity comes with a knife, specifically a thirteen-piece Swiss Army Knife that my father presented to me one night of this same summer, along with a braided rope lanyard.

"The lanyard will keep your knife from sinking to the bottom of the river," he said. "If and when your knife slips out of your hands. If and when you remember to tie your lanyard to the belt loops of your pants."

This afternoon, I check my knot on my belt loop. Then recheck it. Off Dad goes, up the hill to start filleting in the garage.

"Get a move on!" he says, no need to even turn around.

I kneel down in the mud, stick the blade into a fish's egg hole, and bring it straight up the belly and around the gill cover, sawing down around the head. The next step is snapping and yanking off the head, then peeling away its dangling heart and intestines and stomach. Then I scrape off the kidney—a layer of blackish gunk along the spine—with my fingernail.

The first fish or two are fun. After that, gutting is no different from mowing the lawn or doing the dishes: egg hole, belly, head, guts, kidney, egg hole, belly, head, guts, kidney, eggholebellyheadgutskidney. A process that gets, at first, faster and faster, then slower and slower. A process that begins to stall mid-process, when I wander over to the fence to watch the neighbor's mentally challenged black Lab, Wacker, try to gulp down flying bumblebees in the backyard.

Eventually, pretending I'm done, I head up to the garage and hang onto Dad as he industriously fillets fish after fish, wrapping each one in plastic, labeling it with masking tape, and shoving it—with a great deal of effort—into our overstuffed freezer.

Dad takes one look at me, puts down his knife, and says, "Let's get the rest of that catch up here."

I smile. I slump, as if to say *Look at me, your cute, towheaded, helpless daughter.* As an extra flourish, I add, "But I can't finish them all. There's too many."

Even as I say these words, I wonder why I bother. I know what my father is going to say. He knows what he is going to say. Finally, he goes ahead and says it. "Can't lives on won't street, Leifer. Check your home address."

No matter what happens, I know better than to bring up my mother. By August, though, stray objects remind me of her—a plate with little blue cornflowers I find hidden under the sink, the smell of my just-washed pillowcase, forgotten opera records in a milk crate in the crawl space. I'm careful to call her at night, after Dad has fallen asleep.

"Do you miss me?" she mumbles, never mentioning it's three in the morning her time.

"Every day," I say, even though I don't miss her. She's my mother. I love her. I love her long delicate fingers and her slender gold necklaces and the *shush*-sound of her silk work blouse when she bends over me to say good night. But every time I shut my eyes, I can't really see her face. All over Anchorage, thin jagged cracks cut through the sidewalks and streets, left by the Great Alaskan Earthquake that leveled the city in the 1960s. It's as if she and Baltimore and our lives there have fallen into one of those cracks, way down into the deep dark melted center of the earth.

A few times, I ask to go see our old house, the one Dad sold right before my mother and I left. The house is way across Anchorage, in our old neighborhood by the mountains. I try to invent reasons to stop by: Maybe we can go pick the raspberries that we planted in the backyard, maybe we forgot my bike in the garage.

"I sold the Schwinn, Leifer," Dad says. "It was way too little for you. We'll get you a new bike. With a banana seat."

I bring up Baby, my husky puppy that Dad said had run away while I was gone. Dad's own dog, Chrissy, is a hunting Lab. Maybe Chrissy could sniff Baby out from the bushes, I suggest, if we went back to our old house. Maybe if we drove up and down our old streets and called Baby's name, she would come.

My father gets a far, irritated look in his eye. I vaguely understand what it means: Baby peed in the house. Baby chewed up a fly rod. Baby got taken out to the woods and sent off to that great invisible dog cabin in the sky. I run up to my room. There is no bed to hide under. I hide in the closet.

"That's enough, now," Dad says, somewhere in the muffled distance. "Cut that out. We've had enough theatrics for one summer."

I hold the door handle shut from the inside.

"You didn't even like that dog," says Dad. "It stank. It crapped in the house."

He is right. Baby did stink. And she did poop in the house, one time in my bed on my pillow while I was sleeping. I never walked or fed or bathed her the way I'd promised. I never even played with her very much. But I want her back all of a sudden. I want her and I want her old outdoor kennel, which was next to our old garage, which was next to our old laundry room, which was next to our old family room with the leather couch and the rocking chair and the cabinet TV and the thick, dusty carpet that you could draw pictures in with your fingernail: flower, tree, bird, stick-house, stick-me.

Dad's boots thud across the room. "I'm going to count to three. Either you come out or I'm going to rip down the goddamn door."

I wipe the crying off my face. I crawl out of the closet.

"Get in the plane. Now. Hop to."

Off we go to Deep Creek. The silvers are running there, fast and thick. We catch a planeful. We catch a mountain of fish.

Just opposite our house on Campbell Lake lives Lou Gallagher, Dad's surgery-practice partner and best friend. Lou is new to the neighborhood, too. He has purchased himself a split-level house with a leather-walled, fully stocked bar downstairs and, in the entrance, a waterfall fountain made from giant clamshells terraced into a grotto of petrified coral and cement.

For the past ten years, a seemingly endless supply of money has flowed into Anchorage from the oil companies and contractors that are building the Arctic pipeline. This, Dad says, combined with the fundamental Alaskan love of individualism, has led to some lavish, one-of-a-kind décor choices.

Personally, I love the clamshell fountain. I harbor certain classified plans about peeing in the upper tiers and watching the golden waterfall tumble down over the embedded starfish and faux pearls. Lou, however, is not at all enthralled. He's decided to tear the rancher down to build a bigger, more tasteful home. He invites us to a demolition celebration barbecue, right on the rubble of the old foundation.

By the time we arrive, the yard is thick with cigar smoke and random black Labs. Watermelons lie piled up by the coolers. Whole salmon, wrapped into tinfoil logs, sizzle on the grill. Lou, a tall, dark, and charismatic version of my blond, smaller, quieter father, waves us over with one giant lobster-claw pot holder. When Dad stands back, rocking on his heels, Lou bear-hugs him. When Dad says we have to be home early, Lou says Dad has to wear a ruffled apron that says KISS THE COOK, plus finish up grilling the salmon, plus finish up drinking Lou's beer, plus put on the goddamn lobster pot holders that his lovely wife bought him for Christmas. Then Dad can go home and be a party pooper. You bet.

To my surprise, Dad neither thunders back at him nor tells him to *redirect his misguided energies.* He blushes, the way I would. Then ties on the apron. Lou sticks a few beers in the front ruffled pocket, plus an unlit Roman candle.

Over on the half-built deck, Great Alaskan Moms are sipping jug Chablis and nibbling on canapés made from Triscuits and spreadable port wine cheese. They wear silk blouses and teetering heels

and gold hoops straight from the disco-dancing photos in magazines at the supermarket. The poetry of their outfits is lost on their
husbands, all of whom have gussied themselves up in JCPenney and
hip boots, as usual.

I sit in the mud by a broken patio chair. My job is to listen and
worship and not, under any circumstances, be noticed. I can do this
until the end of time. Gesturing with his hands, then his spatula,
then a raw moose sausage, Lou explains how to land a plane on a
moving glacier. Rudolph Deer (his real name) enacts his escape from
a bull moose that charged him down his own street.

Beer flows. The grill sizzles. Stories curl and wind around us.
Dad joins in, finally, pausing at just the right moment and stroking
his mustache for effect, as if he just can't seem to remember how he
fought off that grizzly with a butterfly net, a canned ham, and a
broken paddle.

"I used a can of Cutter once," says Four-Finger Dick. "A blast of
bug spray, straight to the bear's face. Gave me that thirty extra seconds."

A high-pitched scream cuts through the laughter. All ten male
heads swing around, evaluating the landscape of the lake for a possible drowning or discharged firearm. Down on the beach, ten girls
freeze in instant, identical states of paralysis.

Oddly enough, in a state whose population averages 65 percent
male, all my father's friends have daughters. Lou has the one and
only son in the group, a six-year-old boy named Timmy. But he
knows which of his kids causes most of the excitement when left
unsupervised. "Mary-Frances," he roars. "There's enough goddamn
pantyhose for everybody to catch a minnow. Share the wealth! Or
no firecrackers after dinner!"

Lou's wife, Caroline, calls me over with a little wave. She smells
of bath oils and perfumes in curvy glamorous bottles with jeweled
stoppers. Her hand feels soft on the back of my neck—creamed and
cool. "How is your mother?" she whispers.

Before the divorce, she and Mom were best friends. Are they still? How can they be when Dad and Lou are also best friends?

"She's great!" I say.

"She told me she bought you guys a nice house."

"It's white," I say. "And black."

Caroline seems unimpressed.

"It's got a lazy Susan. And—" I'm not sure what to say next. That Mom misses her? That Mom is sick a lot now? That we have been away since January, but I'm pretty sure that if Caroline called her up and told her to come home, Mom would do it? Except I don't know if Mom would. She loves Baltimore.

Caroline gives me a hug and nudges me downhill toward the other kids. "Go on," she says. "They're all waiting."

I trudge down—struck mute by shyness as always, only more intensely now that I no longer go to school up here. While the other girls dare one another into eating mud or plot how to get the ducks drunk on gin-soaked corn, I stand on the edges, pretending interest in the dog-kennel trash cans.

"Let's get our dads drunk instead," says Francy, which is her name whenever her parents aren't mad. She, like her father, is smarter and wilder than the rest of us. Her brown ringlets bounce down her shoulders. Her lips jut at a naturally flippant angle. Before the divorce, we were also best friends. Caroline and Mom dressed us in matching outfits—terry-cloth short-shorts, rainbow-embroidered jeans. We're sisters, Francy and I always told people.

Like any good sister, Francy doesn't ask me if I missed her in Baltimore or if I like my new school. She bosses me into stealing the beer. I sneak up through the woods and over the fence, and grab a six-pack from a cooler. Then another.

The rest of the girls turn themselves into eight-year-old waiters, nudging fresh full beers into our fathers' hands the instant their cans go empty. Soon Lou is lurching over the yard. Soon my dad is joining him. "Now," they say, their slurs overlapping, "what about those flipperabuggits? Those whatchmacallits turnoverupsand-arounds?"

"Round-offs?" says Francy, sweetly. "Or cartwheels?" She executes two perfect demonstrations, straight out of gymnastics class. Swaying and tumbling, we all follow her—upside down and right-side up, men and girls and dogs—across the rubble and grass.

Night comes on. Bottle rockets are set off, their exploding colors invisible in the white sky. Ornate, never-to-be-realized plans are made to dynamite, then trap, then poison the weasels that keep stealing the wild duck eggs down by Lou's dock.

The Gallaghers are living in a trailer while their new house is being built. I sneak into the back bedroom and hide underneath the windbreakers on the bed. There I lie very still, as if I might be mistaken for one of the white feral cats that hang around the building site looking hungry and lost, until they are eventually adopted as part of the family. But this is an old trick of mine. My father feels through the pile of coats and finds me. Time to go home.

One week later, Dad and I start building smokers out of three old refrigerators from the Anchorage town dump. If we don't have enough room in the freezer to store all our fish, we can do like the Natives do and dry it out for jerky. We saw holes in the tops of the refrigerators to let the smoke escape, insert pans of burning hickory chips in the produce drawers. On the racks, we lay out strips of fresh raw red salmon. That thinly sliced, the meat turns jeweled and see-through. I hold a piece over my eyes, thinking it will turn the world pink like sunglasses.

"You're going to go next door and spend some more time with kids your age," says Dad, shaking his head. "You'll play there tonight. And I'll pick you up at eleven."

He uses shampoo that evening. And combs his mustache. And pulls on a sweater. I watch him in the mirror. Where did my father get a sweater? It is a soft, fancy sweater in a fancier lord-and-lady color that he refers to as "burgundy."

He walks me next door and drops me off at the Bardells' porch. The Bardells have four kids—all one year apart—and a wall-sized TV in its own wooden cabinet. They are louder, older, far wiser children than myself, and have rigged up their antenna with elaborate tinfoil antlers in order to capture porn off an unsubscribed cable channel. As we study various body parts thrashing through a blizzard of static, the oldest boy, Shawn, leans over my way and says, "So. Have you met your dad's girlfriend?"

Legs writhe over the screen. Moans filter through the crackles. "Girlfriend?" I say, staring at the TV, swallowing hard. "Yeah. Her. Sure."

But I begin counting chimpanzees until it's time for my father to pick me up. One chimpanzee equals one second. Sixty seconds equals one minute. Sixty minutes times sixty seconds equals thirty-six hundred chimpanzees, which equals an hour. Dad won't be late, will he? He promised to come at eleven o'clock. Luckily, nobody can hear my mumbles over the blasting sex sounds and the crunching mouthfuls of Jiffy Pop.

My father is late—by 1,789 chimpanzees. I don't speak to him. I pretend to be asleep in his arms and let him carry me home and tuck me into bed. In the morning, over our matching vat-sized bowls of oat bran, I finally figure out how to ask him about the girlfriend without embarrassing myself. "If there's some girl you like," I say, slow and casual. "You could take her out maybe. Like on a date."

"Actually," Dad says. "I've seen a very nice lady a few times. She works with me."

I spoon through my cereal. I think about how much I hate oat bran and how it gets gritty and soggy as soon as you pour on the milk. My dad's girlfriend doesn't like it, either, maybe. And right then I invent him a girlfriend. She is perfect. She lives in an apartment. She has short dark hair and diamonds in her ears and looks a lot like the figure skater Dorothy Hamill, which is how I want to look, too. The best part about my invented girlfriend is, however, that she is a stewardess. She flies away to foreign countries all the time, and stays there for months and months.

The last week of August, hot black clouds billow over the roof of our house and our backyard starts sliding into the lake. The smokers are going full blast on the driveway, puffing salmon grease into the cool, autumn-smelling wind. Meanwhile, the muddy lot on which our house is built keeps slipping inch by inch into the water. We forgot to plant grass. Or trees. Or anything with roots to prevent erosion. As the mud moves, long thin cracks split up our kitchen walls. The tiles on the floor buckle.

My father puts me in charge of the smokers, then goes back to the dump for railroad ties. He drags them one by one—each an eight-and-a-half-foot-long tie weighing about 250 pounds—down to the lake himself, rolling them into the water off the bank.

Up in the garage, I sit around lonely and bored. My hands stink of rotten fish. Flies bite my ankles. "The smoker door is stuck!" I call out to Dad, who is now diving into the lake, trying to lift the railroad ties on top of one another, underwater, to build us a retaining wall. "I can't find the spatula!"

"Look by the ice auger."

"I can't find the bag of hickory chips!"

"Honey," Dad says, standing up with weeds hanging off his ears. "For Christ's sake, imagine you're on a desert island."

I stomp off to the kitchen, leaving all our fish to burn. My father is stupid. My father is a jerk. I look up at the fridge. My airplane ticket is still there, under the calendar magnet, where it has been all summer.

Dad and I are already on a desert island, aren't we? We've been there for a while, fishing and flying and eating and smoking and grilling and piling railroad ties into walls. While the rest of the world has been buying new backpacks and hemming new jeans, plus doing all the summer reading that I haven't even looked at yet.

I jump up and slide the ticket down to eye level. NORTHWEST ORIENT, it says across the thick red packet. In a few days I will be going back to Baltimore, back to my mother and school and my new life Outside. And Dad will be staying here in our house, sleeping in his down bag, eating all our salmon, all winter, all by himself.

Inside the packet is a bundle of thin, bound, smeary carbon paper. The ticket. I sniff it. Then lick the purple-black ink that rubs off on my fingers. The ticket cost a thousand dollars. If I rip it up, I'll have to pay Dad back that thousand dollars, the way I had to pay him back the nine dollars for the Bonne Bell lip glosses that I stole one time when I was seven.

I slide the ticket back under the magnet and leave it on the fridge.

When Dad takes me to the airport, he walks me all the way onto the plane and straps me into my seat. His face goes red and squishy. Huge, racking sobs burst out of him. He hugs me. He hugs me again. It's not even like in the bathroom when he cried and it was only us two, and we could pretend it wasn't happening. I look around the airplane. An old lady is staring at us. Another one is looking straight ahead so as not to stare at us.

The stewardess tugs on his arm. I try to hug Dad back, but that only makes him hug me harder. I have a horrible feeling about what's about to happen. Already, in fact, I can feel it happening—the smile widening across my face, a huge toothy zinger.

The last—and only—time I ever smiled like this was two years before, the night our old house caught on fire from the stove and the kitchen burned down. Dad ran around, beating the fire out with blankets, while Mom cried in the corner and I smiled like a jack in the jack-in-the-box and didn't move and didn't run and did nothing to help. I wanted to help. A voice in my head was saying, *At least stop smiling. You look like you think this whole situation is funny—or like you're glad about it.* But my face was rubbery and stuck, and when I tried to move I couldn't figure out what to do: run to the closet for coats, or run to the bathroom for towels, or fill some cups and throw water, or hide from the fire and Dad and Mom in the family room, under the afghan on the couch.

This time, though, I can do something. Because I'm coming back to Alaska—and not just for Christmas or next summer. There is a clause in the custody agreement that requires me to come up to Anchorage and live with my Dad for one full year when I'm twelve. After that year, I'm supposed to go back and live with Mom again. But I'm not going to. I'm not sure how yet. I've been working on some scenarios—like getting "lost" in the bush and then hiding out for a while, just long enough for everybody to give up looking for me. Except for Dad and Mom.

A few of the specifics need ironing out. Fact one: Twelve years old is a long way off, four huge never-ending years from now. Fact two: I'll have to get lost in early June, so I can get back inside a house by September. Fact three: I'll have to figure out how to protect myself out there, with a gun maybe, which I don't know how to use and I'll have to steal from Dad. Not to mention, where in the bush should I hide? Somewhere like Chugach National Forest, outside Anchorage, which I can get to on my bike? Or someplace farther out, like Beluga, which means getting lost from Dad while we're fishing? The latter seems a little too scary. Then again, it would be the ideal setting for Dad and Mom to realize—as they chop through the alders, calling out my name—that they made a mistake, that I have to live in Alaska, and Mom has to live here with me, and Dad has to live with the two of us, the way we did before.

None of which I can tell Dad. Not while he is sobbing still. And I'm smiling, smiling like his crying is funny instead of loud and embarrassing and scary. I unbuckle my seat belt and stand up. I start to hug him one last time, but that won't work; if I hug him, he'll only hug me back and not let go. So I stick out my hand—an unconscious and unplanned gesture, a firm, welcoming handshake of the kind that my Swiss headmistress in Baltimore gives to each girl in the morning as we enter the double doors of school.

CHAPTER 3

Homeland

I't's impossible to miss. Something wonderful happened to my mother while I was in Alaska. Before I left, she did two things: go to work and lie down to rest. Now that I'm back living with her in Baltimore, she buys daisies at the grocery store again. She lemon-polishes the furniture. Our first weekend together, she wants to walk through our neighborhood instead of staying in bed with the blinds pulled down.

"What we need," she says, "is some fresh perspective."

I'm looking at the sidewalk, not breaking her back on the lines between the squares of cement. Sidewalks don't exist in Alaska. There are gutters. But nobody walks on them. Everybody drives. Things are too far apart there, miles and miles and miles—usually interrupted by patches of unpaved gravel road or ice-splintered asphalt.

In Baltimore, the windows have little green doors hanging on either side of the glass, usually with designs of sailboats cut into the wood. Garages are whole separate miniature houses. I'm still not over the wonder of these "architectural details" as Mom calls them, leading us down Goodale Road, studying ground covers, debating ivy versus pachysandra. She points out French doors and hammocks and the elegance of a flagstone patio. She loves historically accurate touches. She grew up in Baltimore, which "for the record was founded in 1729, as a port for shipping tobacco and sugar."

There is another record, of course. Anchorage was founded in 1915, and only three thousand people lived there until World War II. The really old houses there were built in the 1960s. They are trailers.

"Oh," says Mom. "A portico!" I hang on her as she leads us left toward Springlake Way. She smells of a heady mixture of department-store creams and shiny, worn purse leather. Her sweater is soft against my cheek. We pick out houses to live in one day, ones bigger and better and more beautiful than ours—a witch's stone cottage, a brick Colonial, a rambling mansion with a real Rapunzel tower, decorated with panes of rainbow-colored stained glass.

"I find the Victorians a bit overdone," Mom says. "Don't you?"

"Let's get one with a tennis court!"

When a car meets another car in our neighborhood, one of them has to pull over and let the other drive past, as if the streets were built for horses and carriages. When the wind blows, the air glitters gold with sawdust.

The elm trees are sick, my mother says. The sawdust comes from cut-down stumps. But I don't believe her. There is no visible evidence of it, other than the occasional pink slip from the city, nailed to a still-standing trunk.

At the entrance to our neighborhood stands a wooden sign. HOMELAND, it says. In black, gilt-edged letters. On white land-marked paint. It looks like the title page to a book of Outside fairy tales—stories filled with bugs that light up like stars in the dark and flowers filled with edible honey and long, twisty slides that spit you into pools—outdoor pools, in backyards, with water the color of melted blue lollipops.

That night, after a shower, wearing only a towel, Mom dances through the living room. She's singing, "I'm going to wash that man right out of my hair." I sing along, stumbling through the chorus I don't know.

Mom's previous song was "Tea for Two." She sang it sometimes laughing, sometimes crying as we drove off the ferryboat from Alaska to Seattle the previous January, when my parents' marriage came officially to an end. Then she sang it as we headed across the country to Baltimore.

This was a trip that, by most maps, takes 2,764 miles and forty-one hours. It took us five thousand miles and the entire month of January. We roared down into Mexico, up into Kansas, over to Louisiana—my mother at the wheel, muttering that we could not go the direct route because the direct route was northern and off-limits due to snow. "What if we slide off a highway and end up in a ditch?" she kept saying, very fast, very loud, speaking into the rearview mirror. "What if we get stuck? We can't get stuck, honey. Not now. No getting stuck. Full speed ahead."

I did not bring up all the times we'd driven in the snow at home. And she did not take her foot off the gas, zigzagging over the southern areas of the country—that vast anti-Alaska of waffle houses and sunshine, cattle ranches and swamplands. "Tea for two," Mom sang in a trembling voice, looking out over the burnt plains of Oklahoma. "You for me. And me for you."

As the landscape and truck stops passed, I sat in the back playing with Kleenex—fashioning a head out of a ball of tissue, wrapping another loose tissue over that head, tying off a neck with a thin, torn strip. When my ghost was finished, I drew a face on it with a pencil. These were always girls' faces, with curly eyelashes and pouty lips.

As soon as we came to a hill, I released my girl-ghosts into the wind, watching them float for a moment in the hot, dead pocket of our speed, then spin off and drop behind us to the side of the road.

Somewhere between Texas and Georgia, we stopped off to see my grandmother in the panhandle of Florida. Back in Alaska, she existed only as a picture in a silver frame on the nightstand. Mom didn't talk about her very much and she lived too far away to visit. "Your grandmother is either a borderline personality or schizophrenic," Mom said in the car as we turned down an unpaved road that bordered a bayou. "The doctors have never been able to make a clear diagnosis." Long pause. "She's also an alcoholic." Long pause. "And there are some medication issues, but I expect you to be respectful."

I shuddered. I didn't know what *borderline* meant, but *schizophrenic* had something to do with having dry white scaly skin, like the girl in my old school who had to take oatmeal baths and flaked all over her desk.

Through the windows, the road smelled of wet salt and lizard. Little shells from the sandy soil popped and splatted under our tires. It was midnight or after. The only thing on in the house I could make out were the yellow windows, lit from the kitchen. My grandmother was inside, we could see by her shadow. But nobody came to the door, even when we banged and rang the bell.

Finally, a neighbor-lady came over and talked to my grandmother through the mosquito screen. The door opened. Mom went in first, me behind her. Face-to-face, my grandmother didn't look much like a grandmother. She looked sexy and scary and old, with curly black hair and a little bow-tie mouth and rubies in her ears that made me think of *The Wizard of Oz*. Her name was perfect: Maybelle.

"Dolly girl," said Maybelle. "You never come visit." She had a thick, dippy accent like clear melted jelly all over her words.

"Mom?" I whispered. "My name's not Dolly."

"No," said Mom. "Mine is. That's my nickname from when I was a little girl."

In the dining room, a wall of dishes towered over the sideboard. Maybelle had been cooking for us for the last week: a pork loin, a whole turkey, a coconut cake, a lemon meringue pie, all of which she'd forgotten to put in the refrigerator. Flies swarmed over hard crusty gravy, a fan turned limply, and a hole gaped across the ceiling where the roofer had started to fix the roof then quit when Maybelle paid him in full on his first day of work, using my dead grandfather's two-hundred-year-old Baltimore family silver.

"It dated back to the Civil War," Mom said. She kept staring inside the little coffin-looking box that the silver used to be stored in, touching the empty velvet. Then she started to cry.

"Dolly girl," said Maybelle, her voice suddenly turning from slurred and southern to sharp and flickering—a dark, smiling hiss. "What else was I supposed to do? You don't want anything to do with me. You'd leave me to die on my feet."

Mom's face went blank. "No, I wouldn't, Mother."

Maybelle laughed. "I know all your ways. Your backhand tricks."

Mom just sat there, her face going blinky and trembly and pre-school. Why didn't she do something, I wondered. Why were her eyes so empty—like she wasn't even there?

"Shut up," I said, but in a tiny, quiet voice.

Maybelle kept laughing.

I took a step forward, but Mom pulled me back. "Leigh," she said.

"Look at what you raised, Dolly! Look at that trash!"

"Time to go to bed," Mom said. But she came with me to the dark back room. We lay side by side in a fancy carved bed, which had also come from my dead grandfather's family, kept awake all night by Maybelle wandering the halls talking about ingrates and muttering "Lord have mercy." I snuck out to get a glass of ice water, but the freezer and refrigerator were packed with chocolate-covered cherries, hundred and hundreds of shiny gilded boxes.

"Your grandmother has some spending issues," Mom whispered.

For the rest of the week, Mom went around town paying off credit card bills and talking to caseworkers and the bank, while I sat on the black vinyl couch with Maybelle watching *Tic-Tac-Dough* on television, eating chocolate-covered cherries, and looking out for "coloreds" who might want to come into our yard and "touch" me. Finally, we got back in the car and got out of there. I wanted to tell Mom that we should go back to Alaska, where it was too far away to see her mother ever again.

But Mom was driving. She wanted quiet time. It was states and states and states before we stopped this time. I held my muscles or peed in soda cups. When I was hungry, I ate baked chicken from the cooler, wrapped in tinfoil. Mom kicked off her sandals and stuck her bare foot outside the driver's-side window, so the fresh air on her skin would keep her from falling asleep and crashing. "I'm adopted," she said, over and over. "Just so you know. You can't inherit any of my mother's mental issues. We're immune."

Once we actually got to Baltimore, Mom bolted out of the car and kissed the street. "I'm home!" she said. "Hallelujah!" Back at the wheel, she honked at the brick buildings and opened the window to wave at strangers.

I slunk down between suitcases.

At the empty house, we unpacked the car. Mom showed up to her first day of work. I showed up to my first day of school, in February. And then Mom got a migraine. She had to lie down at night as soon as she got home. She had to lie down on weekends, too, to rest.

It was a little scary, the first time I saw her on the bed with a washcloth over her eyes. She looked dead, only breathing. Was she going to be this way forever? Was it Baltimore that had changed her? Or all the driving? Or Maybelle? She must be really tired, I thought. Because my mother in Alaska did not lie down. She made soggy moose meat spaghetti and vacuumed the house and hugged me even when I left wet glasses on the living room table. On the weekends she read thick James Michener paperbacks while Dad and I fished, and then, on the weekdays, she picked me up from school and—over and over— more times than anybody thought was possible, drove our car into the ditch on the way back home, missing the driveway to our house, as if she did not know where we lived at all.

Now that I'm back in Baltimore, Mom listens to me talk about Dad and the salmon smokers. But she's not really listening—or it's too upsetting for her to listen, I can't tell. Finally, she leaps up from the table and just starts measuring the dining room walls with my math ruler. All summer long, she says, she's been thinking about French doors. We need a pick-me-up. We need to get our life back. What we need are a few subtle, sophisticated touches around the house and yard.

"Hmm . . . ," she says, "I'm thinking, let's play hooky and go to the National Gallery of Art? We'll look at some books on architecture."

It's September, the first tender month of fourth grade. I'm thrilled. I don't want to go to school. Except that I also don't want to *not* go to school. At the end of the year, the teachers there give out trophies—golden angels on marble bases. This year, I'm desperate to get one. Due to my poor performance in almost every area of study, the only hope I have of getting one is by showing up, the Perfect-Attendance Angel of Excellence. Not to mention, I'm worried about Mom's job. She's a social worker, and, as she says, just about to be laid off.

"What about the federal budget cuts?" I say. Then add, in more specialized Mom-language, "Reagan's administration has no compassion for the underserved."

"Honey, we need to recharge our batteries." Mom sips from a

fine-china mug from before the divorce, painted with English orioles. (On the bottom is a tiny gold stamp saying FINE-CHINA that I've tried many, many times to scratch off.) "Besides, I already called in sick."

I slump on some jeans. There's no point in arguing, not with the new, improved, radically energized version of my mom—a version that I have finally come to realize is a product of the steamy viscous elixir that lurks inside her mug. Mom has discovered Taster's Choice. Mom has turned into the Great American Instant Coffee Single Mom.

I don't know if there are other mothers out there in the world of this species. In Alaska, the other mothers were my friends' mothers. They were married. They drank Tab and told us to go outside and wear a life jacket by the lake or we'd get grounded or drown. In Baltimore, I don't know any other mothers, but the ones I see in the neighborhood do not drive hatchbacks and rant about free child care in Sweden. Mothers here drive station wagons. They honk in the car-pool lane at school and zoom off with girls stacked across the seats, sucking on Popsicles and bottles of Sunny Delight. If they drink coffee, I doubt it has to be black in order to keep them thin and ready to meet a fresh, exciting, romantic, imaginary man who doesn't mind that they have a child or no time to date him. Nor does that coffee have to be instant due to the fear that if they take the five minutes needed to wait for coffee to drip through the filter, they'll fall asleep on their feet, get a concussion, and end up in the hospital, leaving their child without a parent to supervise her.

On any given day, Mom is now up at 5 A.M.—a flannel warrior in a lace-necked nightgown with a cup of Taster's Choice and a bucket of vinegar, washing the floor to keep our kitchen looking like my friends' houses with housekeepers, allowing me to have friends over and not be ashamed. By seven fifty-five, she's at the wheel of the car, with me in the seat beside her, holding her second cup of Taster's, the scalding liquid sloshing onto my uniform as she weaves into and out of traffic, veering through yellow-red lights (because the police should give working mothers a break in this day and age). By nine fifteen, she's at her desk, gulping Styrofoam cup after Styrofoam cup, the brims of each smeared with kisses of work lipstick, as she races to different Head Start centers to do her job, saving preschool kids from ignorance and worse—sometimes their own mothers, who lock them in closets or try to burn them with cigarettes. By six twenty, she's back at home, scooping cottage cheese onto a plate, lighting candles at the table so that we will have a family dinner just like any other family. Then she's back on the road at eight thirty to work her second job at a nursing home, where usually I come with her—sitting in the lobby, with old people who want to touch my hair (until 10:30 P.M.).

She will not be defeated, not by ex-husbands or poverty or Republicans or budget cuts or her feet—which I rub with Bengay at night as she moans into her pillow. So me and my stupid Angel of Excellence trophy versus a day at the National Gallery of Art? I'm toast. I get in the car.

She revs the engine. "I feel so free!" she says. "Don't you?"

I smile, then look out the window as we blast out of Homeland.

Every species of creature has its subspecies, of course. And though my mom is now a Great American Instant Coffee Single Mom who can hang up a picture frame with dental floss and a tack ("See? We don't need a handyman!"), what she can't or won't or doesn't seem to know how to do is all the Great American Boring Parent stuff: toothbrushing, high fevers (we don't even own a thermometer), bake sales, school play costumes, helping with homework, or even nagging about homework.

We don't go shopping together for school clothes or talk about friends over chocolate shakes. I don't have to go to bed or come home at any time in particular. I have never been grounded or sent to my room. Not that all this started after the divorce, either. At age five, I used to wander around in our old Alaskan neighborhood thinking, Where is everybody? Why are they always taking a nap? Wait . . . am I supposed to be taking a nap?

At the time, this seemed like a pretty good deal. I usually found some kind of left-loose, open-minded dog wandering around to play with. But that's the thing about Baltimore: Nothing wanders. Even the squirrels hustle by as if they have a piano lesson to get to.

"Now that we're no longer stuck in know-nothing Anchorage," says Mom, shifting gears and powering over to the fast lane on the Baltimore–Washington Parkway, "I want to show you a few things."

As it turns out, my mother has artistic interests, thwarted by all those years of hunting and fishing. She wants to educate me, specifically about: Puccini Operas, Civil War Battlefields, Volkswagen Beetles, Chippendale Furniture, Fabergé Eggs, Jungian Philosophy, Siamese Cats, Girl Detective Mysteries, Rodgers and Hammerstein, Civil Rights, Frank Lloyd Wright, Swedish Films, Emily Dickinson, and the historic city of Williamsburg.

Today, however, we will start with the National Gallery of Art.

It takes me about 42.7 seconds to fall in love with this particular interest of my mother's. The National Gallery of Art is huge, towering and marble, with a tearoom at the center featuring a harp player and splashing fountain. It's beyond a fairy tale. It's England or some other place that's black-and-white with grown-ups wearing gloves.

I float through the rooms, ignoring Mom's mandate to look for "classical architectural details," stopping mostly at scenes of French court life—young, wigged girls on swings, pushed by counts in frock coats. If only I lived there, in the painting; if only I got to wear a corset and serve as Lady of the Hairbrush.

There was only one museum in Alaska. It had baskets and totem poles. Mom and I went a lot, mostly on crafts day, when the curator gave us a bar of Ivory soap and showed us how to carve it into a little Native man in a kayak. The Ivory was supposed to look like ivory.

"My parents never took me to museums," says Mom. "I was

eighteen before I saw one." Her eyes go distant and dreamy. "I took the bus. I remember it took me so long to get there. I don't think I'd ever have known such things existed if it hadn't been for my girls' school." Her father, she explains, came from an elite, dead Baltimore family. They disowned him when he married Maybelle. But they paid Mom's tuition until she was eighteen. "Just like your father," says Mom. "He's going to pay for your school. Don't think he wriggled out of *that*."

I slide over to another painting: a bowl of fruit with what looks like a caterpillar creeping over a pear.

"You'll see it all," she announces. "Art, ballet, culture . . . you'll experience everything!" Then she gives me a long, squeezing, eyeball-popping hug.

Right then a thought flops through me. It's the wrong time for such a thought. But I bring it up anyway. I ask about Dad. If Mom was off at museums all the time, how did she and Dad ever meet and get married?

Mom laughs. "You don't know?"

"Know what?"

"Our story. Your father was in medical school at Johns Hopkins. He was from California." She lets out a giggle. "You can't imagine just how thrilling that was to a girl like me from Baltimore. I mean, I had the covers of my Bermuda bags dyed to match my sundresses. He didn't know a napkin from a handkerchief, and he didn't care, either. But we were set up on a blind date, then—two months later—engaged."

She's still talking—she was twenty-three, Dad was twenty-one—but right there I stop listening. My eyes are closed. I want to see if I can see Dad—his face has to be in there somewhere, like a painting hanging in my brain. But the same thing happens to him as happened to Mom over the summer. He's gone. All that's there is black, and the sound of the echoing footsteps on marble.

———

Back at our house, Mom patrols the yard, making more detailed renovation plans. She has a yellow legal pad and a ballpoint pen. She points to a window in back. "Right here!" she says. "We'll put in the French doors."

I'm more than happy to follow her around outside. Why did nobody ever tell me about fall? It's incredible, the magnum opus of seasons. In Alaska, the only deciduous trees are aspens and birches, the leaves of which turn a flat pale yellow and blow off in about two days. In Baltimore, the leaves turn red! A deep burnt red! And orange! For weeks! The brightest I've collected in a plastic bag, which I keep stashed under my bed like a bucket of Halloween candy.

Our house is perhaps the smallest and most modest in Homeland, but made from white painted brick, and decorated with black shutters and a screened-in porch. My father gave us the down payment as part of the divorce settlement. In the backyard, Mom draws a deck on her pad. She makes a sweeping gesture—to indicate a tree that is not there. "Look at this greenery. Here's where we can put in that patio. With wrought-iron loungers."

I try to see what she's seeing, as she plants imaginary Japanese maples and springtime forsythia. But what I really see is her, gesturing to parts of our house. She is tiny, a hummingbird, her whole body vibrating with some kind of breathless, musical energy, her green eyes shot through with gold. She stops and looks down at her clipboard. Her face is so fragile, so delicate. You want to bundle it up in soft white tissue paper. You want to press your hand against all those graceful angles—the cut of her jaw, the narrow slope of her nose. My mother is beautiful, I realize for the first time.

And now that I'm noticing, why is she wearing a fluffy pink sweater all of a sudden? I've never seen her in a fluffy pink sweater with little pearl buttons, or in a tweed skirt, either. She has frosted lipstick on. And a gold bracelet. She looks like the mother from 217 St. Dunstans Road or the mother from 89 Homeland Avenue—both mothers I now regularly stop and watch on the walk home from school, spying on them from behind their boxwood hedges as they plant bulbs and order their kids not to dump each other off the hammock.

I'm not sure what to make of this. In Alaska, my mother had droopy bags under her eyes, which are no longer there. She sang off-key, very, very loudly. She wore scarves over her hair—one greasy bang swooping out—and a baggy down vest and jeans.

Where did she get shiny blond streaks in her hair? Where did she get a pair of shoes like velvet dancing slippers? Why does she get to change all of a sudden? Why does Dad? Where did all these sweaters on both of them come from—in burgundy and pink and all the other go-out-for-dinner colors that, evidently, my parents have owned all along?

Not that Mom is dating. Yet.

"After we get the Black Watch plaid cushions," she says, jotting down something on her pad, "we'll deal with the loungers and gutter issues."

"I hate Black Watch!" I say. "I don't want any stupid cushions."

Her face falls. She stops dancing. "Okay. It was just an idea. You know, for next summer."

"I won't be here. Do what you want to. You'll be all by yourself."

"Thank you," she says, "for that loving reminder." Then she marches back into the house and shuts the door to her room—with a loud final *click* of the knob.

A few hours later, I sneak in and stand by her bed, in the murky drawn-blind darkness. The air smells of bad coffee breath and sweat. Her chest moves rhythmically under the covers. A damp washcloth covers her face. She has a migraine, again, a bad one. I think about apologizing for giving it to her. Instead I go back to my room to pick at the rash scabs on my legs.

CHAPTER 4

Sweat and Pencils

Monday is a school day, but this time I'm actually going to school. Mom drops me off by the bench at the entrance. The willow branches leave a delicate, riffled shadow pattern on my skin. Then come the chestnuts. I look up as I walk under them, watching the veiny, golden trembling of the leaves. It's quiet except for the wind and birds. The double doors to the school are already shut, leaving the great gabled stone building looking like what it once was—a mansion constructed for Napoleon's great-nephew, who threw off his tyrannical uncle to marry a Baltimore socialite in the 1800s.

Roland Park Country Day for Girls smells of sweat and pencils, wool and damp chalkboard, an odor that the antique radiators boil into a heady indoor mist. I'm late again. I walk slower and slower through the twisting halls. By the time I drift my way to the door of my fourth-grade classroom, the girls are standing at their desks, chanting out the Lord's Prayer.

Everybody stops before Amen and looks up.

During the four months of third grade that I spent at the school the previous year—from February to June—I learned to mumble through the forgive-us-our-trespasses part, as well as hitch up my bloomers under my tunic while running around with a stick with a leather woven pouch at one end. The specifics of what I'd been doing—playing lacrosse, wearing a uniform, asking for Protestant forgiveness—felt a little murky, but nevertheless entrancing. Books, binders, pencils at Roland Park Country all came stamped in a gilt version of the school's symbol: a laurel leaf. Windows were thrown open in winter, under the belief that gulps of frosty fresh air strengthened our lungs and IQs.

I rarely had to interact with my classmates, though. During recesses, lunch, and after school, I sat inside with Miss Pendleton doing flash cards to catch me up to the rest of the girls. In Alaska, I had gone to "a wonderfully progressive" public school, as my mother always described it to other mothers. To me, it had been just plain wonderful. The teacher there had pointed out the math corner to me and the reading corner and said that we students could go to these corners and do worksheets whenever we "felt like doing math or reading." I did not ever feel like doing math or reading. I felt like playing with the bunnies in the pet-the-bunny corner, which is what I did. Every day.

At Roland Park Country, unfortunately, illiteracy didn't have a corner. Miss Pendleton sat with me during all her free periods, nodding and listening to me stumble through kindergarten picture books like *Sylvester and the Magic Pebble*. Mom had tried these tactics, too, but lacked Miss Pendleton's *je ne sais quoi*—a mixture of vanilla extract and grim spinster determination.

Soon she discovered my lack of math. She drilled me incessantly with flash cards. Three times four? Eight times seven? I loved Miss Pendleton and her cardigan sweaters and long pearl necklace with little wire Mrs. Claus glasses dangling off the end. I loved not having to go outside where all the other girls were laughing and running and trading puffy stickers from their extensive collections housed in heavy leather photograph albums.

This year, though, I am under the supervision of Mrs. Chantal-Romanel, who wears her long brown hair tumbling down over her shoulders and her husband's old shirts as "learning smocks." Over the summer, while I fished with my father, she assigned us Shakespeare's *Romeo and Juliet* to read, as well as Ovid's *Metamorphoses*. This is not typical lower-school curriculum. But Mrs. Chantal-Romanel has higher goals, she explains to us, when it comes to primary education. Despite her poetic outfits, she does not appreciate tardiness, ignorance, or misleading questions—my specialties. I slink into the room.

"Everyone," she says, "kindly pull out a fresh piece of paper."

We are having a pop quiz on mythology. Some of the girls in the front row begin to cry. They didn't know that they had to memorize the spelling of Sisyphus from last night's reading. "Pop quizzes are standard procedure in university," says Mrs. Chantal-Romanel, who is American but refuses to use American words like *college*. "Are you going to cry in university? My job is to prepare you for your educational future."

The great yawning blankness of my paper stares back at me. While the other girls scribble away frantically, I use the time to study their uniforms. Something is wrong with mine. It had been wrong the year before, but I had been too confused at the time to pinpoint the source of the issue. We're all wearing blue tunics with white shirts and brown shoes. And yet, as I now see, my tunic has darts for breasts I don't have. It has a flared poodle-skirt. My shirt sports a round, high Peter Pan collar and is a brittle yellow, papyrus shade. My mother bought it used—unaware that in the eighty-odd years of Roland Park Country, no one had ever bought a used uniform. Mine had been sitting in the school closet since the 1950s.

"Prometheus," says Mrs. Chantal-Romanel. "Pro-me-the-us."

Scribble, scribble go the other fifteen pencils in the room. I draw pictures of my classmates' matching clothing—their shapeless, new tunic sacks, their slouchy leather shoes, their oversized Oxford shirts. Then add a daisy on the margins.

A few periods later, we line up for recess. Mrs. Chantal-Romanel's rule is that you have to hold your partner's hand on the way to the playground. And the girls' unofficial rule is that you have to play with your partner, too. In fact you can play with or talk to *only* your partner, who is also known as your "friend for the day."

Down the line I go, looking for a girl to stand beside. One by one, each one says:

"I'm friends with Chandler today."

"I'm friends with Eleanor today."

"I'm friends with Libby today."

I don't know why I do this every day. Miss Pendleton taught me sufficient division. There are seventeen girls, which adds up to eight pairs of girls and a remainder of one girl, standing alone in the back of the line.

Down the hill from the jungle gym stands a mass of thick evergreens and spruces—vestiges of the forest that sheltered Jerome Bonaparte's house a century before. A small creek burbles on the other side of the gravel road, continuing past a dilapidated barn that leans off its foundation, filled with broken lumber and bats.

I pitch a camp nearby under a pine tree, building up walls of boughs, collecting pinecones for kindling. I'm a settler on the wagon trail, with my trusty pinto pony, Samson. We're living on griddlecakes and honeysuckle sap. And winter is coming on quick.

This is a new game—one that's also real-life training for when I get myself lost in the Alaskan bush. Which I know probably won't happen. But other things could happen: Dad could slip under the plane and the propeller could cut off his hand. He'd lose his job at the hospital. I'd have to stay and take care of him, earning us a living by working at a salmon-canning plant. Or maybe, I'd lose *my* hand. Moving me back to Baltimore—with my injuries—would be out of the question.

Two girls from my class approach in the distance: Heidi Tompkins and Marcie Lerner, two loud, confident, bossy girls I've secretly worshipped for months.

"You're the one that lives in an igloo, right?" says Marcie, but not in a mean way. Almost curious.

I look down at the pine needles on the ground. Say something! Say anything! Pine needles, pinecones, dirt. Say anything! But nothing about Marcie being black or there not being black people in Alaska or about touching her hair, which I've almost touched in class, just to feel the shiny, tight ridges of the curls. When I look up, both girls are still looking at me, but more intently. Say anything! Instead I run down the hill and hide behind the barn until the bell rings for class.

In the dining room, at the ball-and-claw-foot Queen Anne table, next to the mahogany sideboard that holds china and silver service for twelve—all purchased before the divorce—Mom is chewing on a pencil, punching numbers into her electric calculator, watching the totals spit out on a roll of white receipt paper. We have money problems. Dad pays for my school and my books. But Mom's salary isn't enough for food and the mortgage and . . . new shoes.

I slink in. I clear my throat. But how can I ask for the slouchy, sloppy brown shoes that all the girls at school are wearing? The totals on Mom's calculator tonight are in red ink—again—and a cut-glass goblet of Chablis sparkles on her coaster.

I slink out, making it only to the kitchen doorway.

She looks up. "The least you could do is keep me company."

"The budget is boring. I want to watch TV."

She nods, then explodes, throwing the legal pad off the table, followed by the calculator, which bounces against the wall. She's crying. "How selfish can you be!"

I study the Oriental carpet—curl, flower, fringe.

"I worked fourteen hours today! Fourteen hours. All you ever do is take and take and take."

It's true. Mom had worked fourteen hours. All I'd done was go to school and watch cartoons in the basement. Last year, a high-school girl took me home to her house every afternoon and made me hot chocolate, but this year Mom said babysitting was too expensive.

"You got French doors," I say, pointing to them. A man came in October and cut a hole in our wall. I got to hand him nails.

"That was for us. That was an investment." She picks the bills off the floor and begins to stack them, evening out the untidy ones, forming neat, equal piles. One stack. Two stacks. "And by the way, don't think that we wouldn't be fine—just fine—if your father hadn't cheated on our taxes." Three stacks. "I'm not the one who got the big-deal accountant. I'm not the one who lied. But I signed the joint return. Like a dummy! And here I am, paying all the penalties."

I back away—not just from her, but from the stacks, which are huge, looming.

"I'm just telling you so you know," she says. "I'm not sure how much longer I can keep us afloat. Not with you and your clothes and your ballet lessons. Not with your father bleeding us dry. He wants twenty-five thousand dollars to make the IRS leave us alone. That's what I make a year in salary."

I head for the stairs. But Mom follows me to the landing. "At least I turned down his alimony," she says, with a broken sound in her laugh. "I wasn't that desperate. We still have our pride, don't we? We still have that."

In my bedroom, under the layers of covers, I feel sick. Where are we going to get twenty-five thousand dollars? Are we about to be kicked out of our house? Where will we go? Will we have to live on the street, in our car, the way Mom always says happens to women with children in Reagan's pro-gun, pro-life, pro-capitalism society? Or will we have to live down south with Maybelle, with the hole in the roof and the splatted dead roaches in the bathtub and kitchen?

Would Dad even care? I wonder. But only for a minute. Then I curl up in a ball and try to go to sleep. I face the right wall. This is a rule I've recently made up, with my own blend of religion and logic: If you face the left, you go to hell if you die in the middle of the night. If you face the right, you go to heaven if you die in the middle of the night, and even if you don't die, everything will be okay and perfect.

"Hello," my father says. "Hello? Who is this?"

I hang up.

"Hello?" my father says. "I'd start talking if I were you."

I hang up.

"Hello," my father says. "Ellen, goddamnit, it's you. I know it's you. Leave me the fuck alone."

I hang up. It wasn't my father's fault he didn't know that was me on the line, not my mother. When we breathe, we sound like the same person. If I had talked, if I had said, *Dad, did you steal twenty-five thousand dollars from Mom?* he would have said, *No, honey, that was all a big mix-up with the lawyers.*

Behind me, my mother stands in her old flannel nightgown. My hand is still on the hot receiver of the phone. She opens the fridge, pours a glass of Chablis. The crystal twinkles in the refrigerator light.

She has to know that I called Dad. What if she knows what I was going to ask him? "It was Dad," I say, very fast. "I only called to say hi."

"That's wonderful," Mom says. "You and your father have such a good relationship. I never wanted to stand in the way of that. No matter what he's done to me personally." Then she smiles. But a smug, phony smile.

I stand there, hating her chin, which has a little flap of skin under it that jiggles. Then I hate her Adam's apple and the way it bobbles in her throat when she sips. She sips and sips and sips. Her face changes. It gets hard and funny and I don't even recognize my mom for a minute—until I do. She looks like her mother. She looks like Maybelle.

But she can't look like Maybelle. Mom is adopted. Mom has brown hair and Maybelle has black hair. They don't have the same DNA or noses or cells.

Then her voice curls, low and hissed. "And how is your father—with all his planes and all his money?"

I just have to go to bed. When I wake up, Mom's face will be her face again and we'll drive in the car all the way to some museum in Delaware or West Virginia to learn about Japanese pottery or the cooking habits of eighteenth-century kitchen slaves. This is the problem with Baltimore. Mom is so worried about Dad. But it's all the other people who are scary and horrible—all the crazy or dead people who are seeping into us the more we stay here. We never used to talk about families or the past or even each other in Alaska. In Alaska, we were faraway and safe.

"Did I ever tell you how he called up all the banks in Anchorage, and told them to turn down my application for a mortgage? That's why we had to leave Alaska. I couldn't buy a place for us to live."

I know what to say. *Good night*. Or *I'm tired*. But I'm sick of her talking about Dad. I'm sick of her telling me things that might be lies or might not be, and not knowing which I want to be true. "Actually," I say, "Dad's doing great. He wants me to pick out a bed for my bedroom in his new house."

"Really? That's wonderful."

"I want to get a water bed. Or a canopy bed. We're getting all new furniture. And a pool table."

"That's exactly what your father should be doing—setting up a home for himself." Mom laughs, and takes a sip, sip, sip of wine.

"I can get any bed I want. Even if it costs a thousand dollars. The sky's the limit. Dad said."

She stops, cocks her head.

"Dad's buying us a new cabin, too!" But now everything I'm saying is coming out panicked and stupid and rambling. She knows I'm lying. "A cabin in the bush. With a stove and a canoe and a kerosene lantern. I get to get my own snow machine if I want. He said just to ask."

Mom waits a beat. Then she says in a flat, stabby voice that comes with a twist of a smile, "Why don't you ask him if he's started dating Abbie yet? Ask him that, why don't you?" She turns her back to me and walks out of the room.

I run upstairs, the way I should have in the beginning. How did Mom know that Dad is dating? I found out last summer, when he went out to dinner that one time. But I never told her about it. I didn't want to make her feel bad. And . . . how did she know it was Abbie who Dad was dating? I didn't know. I thought he was dating a stranger, or different strangers—ladies who were hostesses at restaurants or veterinarians. A dark, scratchy feeling zigzags through me: Abbie works for Dad. She is his nurse in his office. She has long flippy blond hair and always makes homemade chocolate cakes for the receptionists' birthdays.

You know how you can stop from thinking? You can break something. You can't break something loud and get in trouble. But you can cut up a shirt with scissors, over and over into tiny pieces. I get down on the floor. I pull out my bag of fall leaves from under the bed. But they are just like wet river pebbles, after the pebbles have dried in your pocket. All the colors are gone—all the reds and golds and oranges and greens and yellows. Why didn't anybody tell me? I reach into the bag. They've turned damp and black and slick. You can rip them, but it's like tearing up a handful of soft molded toilet paper.

Two weeks later I'm busted by the police at the Homeland goldfish ponds. The ponds are dark, mossy stone constructions, surrounded by weeping cherry trees and azalea borders. Fountains shoot up at the center. Little narrow bridges cross them, overseen by green copper nymphs wearing leaf-shaped caps.

I love the ponds. In Alaska, in our old neighborhood, which nobody called a neighborhood, we had a big drainpipe that funneled all the water down from the mountains, under the houses, and out to the town rivers where it went to the sea. I used to put on my waders and fish the drainpipe stream, even though there were no fish and my dad said never to do it. You can trip in heavy waders, hit your head on a rock, and drown.

As usual, no kids are around in Homeland. It's after school, Wednesday, dancing-class day. Creaking white buses from the country clubs pick up the girls at our school in the parking lot, as well as the boys from the boys' school across the street. Dancing class, I imagine, takes place in the ballroom from the storybook that came included in my scratchy old Cinderella record. Chandeliers twinkle overhead, the girls wear glass slippers.

As I walk home through Homeland, I sneak into a few backyards, kicking odd things that the families have left forgotten in the grass: the sprayer from a hose, galoshes, a barrette, a broken half of a croquet ball. Finally, I find what I need—a rake with a long wooden handle, leaning against a porch. I look around to see if anybody is looking, then sling it over my shoulder.

In my backpack, I've already stashed a few loops of dental floss, a safety pin, and a piece of bread. One of my favorite stories of Dad's is the one about the summer when he and his friends poached salmon at the dam, back when he was growing up on a ranch in California. Dad and his friends had used Wonder Bread. Mom doesn't believe in white-flour foods. But fish, I hope, will overlook a little whole wheat.

There is a sign by the ponds. It matches the Homeland neighborhood sign, except that it's smaller. NO FEEDING. NO FISHING, it says in tiny black letters.

Kneeling down, I rig up the rake as a pole, using the dental floss as line and the safety pin as a hook that I bait with balled-up bread. The fish are moving along the edges of the pools, great fat orange monsters with mouths as wide and round as the tentacles of octopuses. I try to cast, but the rake is too heavy. I dangle the line directly into the water, pulling the bread ball over the surface, avoiding the lily pads.

One chimpanzee, two chimpanzee, I count. A fish slaps out of the water, its mouth sucking up the bread ball and safety pin. I jerk back, softly. The fish is on, the fish that now appears to be a goldfish. A large goldfish. But a goldfish nonetheless. A pet. It doesn't even know how to fight. It lets me pull it directly out of the water. It is hooked someplace wrong, too—not in the mouth, maybe inside it, in its stomach. It flops and splashes in the air, desperate.

"Kid!" says a voice.

I look around. There's a police car behind me. I panic, throw the stolen rake into the water, where it, along with my poached fish, sinks into the bubbled mud and weeds.

"Get over here," says the voice, through the open window of the car. The policeman is an old fat man, with boiled skin and mustard on his breath. "What are you doing?"

"I live here?" I whisper.

"Get in the car. In the back."

I think about the fish at the bottom of the pond, still hooked and writhing and dying. I get in, anyway—shaking, my throat dry. The policeman says something to somebody on the radio. "Where do you live? Your parents and me need to have a little talk."

I direct him up the hill to our house. He parks in front and reaches for the door handle.

"She's at work," I say. "My mother. But she's coming home soon."

"I'll have to take you down to the station, then. We'll call her from there."

I know what the station is. It's jail. I'm going to have to stay in jail with all the grown-up men with beards and raincoats. Because my mother isn't coming home soon. And nobody can call her. She doesn't have an office or phone. She works all over the city. And tonight is a meeting night, until 6 P.M.

"She'll be home in a minute," I say. "Promise."

We wait and wait. Calls come in over the radio. The policeman taps his fingers on the steering wheel. "What about your dad? Why don't we call him?"

I start to cry. My dad is going to kill me. Not about the goldfish maybe, but about the stolen rake. Before Mom and I ever left Alaska, I stole more than Bonne Bell lip glosses. I stole Kraft caramels from the bulk bins at Safeway. I stole quarters from Dad's piggybank. He found everything I'd taken when I was seven, hidden under the bed. "You can't call him! He lives far away, in Alaska."

The policeman turns around "Look, kid. There's no need to lie."

"But—"

"Either your dad's at work or your dad's out of the picture. Which is it?"

I gulp. "He's out of the picture."

"Okay," the policeman says. "Okay." He burps, but cups it.

I shrink down in my seat.

"I'll tell you what, your mom's got enough on her hands. You go inside now. And you promise me never, ever, ever to fish in those ponds again."

"I promise."

"And knock off the stupid lies about your family. You don't want to grow up to be a liar, do you?"

"No," I say. "Sir. No, sir."

"Go on, then. Run inside and let me see you lock the door behind you."

I run up to the front door and unlock it with my key and slam and relock it. I run down the stairs to the basement, which is a room that doesn't exist in Alaska. There are cramped tunnels under the houses called crawl spaces, but those are full of insulation and mud and you can't stand upright in them. To get into Dad's crawl space, you have to climb down a hole in the floor in the gun closet. There are no gun closets in Baltimore, either.

Our basement in Mom's house is what Mom calls "finished." It has indoor-outdoor carpet and our old leather sofa. I'm safe down here. I'm okay. As long as I keep the lights off and sit right in front of the television with the volume up as loud as it goes, loud enough to feel the hysterical *Tom and Jerry* music jittering against my face.

Later that night, I don't hear the scrape and click of my mother's key in the lock or the thump of her footsteps on the ceiling. All of a sudden, she's simply there, standing in front of me, blocking the TV. Her curls are saggy. Her glasses have left a deep, red dent over the bridge of her nose. "Do you want to sleep with me?" she says. "Just this once? Just in case you're feeling a little lonely?"

She says this every night. I try to look around her, to see the edges of the car commercial, playing on the screen. "I'm not lonely," I say.

"Okay." She starts up the steps. She sighs. "Good night then."

"Wait!" I say. Then run up behind her. "Wait!"

Upstairs in her room, though, in her four-poster Colonial bed, I lie facing the wall instead of her—letting her wrap her arms around my waist, but holding myself separate from the familiar comfort of her breath heaving softly against the back of my neck.

CHAPTER 5

Snowslide or Glacier?

I'm a little scared about the polar bear. He himself is not scary. His coat is pee-colored. His tongue is a rubber rage of pink that's supposed to look evil and ferocious, but only makes you feel kind of sorry for him, standing on his slab of fake glacier rock, roaring at airplane passengers. His towering glass case, on the other hand, is a little worrisome. It's not at the end of the gate. It's always at the end of the gate. Unless I'm at the wrong gate. Unless the airport people changed the gate and Dad doesn't know and there won't be anybody to pick me up at security.

I turn at a bend in the hall, past The Last Frontier Gift Shoppe, displaying joke paperweights made from shellacked moose turds right beside a pyramid of canned coho salmon. I should have never ditched my stewardess chaperone. People stream by. Knees. Suitcases. Ankles.

I hunch down by a trash can and try not to cry.

"Leifer!" says Dad from the back of the crowd. Beside him is the polar bear. And beside it, Abbie. Abbie is officially now Dad's girl-friend. He told me last week over the phone. While he hugs me, I give her the once-over. She looks just like she always did while work-ing at his office—slender, pale, her long straight hair falling in loose, curling-iron waves around her face. Her nose has a slight, snorty flare at the tip. Her chest looks bony. But these are cheap details to notice, even for me. She is pretty, the soft, gentle pretty of kinder-garten teachers. She smells like mints and roses-of-milk lotion.

Behind her stands Francy Gallagher in pedal pushers and a blue satin roller-skating jacket. She sticks her tongue out at me, stained watermelon red from Jolly Ranchers past. I stick out mine, then grab her hand. If Francy is here, we are going fishing straight from the airport or—please, God, make it true—going to Baskin-Robbins for double dips.

Our first step is loading into the Suburban, Dad's shockless, semi-brakeless Great Alaskan Dad Tank, a Neanderthal version of the vehicle that will one day be the SUV. A heady cloud of antifreeze fumes and WD-40 hangs in the air. Construction dust billows from the heating vents. Francy and I sit in back, wearing no seat belts and bouncing almost up to the ceiling every time we hit a bump in the asphalt.

On we go down Jewel Lake Road—past the turn onto Dimond Boulevard, which hasn't changed, past the Taco Bell that hasn't changed, and the Quik Stop that hasn't changed, either, even if somebody misspelled it. The streets are big wide boulevards, with sexy-lady bars and supermarkets and trucks bouncing all over. Everything is exactly the same as always, exactly perfect as far as I am concerned, down to the black, scrawny Alaskan spruces on the sides of the road instead of East Coast oaks and maples.

The only thing that could make this moment more sublime, in fact, is . . . a cat. Francy has a cat, a white fluffy cat. She has white cat hair on her satin jacket right now, squiggling all over it. I know my dad and pets, and I know I'm not going to get one. Because even if Francy's dad and my dad are best friends, they're different kinds of dads, meaning that Francy gets to drive her own snow machine (sometimes without a helmet) and open all her presents on Christmas Eve instead of Christmas Day (sometimes before calling aunts and uncles). Nevertheless, I begin to chant "Can we get a cat, Dad? Can we? [bump on the road] Can we? [bump, bump] Can we [bump] please?"

"Let's talk about it later," he says. But in a tone that's almost angry-sounding instead of just annoyed. He's in the driver's seat. I can't see his face. Or Abbie's face, either. She's in the passenger seat, but studying the road. Something in the car feels tight and hard to breathe.

"Can I get a cat," I say, my voice trailing off. "Can I please?"

"Well," Dad says, in a flat, determined voice, "Abbie has a cat. And she lives with me now. She's going to be my wife. So you have a cat already."

I look at the back of his seat, at the pocket where the driving maps are stored. Then I look at the floor and at the carpet on the floor and the crumbs in the carpet. And then I make the mistake of looking at Francy, who, despite her freckles and baby-fat cheeks, is looking at me as though she is a grown-up. She knew about Abbie and the marrying already. Plus other things that she's trying to tell me now by staring.

I can't stand her kindness, or the pity in her eyes, either. I pick at the torn vinyl on the door handle, pick, pick, pick, digging a little hole there, a little channel, a stream. We pull into the driveway. Dad hits the garage door opener. Against the walls, all our tackle boxes and camping equipment has been shoved aside. Boxes marked CHINA and KNICKKNACKS and RECORDS stand piled by the freezer. But not in Dad's handwriting.

I make it past them and get inside. I still have to walk through the downstairs, though. I do it slowly, running my hands over Abbie's rocking chair in the living room, Abbie's crocheted afghan on the sofa, Abbie's dishes in the cupboards. Our empty house is full now, full of Abbie's spider plants and potpourri and mixing bowls and spices. Abbie's china and knickknacks and records.

I'm not as smart as Francy. But I understand all of a sudden that Abbie has been living here for a while, probably as soon as I left Alaska last Christmas. It wasn't that bad of a Christmas, was it? Dad and I chopped down a tree in the bush and flew it home, tied to the plane struts. Abbie came over for goose dinner—because Dad had told me by then that they were dating. But just casually, nothing serious.

Only six months have gone by since I left. How did Dad fall in love with Abbie so fast? I slip into the downstairs bathroom, where I turn the diamond faucet knobs on and off, on and off. They are thick round knobs, the size of my whole hands. On and off . . . on and off . . . oh. Maybe Dad has been in love with Abbie for a long time. Maybe, I realize, even before the divorce. Maybe Abbie is the real reason my mother and I had to leave Alaska.

I rest my head on the cool, marble sink counter, all these conclusions just scribbling through me, scribbling and scribbling in a black, penciled scrawl inside my head. The faucet drips. Pans crash in the kitchen. Through the door, I hear Abbie and Dad laughing by the barbecue grill. But I don't cry. And I won't, either. Dad already picked Abbie over me once. And if I cry, if I yell, if I make a stink downstairs at lunch, he'll pick her again.

You know what you do to not cry? You picture patching a sleeping bag—holding the lighter up to the edges of the tear, watching the plasticky fabric curl up so that when you blow the flame out, all that's left is a hard melted seal.

I look in the mirror. My eyes are dry. There's a lump in my throat, but you can't see it on my neck. I turn the faucet off. I walk slowly out to the deck. And I sit down at the picnic table and eat my salmon and drink my Fresca, along with everybody else.

Abbie's cat is named Rita. I never see her. She stays upstairs, hidden under the bed.

———

There are a lot of new rules in the house. I'm supposed to knock on Dad's bedroom door before I enter now. And I'm supposed to knock on the bathroom door. And I'm not supposed to dig through the drawers in Dad and Abbie's closets. This is about privacy, Dad says.

I don't remember there being privacy when Mom and Dad and I were a family. Everybody was always walking around naked or sticking their head into the bathroom while you were peeing to tell you to "Hurry up and get your hip boots on! God Bless America!"

I feel pretty stupid at night after one of my nightmares. I never remember them but I always wake up sweaty and lost and cold. One night, I go right up to Dad's bedroom door before I remember I can't open it or crawl into bed with him and Abbie. I think about curling up in the hall, but it's pretty open out here with all that carpet and the little face-nibbling things that might live in the carpet and come out when it's dark and you're alone. Going back to my room isn't wise, either. My nightmare is hanging over the bed, waiting to suck me in.

What I do is go outside and climb in the kennel with Chrissy, Dad's old duck-hunting dog. She sleeps in a plywood doghouse filled with hay and a little red heat lamp mounted on the ceiling. It's scratchy in there and stinky, but I don't mind. Chrissy is warm. She lumps her heavy gray muzzle on the top of my head.

I'm not sure if dogs can remember, but I'm remembering less and less. There are facts about our old lives that I'll always know, pasted into my mind from what Dad and Mom told me or told other grown-ups who came over for dinner parties. In 1971, they moved up from Los Angeles so that Dad could do a community service job at the Native hospital and not go to Vietnam. When I was five, Mom started working, too, organizing the first chapter of Planned Parenthood in Alaska.

My own version, though, is more like a movie: Mom making me caribou stew in the Crock Pot and slapping FIRST COMES LOVE,

THEN COMES CONTRACEPTION! stickers on my kindergarten book bag; Dad leaving for the hospital or Merrill airfield to get his pilot's license; me wandering around the living room touching all the vases and lamps. All those years, Mom kept redecorating, adding more and more Baltimore stuff that I didn't know was Baltimore stuff yet—embroidered fabrics and brass candlesticks and furniture with long, foreign names like ottoman and Chippendale that she had to get shipped up on cargo boats. Meanwhile, whenever he was home, Dad was ripping out our clipped subdivision grass and planting his own forest in the front yard with native trees and wildflowers.

Looking back, the differences seem so clear. Mom was building a city in our living room—a city built of mahogany tables and Persian carpets and crystal salt-and-pepper cellars. And Dad was flying off into the wilderness in his new plane to get away from all cities, even Anchorage, the one where we lived.

It's too squashed in the doghouse to sleep for more than a few hours. Eventually, I go back inside, taking Chrissy with me. It's not fair to leave her out there by herself. Being alone in the dark feels so much lonelier once somebody's already been curled up with you.

Over the next few weeks, I do some investigating. Abbie, I find out, has her own pilot's license. She likes to fish the river, instead of sitting on the bank like my mother, reading books. Coming from Ohio, from a little paper-plant town with a drive-in and a penny-candy store, she claims she's always dreamed of living in Alaska. She drove up in her Dodge Rambler American looking for excitement and adventure.

I'm skeptical. What's so exciting about Alaska? A drive-in sounds pretty cool. So does penny candy. Abbie will say anything to suck up to my dad. She is sucking up to me, too, the faker.

Unfortunately, however, I happen to be a sucker for sucking up. All that June and July, Abbie is either in the kitchen, in an apron, showing me the secret to her chocolate cake recipe (mayonnaise). Or she is teaching me how to sew on a sewing machine, helping me make a clown costume in advance for Halloween, so that, for once in my life, I won't have to march around in a torn, drugstore plastic Wonder Woman outfit. Or she is making me a lunch like the ones that the girls at school in Baltimore always have: ham and American cheese on white bread, wrapped in tightly cornered waxed paper.

Or she's kissing my dad—one afternoon, in particular, in the back of the Avon raft as we putter around Campbell Lake. I'm supposed to be practicing how to handle an outboard motor. I take my eyes off the reedy shoreline and glance in their direction. She has her hand on the fly of his jeans. She is laughing. So is he. I take my eyes off them, quick, my face burning. They are disgusting—gross and disgusting and nymphos.

But is that what people in love do?

My dad is old. So is Abbie, not as old as him, but almost thirty. Dad bought her, as a surprise, the clunky kind of pottery cups she likes. She planted him raspberry bushes. At night after dinner, they sing lounge-song duets—Dad bashing the notes out on the piano, Abbie's voice floating over his, soft and tinkled. Except for her blue eyes and his brown eyes, they even look alike: blond, tan, competent.

Guiding the raft toward the dock, I think about my mother's lunches: the two-inch-thick slab of peanut butter, topped by the two inches of runny historic crab-apple jelly (bought at the gift shop of a restored tobacco plantation) smeared on wheat-and-seed bread, massed into a bundle of tinfoil, positioned under an apple, where the sandwich gets pounded and scrunched into a kind of leaky PB&J meatball at the bottom of the paper bag.

I love these lunches, I tell myself. They are original. They are spunky, independent, Democrat, social-worker lunches. Not vanilla-wafer, tongue-kissing, husband-stealing lunches. When I get back home to Baltimore, I'm going to eat them instead of throw them in the trash.

From Judy Blume novels, I know what my newly divorced dad is supposed to do next: invite me over to his rental apartment where I get to eat all the sugar cereal and pizza I want. Clearly, this is not going to happen. Nor are he and I going to go fishing together alone anymore. Abbie fishes next to him, trying out every lure and fly he suggests. I fish as far down the river as I can. And I don't really fish. I play openly with minnows, corralling them toward the shoreline with the looming shadow of my boot.

One Saturday at home, after breakfast, my father looks over at me and smiles. "How old are you, anyway?"

"Dad." I scowl. "Cut it out."

"Ten's old enough for a little fun, isn't it? How about you and me go blow up some cans?"

I nod, carefully casual. He unlocks the heavy, wooden door to his sacred gun closet and hands me the .22 his dad once gave him. Our new quality-time occupation is decided: firearms.

Dad does not fool around with guns. All I have to do is look at the engraved metalwork on a wall-mounted shotgun for a warning to thunder forth: Never pick up a firearm without permission! Never pick up a firearm without knowing if it's loaded! Never trust anybody who says it's unloaded! Never get snow down your barrel! Never believe your safety is on when it's on! And never, ever, ever point your weapon at anybody unless you're prepared to kill them! "Are you prepared to kill somebody?" Dad finishes that first afternoon, in a crescendo of bulging eyeballs and forehead veins. "Are you?"

"Uh," I say. "No?" I look down at the concrete floor of the garage. I'm not sure what killing means exactly. I know what dead is. But killing—not a fish or a mosquito, but something with a face and lots of blood? I don't know. And this is clearly not the correct answer. The person you're pointing the gun at is supposed to be scared, not the person holding the gun.

Dad lifts up my chin. "It's good to be scared, Leifer. Fear keeps you careful."

What he doesn't say is that guns are the greatest thing since firecrackers and water balloons and the birthday candles that fizzle but don't blow out. I can't get enough. On the weekends, Dad and I fly out to the cabin and shoot beer cans lined around the trash pit. We shoot up bottles balanced on hay bales. One time, we shoot up a life jacket that we drape on an oar and stick in the tundra—causing a Native man, rightly, to three-wheel over from his village and yell at us. On rainy days, we drive to the range outside town to shoot holes in bull's-eyes and blast clay pigeons from the sky, checking in at the counter manned by potbellied Old Great Alaskans who pat me on the head and give me chocolate bars free, along with the purchase of a box of ammo.

We are the same as always, the two of us in hip boots, trudging through the mud and alders with overloaded duffels of outdoor equipment. But something feels different about shooting. We do it next to each other—shoulder-to-shoulder, gun-to-gun—but not with each other. I don't mind so much, not really. Something funny always happens to me, especially with a rifle—lining up the bead, then the bead in the loop, then the bead in the loop and the center of the target, easing back on the trigger slowly, so slowly that time turns smudged and runny and everything outside the narrow range of focus fades away. There is no sound of the wind or leaves or birds, no sound of thoughts even, including the dull chant that plays in my head, leadenly, relentlessly—about Dad and Abbie, about Mom and the IRS money, about Mom and me going homeless and Dad living in a fancy house, about not crying, not talking, not asking, not thinking. There is only quiet, then a distant, alien *crack*.

———

Like most Alaskans, Dad is an outdoorsman. That means he and I will walk for miles, loaded down with packs and equipment, just to find the ideal spot to cast. But to walk just to walk? To climb just to climb? This is like people who go into the bush and set up a tent and just sit around, calling it camping.

Abbie, though, has a nature-girl streak. She makes salads out of weedy-tasting herbs and brown kernels. She grows ferns in macramé holders. And this August, three weeks before I'm due to leave again, she wants us to hike a few mountains.

Crow Peak is our first big trip. The trailhead begins only an hour's drive from Anchorage. We start at sea level, crossing a narrow valley that runs along a stream. Up we push between two mountains, and set up a small camp by a glacial lake. Against the hot sun and white sky and black shale, that glacial lake looks so eerily, so strikingly phosphorescent—a blue, liquid version of the green glow inside fireflies. I feel a rushing need to crash into it, to break it by plunging in my hands. At which point the cold strikes, and I scream.

The next morning, we start up the peaks, crawling over boulders and along a spiny ridge. There is hardly enough room for our feet to fit on the trail. We stop only to guzzle water. For hours, we pick our way higher and higher. "I can't do it," I say, flinging myself on the ground. "And don't say can't lives on won't street."

"Suck it up, now, honey," Dad says, pulling me up over a boulder. Then another. Abbie holds out bribes of sugar-covered jelly orange slices, patting me on the back.

At the summit, we all collapse. The lead-colored waters of Turnagain Arm and the massive Chugach Mountains spread all the way to the horizon. I crawl forward, leaning over an outcropping, imagining the fall, the scream, the splat on the craggy boulders fifty-five hundred feet below. A strange, scary, but excited part of myself wants to do this.

"Hiking's not so bad," I say to Abbie, but into the wind where she can't hear it.

A few hours later, it's time to head down. The light is failing. The temperature is dropping. We work our way along the ridge, trying to maximize the amount of daylight left by taking the shorter route down the opposite side of the summit.

But the ridge gets slimmer, steeper, higher. Did we end up on the wrong trail? Far below us, in the shadows, our tent hunches ever so brightly, a dome of fluorescent orange beside the lake. But directly ahead of us lies a snowfield. Our options are: Cross it or retrace our steps all the way back to our original route.

Dad and Abbie huddle, but I can hear.

"What about hypothermia?" Dad says. "Not to mention falling in the dark."

"We don't have ropes," says Abbie, in a worried voice. Contrary to the basic rules of outdoor Alaskan life (pack for panic! pack for disaster! pack tents, food, jackets, ropes, matches, guns, bungee cords!), we have brought only day bags, loaded with water and granola bars. "What if it's not a snowslide? What if it's a glacier?"

"I don't know."

"That's not good enough, Jim."

I try to not think about the snowslide, which looks so harmless, a gentle slope of glowing white. Do crevasses plunge below it? What if we fall in? What if we break our legs and have to lie at the ragged icy bottom, simultaneously freezing and starving to death?

"We're too tired," Dad says. "Not to mention dehydrated. The snow's shorter by hours." He buckles all of our belts together, plus ties together all of our jeans, hoping that the improvised line will be sturdy enough to hold our combined weight if one of us falls through. Off we go in our underwear and jackets, crossing ever so slowly: Abbie in the lead, me in the middle, my dad anchoring in back.

"Feel out each step," he shouts. We shuffle onward, easing our boots over the snow. With a branch, Abbie pokes each patch ahead of her, testing whether or not it will hold. I step exactly where she stepped, Dad steps where I did. Our progress is slow, clumsy, nerve-racking. Nobody asks how you're supposed to feel out your step if you're falling already.

At last, we come to the end of the slide. We throw down our packs, whooping and dancing. Then we pull our jeans back on and slide down the loose crumbled shale, all the way back to camp.

After dinner, by the fire, Abbie asks me to wash the dishes in the lake. I do it, but not without first thinking, *Wash your own stupid dishes and find your own stupid family.* It's strange to hear that hateful, singsong voice in my head, a voice that pipes up all the time back in town. Up on the mountain, it had disappeared. I had tethered myself to Abbie, without question or pause or commentary, trusting her the way people normally do with only their closest family.

Six months later, I come back for Christmas. Winter is one of my favorite times in Alaska. It's not what people from the Lower Forty-Eight expect. Twenty hours of daily darkness isn't actually that dark. What soaks through the sky is a hushed, dense purple that glows from the light of the snow, even as the snow glows from the light of the moon. People speak more quietly during these slow, secret-feeling months. Errands are postponed in favor of naps. Whole days go by where you never change from pajamas into jeans and snowsuits.

Except during Christmas. For two weeks, the world wakes up and blooms. Sledding parties whoosh down the backyards. Lights blaze through the trees, massive Alaskan-sized light displays, as if designed to spread the visible cheer all the way over to the gloomy Soviets across the Bering Strait.

This particular Christmas is no different, except that Dad and Abbie are getting married. At the end of last summer, when I'd left to go back to Baltimore, they'd told me that they'd set a date—New Year's Eve. At the time, that seemed far, far away, like Easter or college or the black, burning end of the sun. All that subsequent fall, living with Mom, I just didn't think about it. The wedding disappeared, along with Dad's face.

Now that I'm back, I find a dress waiting on my bed. It's my dream dress, a Gunne Sax with white puffy sleeves, perfect for a flower girl. I lift it up, rubbing the soft red velveteen fabric against my cheek. But even so I'm crying; I'm going to stain it. I'm going to ruin the wedding—and my dad is never going to forgive me or speak to me again.

I have to pull my face together.

Luckily, the house looks more like Christmas than a wedding. The kitchen is filled with gifts prepared by seasonally manic neighborhood friends: blueberry jams, cured salmon, caramel popcorn balls, a homemade beaver-fur hat. Moose wander through our backyard, stuffed and stunned on pickings from the garbage cans, the delectable twigs of our landscaped blue spruces.

Dad and Abbie have bought a huge tree at the feed store. "This is going to be a great Christmas!" Dad says. "Just terrific!"

In the living room, Abbie gets on the ladder and I hand up ornaments. They're chintzy, supermarket items—generic sparkles, bland silver balls. I miss all our old decorations, wrapped in tissue paper, stored in the cardboard trunk. Mom took them when we left: the squirrel with the fluffy real fur tail, the little Jesus asleep in a cradle made from half a walnut shell, the Alaskan Santa on cross-country skis.

According to our phone conversations, Mom is spending Christmas Day feeding the homeless. I don't know what she does all the other days. Except that I do know. She's probably sitting alone in the living room, listening to opera. Or sitting in the den, looking at old pictures of us together in her thick, huge scrapbooks: The three us by a glacier! The three of us by the pop-top VW camper! The three of us in our first apartment in Anchorage, down by the port!

"Isn't this great!" says Dad from the sofa.

I turn around. His eyes feel like cameras, waiting to pop the flash. And I smile, oohing and aahing over the handful of boring box tinsel that Abbie holds out. Later, in the kitchen, I make sure to laugh while she and I bake sugar cookies, laugh loud enough for Dad to hear us, tying flies in the living room. I know what he wants. My first night back home, he came up to my room, sat on the edge of my bed, and asked me, "Do you like her?"

I waited—carol music tinkling up from downstairs, my dad's face looming over me, pale and anxious. I didn't know what to say.

He took my hand. "I love you," he said. "It's important to me how you feel."

Inside me—a long, white whistle of silence.

"My parents never talked to me about anything. Not even when my dad died. Or my sister. I want us to be different. I want us to talk. Do you like her?"

More silence.

"Leifer?"

I looked in his eyes. I said, "Yeah, Dad. I like her. I like her a lot."

He hugged me. His eyes got wet, as if I'd given him some huge, sparkly present.

Days pass, full of fires in the woodstoves, snow up to the sills. I'm tired, for no apparent reason. I sleep ten hours, then go back to bed for a nap. I don't skate, I don't sled. I don't call Francy. I don't go to the grocery store with Dad and Abbie to load up on low-fat eggnog. But I'm relieved when they're gone. I pull down Dad's address book. I find the number under M for Mary and call my nana.

Nana lives on an island off Seattle, deep in the forest. She has a little red house on the beach where we collect seashells. Even though she's Dad's mother and not Mom's, Mom and I stayed with her for a few months before we went on our cross-country trip to Baltimore. She knows about things: my rash, my lice, my nightmares. She says there's nothing you can't fix with a martini or a peanut-butter-and-butter sandwich. She wears her dyed-silver hair sticking straight up and her go-go pink lipstick all over her face, except for her lips. She has a booming voice that's louder—and deeper—than Dad's. All the grown-up relatives call her "a character."

"Love!" she says.

"Nana?" I say. "I wish you were here!"

There's a long crackled quiet.

"I'm going to be the flower girl at Dad and Abbie's wedding. I get to throw rose petals!"

A sharp, sudden breath comes over the phone. Then . . . is that crying? It's deep and mangled. It's awful. It's like Dad crying. Why is she crying? She never cries.

"Are you okay, Nana?"

End of crying sounds. "That's my new dog, love. He got attacked by a raccoon last week. I had to take him to the vet."

"Oh," I say. Then I say something really dumb. I say, "That's so funny, Nana. I got attacked by a raccoon, too. He bit me on the arm." But I'm not crying, the way Nana did when she lied, which made her lying okay. I'm just lying-lying. And Nana knows there are no raccoons in Alaska—only wolverines, which I've never seen.

"I have an idea," she says, very kindly and softly, not like Nana at all. "I'll meet you in Sea-Tac on the way back to Baltimore. We can change planes together. Won't that be fun?"

I hang up. I pull open the golden binder rings that hold the address book together, then let them spring shut. I do this again and again, each time listening to that crisp, office-sounding snap of metal on metal. In three days, I have to stand up and get my picture taken at the wedding. I have to be tougher. I have to suck it up and not cry and not let my face or eyes or voice break and go crumpled. If I didn't fool Nana—even on the phone, where she couldn't see my face and only my voice counted—there's no way I'll survive all those guests and neighbors and cameras.

————

Two days before the wedding, Dad asks me to help load the plane. He and Abbie are flying out to our cabin on Shell Lake as soon as I leave for school. The pile of gear in the garage, as always, takes up enough space for a few trucks. All of it has to be dragged down the icy hill in our backyard. And it is dark out already, and one or two degrees below zero.

First comes our beloved emergency box, a cooler-sized plywood trunk with rope handles. Inside it lies everything you'd ever need to live on in the bush: a tiny stove, fuel bottles, containers of coffee and tea and Tang and liquor, salt and pepper shakers, a tube of matches. But we never use it for emergencies. We use it like a wilderness kitchen. A very heavy wilderness kitchen. You need two people to lift it.

Dad takes one end, I take the other. But I'm carrying without carrying—my glove is on the rope handle without supporting any weight. Dad has to feel what I'm doing. He slings up the whole box himself finally, banging his hand against the wall of the house. He cries out. I wander off, ignoring the blood on his knuckles as I drag sleeping bags through the snow (getting them wet), as I drop tackle boxes (losing lures all over the yard), as I go to the bathroom, spending ten or twenty minutes washing my hands while Dad loads up the ice auger, the rods, the duffel bags, the rifles, the shotguns, and probably another two hundred pounds of miscellaneous equipment.

I can feel the ball of frustration in him, compressing, held tight. Even as I pretend to sweep up the garage, tripping over the broom, spilling the dustpan. He sweeps up for me. Then takes out the garbage cans.

As I head upstairs to my room, he stops me on the steps. "Leigh," he calls up. "There's a couple of presents up there in your room, wrap them up for me, will you?"

"Whose presents?"

"Abbie's."

We're on the landing of the stairs. I start to shake. And this rage, it isn't about Dad and Abbie's wedding or their honeymoon or their matching champagne flutes. It's about the subject directly in front of us—the presents. Because it's all of a sudden obvious: My dad is a cheater. A stinky, lying, disgusting cheater! He's going to try to give Abbie presents that I wrapped, as if he'd wrapped them himself. And I wrap presents perfectly, with tight corners and invisible seams and crisscrossing ribbons like people give each other on soap operas, which I watch in the basement in the dark in Baltimore alone, waiting for Mom to come home from work.

Cheater, I think. You're a cheater! But what comes out of my mouth instead is low and wrong and whispered. "You're a bastard," I say.

"What did you say?"

I lift up my face so he can see my mouth. "I said: You're a bastard." Even before it happens, I know what's coming. Dad lifts up his hand, and then it's slamming toward me, fast and hard and big. I'm ready for it. I deserve it. Except. I duck. And Dad misses, his hand slashing right over my head.

Run, I think. Run. But I can't. I crumple to the floor, right at his boots.

Dad swings me over his shoulder and throws me into my room. I hit the bed and roll off it onto the carpet. The door slams. I wait for a while, then pull the comforter off and lie there on the floor, the late-afternoon moon shafting through the slats of the blinds. I'm crying but that's okay, it's just scared-crying, not the hurt kind.

Hours later, Abbie comes in. She has a plate of moose hot dog with her, cut up into little chewable pieces, as if I were a baby. She holds one out. "Just one bite."

I shut my eyes.

She is quiet for a long time. I hear her breathing. I can feel the warmth of her body in the air, even though she isn't touching me. "I guess," she says, finally, "what your dad's upset about is that you think that way about him."

"What way?"

"That he's a bastard."

But I don't think my dad is a bastard. I don't even know what the word means exactly; it's kind of lumped in with *bitch* and *mother-fucker* and all the other words that float over the playground or come tearing out of people's mouths in movies. I don't know why I didn't just call him a cheater, either. That had been the word in my head. My head and my mouth just didn't work together.

There is a pillow by my arm. I roll over on it and pretend to fall sleep until Abbie goes away. I see my dad, though, later that night, when he opens the door and peeks his head in, almost shyly, as if that big, loud Great Alaskan is somehow afraid of me.

One week later, Abbie and Dad get married in front of the fireplace on New Year's Eve. I'm wearing my Gunne Sax dress, the lace-up bodice of which makes me look, I hope, like Laura Ingalls Wilder heading west on the wagon train, from *Little House on the Prairie* to *By the Shores of Silver Lake.* My hair is pulled back in a French braid, which has been braided at a real beauty salon, in the chair next to Abbie. My nails are painted. Only the bottom half of me lacks glamour. Dad and I forgot about shoes and tights—in Alaska, in December.

I walk down the aisle, which is just a cleared path through the living room, in bare legs and feet. Lou Gallagher, my uncle Steven, and I are the only witnesses. Not even Francy is invited. I'm glad about this. I don't want anybody who knows me looking at me. I just have to focus on my immediate surroundings—the cold air on my toes, the warm of the fire, the droning of the judge, the stabbing of bobby pins that hold my hair stiffly in place—then smile.

There, finally: "I do."

I smile some more. I look over at Dad—smiling!—as the photographer snaps the just-married picture. It's funny. Dad is smiling, too, but a happy, terrified smile, as if the world might turn out to be a bubble and pop. Abbie, on the other hand, is floating on the bubble. She is the shiny rainbow on the soap skin of bubbles.

After the ceremony, all the families on Campbell Lake come over for a party, with exotic Mexican enchiladas and guacamole, plus a carrot cake for dessert. I hate carrot cake. I hate the thick cheesy frosting on it. But I eat it and get my picture taken eating it as proof. Then I sneak off with three neighbor girls and three stolen bottles of champagne. Two of the girls, Lynne and Amy, are sisters who only come up for Christmas. Their parents have been going through a divorce involving court actions and custody battles.

"She looked butt-ugly," says Lynne. "Heinous."

"You just wait," says Amy. "She'll steal all his money, then divorce him, too. That's what all new wives do. My mom says."

I nod, even though I know that none of this is true. I take a slug off the bottle and pass it to Christy, the youngest of us. Her mother has made her wear a nightgown to the party. "Maybe," Christy says, "she'll have a baby. Then we could play with it."

Nobody says anything, not even anything about the baby being born deformed or retarded. I take the champagne back, and go into the bathroom alone. I shut the door, lock it. Then I drink and drink and don't stop until I'm spinning. I wander through the party bare-legged and weaving. Does anybody notice? The bricks in the mantel are going wibble-wobble. The spotlights on the ceiling are twinkle stars. I puke in a trash can in the garage and keep walking.

It's midnight. Dad and Abbie are kissing as people clap. I can't stop myself. My face is runny and it won't listen to me. My face is crying and I'm crying and crying, just the way I trained myself not to. I'm huge and loud and stupid and obvious, wiping it off on the sleeve of my dream dress. I want my mother, that's all I can think, I want my mother.

Luckily, nobody hears me. Nobody notices me at all. They're either tipsy or standing outside, watching other fathers set up a firework station at the center of the lake, far from the shoreline and docks so that the falling sparks won't explode and burn holes in anybody's plane. Last fall, Dad went to Seattle and bought boxes and boxes of Roman candles and cherry bombs at the tribal reservation, then packed them in his suitcase and brought them back to Anchorage.

"Hurry it up," a man shouts.

Dad runs onto the lake to set off the bottle rockets first, lighting the fuses with his cigar, racing back over the ice, slipping and laughing and crashing onto the dock.

I rub my face with a handful of snow and slip on somebody's boots. A small box of kids' fireworks lies by the grill, full of ladyfingers and spinning flowers and little paper tanks. I light all the tanks, one after another. They're my favorites. They've always been my favorite. They roll along the deck, shooting sparks from their cannons, falling off into the snow, where they keep going still—upside down and burning, their paper wheels turning hopefully in the air, until you stomp them, flat and ashy, with your boot.

CHAPTER 6

Summon the Strength

The door to the headmistress's office is made of dark, heavy, dragon-looking wood. I knock, but the handle is also complicated: brass and scrolls and a keyhole that makes me think of the grim-toothed jaws of a Christmas nutcracker. Somehow, fumbling, I get it to turn.

Mrs. Geiger stands up, all six feet of her, her hair streaked with gray, her face hard and carved, masculine. I have never spoken with her alone before. She is like a fountain statue that comes to life in order to shake hands during graduation ceremonies. "May I help you, Miss Newman?" she says, in her low, deep, Swiss-German accent.

Can she help me? I have no idea. Next year, I'm going to be twelve. Next year is the year I've been waiting for—the year I will go back to Alaska, the year I get lost in the bush or Dad gets his hand cut off in a propeller, the year I take up downhill racing and do so well the coach orders me to remain in an alpine climate to train for the Olympics or I fall through the ice while skating and, though suffering no long-term brain damage, lose my eyesight or short-term memory. All of which makes my returning to Baltimore, once that year is over, impossible—no matter what the divorce contract stipulates.

Now, however, living in Alaska means living with Dad and Abbie.

A fly pinballs off the lead glass in the window. Outside, a weed whacker throbs along the hedges below the sill. Mrs. Geiger glances at a wing chair in front of her, one eyebrow raised into a gray-streaked lightning bolt. I sit down. I open my mouth. *Alaska* is an easy word. I can make my lips say it. But there is the Alaska made of letters, the one that comes out of your mouth with rich, snappy *a* and *k* sounds. And then there is the one in my head now, the one that isn't a place or even the-place-where-Dad-and-Abbie-live.

Alaska is me—in scrapbook pictures, in daydreams, in family stories I can't remember, in memories I mix up probably, but believe all the same. The baby in a beaded Native papoose on my dad's back, taking the ferry to Sitka. The toddler in a red velveteen parka, sitting on my mom's lap at Christmas. The loudmouthed girl, pedaling her pink Schwinn through the brand-new subdivision of Chugach Foothills, all the way to where the brand-new streets ended at half a million acres of pristine, federally protected forest.

I'm not very loud anymore. Mostly, I try to survive on mute at this school and up in Alaska, too. But I can remember being loud. I can remember screaming all the way down the driveway on my bike, then hopping off at the end of our asphalt cul-de-sac. First came the meadow tufted with fireweed and high wild grasses. Then came the trees, the endless trees where kids were always waiting—ready to burn twigs or play tag in the shadows, all of us rulers of the neighborhood wilderness.

In our pockets lay the survival essentials: pinecones, rubber bands, firecrackers, granola bars, feathers. Across our legs bumped the white faded scars of raspberry thorns and picked-open mosquito bites. Only our smell harked back to civilization: the comforting reek of deet and Vaseline, and the lingering perfume of no-more-tears shampoos.

In the summer, we fished the drainpipe creek, wandering into rushing, shoulder-high water—and didn't drown. In the fall, we raced out into the chilled clear daylight, jumping up to slap the duck carcasses strung across our garages, aging like laundry drying on a line. A poof of falling dead feathers and we were gone—building a spruce-bough tepee, kicking the can, longing for winter and the Iditarod when we cheered the sled teams on from the end of the street.

The whole neighborhood lined up every February to watch those slender, wolfish dogs. When we grew up, we told the adults, we were going to be mushers. After school, we jerry-rigged leashes into whips and tied our trusting but witless family mutts to our Flexible Flyers, forcing them to pull us for a few glorious dreamlike feet whereupon they immediately flipped us, dragging us underneath our sleds across the snow.

Who were these kids? Even then, I wasn't exactly sure. There was Karen Mayer and Dina Lipton and Rodney, the boy I kissed under his parents' pool table. The names were always changing, the faces on the bus seats always different than the month before. This was Alaska, the land of the boom and the bust. Parents were moving out or moving in or moving on. They were coming to work the pipeline, or leaving to work construction in California or Oregon, or coming back to open a business that didn't exist in the state yet (an exotic Volkswagen dealership or office supply store) or leaving again, transferred by the military or the oil companies to a new town in a distant state or country.

We kids moved as a fluid, anonymous mass of freckles and mittens, runny red noses and slightly frostbit fingers. Until some kind of neighborhood drama occurred, marking us as individuals—like the day we almost got trampled by a moose. We were waiting at the bus stop that morning, in the winter-blued dark. I was in kindergarten. I had on my trusty snowsuit and matching puffy boots.

Angela, an older girl, was the first to spot the cow. Our parents had warned us: Moose might look slow and peaceful, chewing on lawn grass, ambling along with a calf. But a moose will charge you, antlers first. Then finish the job with its hooves. Angela, though, had a savvy, sixth-grade toughness about her. It felt like she was always chewing gum, even when she wasn't. A gang of boys stood behind her.

"I dare you," they chanted.

She flung down her books, dug through the snow. The moose was lumbering along, moving down a line of mailboxes and trash cans, its massive antlers lumbering up from its head, dark weedy hairs dangling from its mouth. It got closer. Angela whizzed a rock at its knees, with a flicking motion, as if she were skipping it. The rock soared over the snow—but missed.

The moose ignored her. Angela got closer, skimmed another rock. The moose ignored her. Angela got even closer, threw another one. Hard. The moose lifted its head. And that's all I had to see. I took off running for home, more afraid of my dad finding out that I had stuck around that long than of the moose. From the safety of my bedroom, I heard the sirens screaming down the street. Angela survived, but with broken ribs and legs.

"We might begin with why you are here?" says Mrs. Geiger, rustling some papers across her desk.

On the wing chair, I swing my legs, the piping on the edge of the cushion cutting into the back of my knees. I'm here because my dad loves Alaska and my mom doesn't, because my dad loves Abbie and not my mom, because Abbie is a good-girl wife and my mom isn't, because I am not a good-girl daughter (or not inside where it counts), because my mom loves me, because now my mom is the only one who loves me and maybe she was the only one who ever did . . . and because some of these thoughts are true and some aren't, and some are and aren't at the same time.

Mrs. Geiger is not going to understand that. Not even I understand that. I have a terrible, goofy feeling I might whip myself up to standing and stick my tongue out at her, or kick a crazy can-can dance around the room the way my mom used to do when Dad refused to go to a movie with Italian subtitles. "Every party has a pooper," she used to sing (kick, kick). "That's why we invited you. Party Pooper. Party Poop!"

Our family wasn't all that awful, was it? Dad used to booby-trap the house, popping out from behind the couch or a door to pin down Mom and me during tickle fights. If Mom didn't want to wake up in the morning, we poured water on her head. If Dad didn't want to eat Mom's chewy, tasteless, overcooked caribou stew, we tied him to a chair, stuffed a sock in his mouth, and hung a sign on his neck that said GONE FISHING. Then took a picture with me on his lap.

On the weekends, with no plane, we drove into the bush in our orange VW camper, casting with a crowd of other Alaskan newbies, elbow-to-elbow, for salmon. We rented boats in silt-covered villages and fished for halibut from the icy, kelp-woven ocean. When winter blew in, we cross-country skied, busting herringbones up the hills outside of town. Our Christmas picture: Papa Bear, Mama Bear, and Baby Bear, wearing hats with snowflake pins and corduroy knickers, drinking cocoa at the end of the day, arguing over who got the most mini marshmallows.

The only not-so-good moment I can remember was Portage Glacier. And even then we all got out of it alive. We even laughed and drank Tang with blue glacier ice (which turns white the minute you remove it from the glacier) in the tent afterward.

Portage Glacier was supposed to be our big family winter trip—a ski across a frozen lake, then camping in the snow in a tent. Only the lake was longer than expected. The clouds darkened, then whitened. A blizzard blew in. For hours, we slogged over the endless, flat expanse of the ice, the wind knifing in our faces. Dad went first, then me, then Mom.

"Keep going," Dad screamed back, over and over. The temperature was dropping. I slid forward on one ski, then the other, trying not to whimper or cry with tiredness. Mom, though, gave up. She tried to turn around. Then tried to get me to go with her, pulling on my ski pole.

"Keep going," Dad said, skiing on.

I didn't know what to do. I sat down in the snow.

Dad, at last, figured out what was happening. He skied back and pulled on Mom's arm, hard, pointing toward the glacier up ahead. She pushed him off her. They were screaming at each other, two red faces in the blinding white.

As they went on screaming I waited and waited, getting colder, trying to stamp my burning numb feet, pinching my fingertips through my mittens. Until they stopped, finally. But not because they had made up. Darkness was falling and we were going to freeze out there in the open.

"Miss Newman," Mrs. Geiger says distantly. "Miss Newman?"

I blink.

"You'll have to summon the strength. Sooner or later." She shuffles through more papers on her desk, dust hovering through the sunlight behind her.

I take a deep breath. Then say, very fast, as if by increasing the speed, I'm not really speaking—"According to my parents' divorce contract, I'm supposed to spend the next school year in Alaska."

"I see."

"I'm not allowed, though, am I? To leave here and go to public school in Alaska for one whole year?"

She looks back down at her papers. My file, evidently. She leafs, frowns, leafs. "Essentially, you are functioning on par with your fellow students. As far as your grades indicate."

"I am?"

"Yes." She nods.

Hmm . . . functioning on par. That doesn't sound too encouraging. Am I flunking like Lindsey Mumford? Does the school *want* me to leave? Now that I know how to do math and read, I keep getting moved to different classes. These are the smart-girl classes, the other girls say. But I'm still the dumb one among all the smarties, who not only have been learning and playing together since age five but also get picked for all kind of special "small group" science experiments and art projects. During recess, I watch them covetously, as they skip off wearing lab goggles or carrying paintbrushes. My ability to spend entire classes watching the shadow patterns of the leaves outside skitter across the ceiling no doubt has something to do with this oversight on the part of the teachers. But it's not possible, is it—to get kicked out of school for daydreaming?

"However," says Mrs. Geiger, "Roland Park Country adheres to a fast-paced, advanced curriculum. In a public school environment, you may fall behind." Long meditative pause. "That would be unfortunate." Longer meditative pause. "Should you choose to return."

"Don't I have to return? I mean, do you want me to return?"

"Let me consider the situation. Let me see what I can do."

"So I'm allowed to go? There's no clause in the handbook?"

She smiles at me—a kindly, shockingly marshmallow smile, as if I'm amusing. But all I am is confused. There has to be a clause in the handbook. Girls at Roland Park Country aren't allowed to wear snow boots when it snows. We're given written exams on the words of the school Christmas carols and condemned to after-school study halls if we don't cross our ankles onstage during glee-club performances. Alaska—and, gasp, public school—has to be against the rules.

The whole plan was for the school to say no for me. That way, I wouldn't have to tell Dad that I don't want to live with him and Abbie.

Mom and I fight all the time. We slam doors. We chase each

other around the house, throwing hairbrushes and the slippers with the hard soles. She'll march right into my room at night and pull down the covers and yell at me for not vacuuming the steps after school and sucking the life out of her. And, the next day, I will march right into hers and break her porcelain hand mirror when she's at work, then pretend a ghost did it—or maybe an intruder.

All this yelling and smashing and crying, though, is easier than sitting down at the picnic table, eating my salmon with Dad and Abbie, as if our Great Alaskan World is perfumed with happiness and blueberries.

I made a jerky mistake last time I was up in Anchorage. I put an old framed picture of me and Mom and Dad in Hawaii on my bureau. We were sitting with our arms around each other, smiling like the kind of stunned loonies you become when you go on vacation someplace sunny after eight months of twenty-hour-a-day darkness. Dad had sunglasses on. Mom had a painted umbrella behind her ear. I wore a muumuu and flip-flops. One day, not long after I'd put it up, the picture just disappeared.

I found it a week or so later, facedown, at the bottom of my sock drawer. I stood there, fingering the velvet-covered cardboard on the back of the frame, careful not to flip it over and look at the three of us together, which would only makes the sharp, stabby feeling in my chest worse. I didn't know who exactly had gone into my room and taken the picture down, but a rule had been established. And if there was one thing Dad didn't tolerate, it was a rule-breaker.

After a final nod from Mrs. Geiger, I shut the office door behind me quietly (no slamming, girls!) and walk (no running, girls!) all the way down the hall to the pay phone. My dime jingles down through the machine.

"Dad?" I say. "My headmistress says I'll never graduate if I go up to Alaska next year so I can't go."

There's a crackle of long distance. Then finally Dad's voice, confused and slow. "Well," he says. "I was sure excited about you coming back."

I put the receiver down on my shoulder. Listening feels too much like looking at his face and the puzzled hurt expression that's on it. The silence continues, nothing but crackles and lies and nothing.

"But I understand," he finally says, his voice getting brighter and phonier and speedier and cheerier with each syllable. "You just keep doing a good job down there!"

"Yeah, Dad." I pray for the recorded voice to come on the line and ask me for another dime. I called collect, though, as always. I can talk for as long as I want to—and so can Dad. He has plenty of time to tell me that he's going to call my headmistress up and tell her what he thinks of her so-called educational system; in fact, now that he's at it, he's going to come down there and pull me out of that snot-nosed school himself.

But he only says, "I'm real proud of you. We'll get another year together, maybe. Sometime. If we put our minds to it. Right?"

"Love you," I say—fast, like ripping off a strip of duct tape. "Bye!"

"Bye!" he says.

Then I do what I always do. I listen to the long, hiss-filled silence, waiting to see who hangs up first. It's me this time, for the very first time ever. It doesn't feel the way I imagined. There's no drama or triumph, no angry smash. There are no tears. It's just an everyday action—receiver, cradle, walk away.

PART II

The Middle
of the Woods

CHAPTER 7

Dividing the World

In the open ocean, most of swimming is just keeping afloat. I don't have fins or a wet suit, either of which would help my buoyancy. First, I tread water. A ragged wave slops by, then another, and another—each the dense marine navy that in the Galapagos confirms you have left the cozy turquoise shallows of a bay for the cold deep Pacific. I flip over on my back, breathe, and try to relax.

Above me, nary a seabird, nary a cloud—the sky a sweep of thin, endless blue. The last hour has been one of the moving experiences of my twenty-six-year-old life. And who did I share it with? The passengers on board the rustic ship that I'm writing about for *Travel Time* magazine, who watched me dive off a small raft and into a pod of dolphins, only to resurface fifty feet away, holding on to a dolphin's fin, then disappear again, dragged along beside it, a human ribbon in the wake of its speed.

Dolphins, it turns out, move very, very fast.

Had it been possible, I would have liked to stop right at the instant I hit the water and scooted, frog-kicking, along the sandy bottom. The dolphins were swimming near a small, rocky reef when they suddenly turned and headed straight toward me. There were four or five, all making clicking noises. I tried to make the same kind of noise. The largest stopped and swam directly at me—stopping only a few feet from my face. He opened his mouth, exposing his tongue. I couldn't explain why, but I reached over and very slowly, very gingerly put my hand inside his mouth. Then I left it there, my palm on the ridges of his teeth.

For a few seconds, neither of us moved. Then, suddenly, he swam around me in circles, presenting his fin. I grabbed on, and he surged forward, heading up to the surface. I pulled in a quick breath, and he took us back down. Only then did I see the mother dolphin and her baby swimmingly directly underneath us, another male to my one side, and yet another male on top of us. Some people might think of this as being boxed in. But it didn't feel that way to me. It felt as if I'd been accepted by a dolphin family.

Something about this seemed so comforting, and at the same time so disorienting and dreamlike, as if I'd just jumped up on a stage filled with trained dancers and begun to flit through the choreography of a ballet I'd never seen. The dolphin shifted, and so did I, wriggling slightly to keep in his slipstream. We were moving so quickly, and with the froth of the water and bubbles, I couldn't see above the hump of his body. We just shot forward—faster and faster.

Until we hit the chop of the Pacific. All of a sudden we were out of the bay, and we weren't stopping, either. Only then did I begin to ask: Hey, exactly how far am I going to go with this? And by *far*, I knew I meant more than the distance back to the shore. I had a thing I could do. To other people it often looked like courage or bravado. But it was really the ability to turn my mind off completely and act—without thinking, without planning or making decisions or considering the future, sometimes to the point of what should have been bodily harm or unpleasant consequences, save for the fact that I generally came to at the last second and wriggled out of it.

As if on cue, a wave slapped me hard and flat in the face. I pulled my head above the surface. There was no island up ahead, no boat. I let go of the dolphin. He and the others circled around me, butting my legs with their snouts before, finally, swimming away.

Two weeks later, I'm sitting in my New York cubicle. A few desks away glints a window with a view of the city's Midtown forty-three floors below: black asphalt roofs, the white rectangles of passing buses, the occasional pink flash of day-dulled neon. My own desk is scrupulously clear of signs of life, save for certain key items: computer, half-eaten burrito, hula doll.

The hula doll is our magazine mascot. She's a brown, curvaceous piece of plastic. I continue pulling out blades of cellophane grass from her skirt. She smiles on—a human pineapple.

My article about the Galapagos is due in eight hours. And though *Travel Time* is not exactly the hottest-selling publication in the country—it's not displayed on the newsstand, for example, has lost over a third of its ad pages, and is teetering on the verge of bankruptcy—I'm supposed to do my job: write a fun, peppy piece about three different ways to see this archipelago of fourteen islands so crucial to the theory of evolution. Why not kick it off with my own experience? It's an adventure story with a joyful, life-affirming ending. The driver of the raft found me a few minutes after the pod took off, scooped me back into the boat, and hugged me.

Everybody—no matter how experienced with the animal or jaded by the turquoise rings and new-age dreamcatchers made in its image—loves a dolphin.

But the whole episode is suddenly acutely embarrassing. First off, even though I don't live in Alaska anymore, I'm still from there— right?—and I'm supposed to know better. In the bush, you don't mess with the wildlife. You don't pretend an undomesticated animal is your dog or your friend. You don't offer a depressed-looking grizzly bear a lick off your soft-serve double dip. What happens when people do this is that they get mauled or eaten and, if that happens, the animal that killed them has to be killed by Fish and Game.

True, the dolphins probably weren't going to kill me, and the wildlife there—sea lions to penguins to sharks—has little fear of man, due to the isolation of the islands. But by swimming with one, by putting my hand in its mouth, I didn't exactly set the best precedent for the animals, who might just think the next band of poachers who show up—looking for specimens for their new dolphin show at Funtime Ocean Prison Park—just want to be buddies and hang out.

Then there's the whole reasoning problem. The moment in my mind happened so quickly, a mental sneeze. But it did happen. In the water, I'd thought, *I'm being accepted by a dolphin family,* when I hadn't been accepted at all. Joining the dolphins isn't like joining the circus. They're dolphins, and I'm a human. In the ocean, the lack of a dorsal fin, not to mention a blowhole to refill your lungs with oxygen in a fifth of a second, is a serious barrier to intimacy.

Even worse, while discussing the matter with myself, I'd used the word *family,* when the correct word, so obviously, is *pod.*

At this point in my adult life, I don't see a lot of my far-flung but completely land-bound family. Mom still lives in Baltimore. On Thanksgiving, we get together at a hotel and eat fading turkey off a buffet basked in heat lamps. Dad still lives in Alaska, where he and Abbie now have two kids of their own, boys, ages eleven and fourteen. I see them up in Anchorage for Christmas.

I think a lot about Dad's kids, though. They aren't teenagers in my mind or even children. They're still babies, my little brothers. The "half" part of our relationship never really stuck. Even now, I still don't know how this came to pass. I was twelve when Daniel, the elder, was born. I had dark, elaborate plans. I was going to hate that baby or ignore that baby or at least dislike him a lot, while somehow hiding it enough to keep Dad and Abbie from realizing. I came up for the summer of 1983, sullen and terrified on the inside, smiling like the fourth runner-up for Junior Miss Anchorage on the outside.

In August, via salad tongs and a lot of screaming, the baby arrived. Dad took me to the hospital. Abbie was sitting up in the remote-control bed, straight out of a Renaissance painting—all glowing skin and intricate, folded sheets. Even after twenty-four hours of straight, unmedicated labor, she looked fresher and more put-together than me. And the baby in her arms was so little, so bony, so ugly and helpless. What was with his forehead? It seemed to have extended off his face into a long, gruesome skull funnel.

"You can hold him," Abbie said.

I stepped back. If I were a mom, I'd be thinking, *Get away from my delicate, deformed-headed baby! And by the way, I know you never wash your hands after you go number one!*

But to my surprise, she held him out, still wrapped in a blanket. It was like holding a fluffy human chick. Don't squeeze him, I told myself. Don't drop him, either. He was so warm. How did babies get so warm? I held him really close. I looked into his eyes—two little blue yawns in the middle of his face.

He looked back, blinked.

"Hello," I said, but in my secret voice, the tiny, squeaky one I used with sleeping dogs, to make them thump their tails on the carpet with dreamy contentment—but without waking up.

One year later, Daniel was a lot better looking. He had blond hair, baby chub, and an acceptable-shaped head. Strange new grown-ups were always coming over with presents for him. These were Dad and Abbie's new friends—lawyers, accountants, neighbors who arrived with bottles of Hansen's Natural boysenberry juice instead of a six-pack of Oly Gold. They wore khakis instead of jeans and hip boots, not to mention plush, outdoorsy Patagonia pullovers. When in town, they played tennis instead of tied flies, and talked about weekend camping trips where they had charted Arctic stars and cooked Asian noodles over the fire.

Not one of them carried a Roman candle in a pocket, much less an electric-shock remote control for their duck-hunting dog, should it attempt to hump our living room sofa. This was because they left their dogs at home—in favor of their babies, which they wore, slung like canteens, in quilted bags around their chests. There was Jill with the seven-month-old and Russ with the toddler and Dee-Dee with the fraternal twins.

All of them said the same thing, as soon as they saw me at the front door: "Jim, I didn't know you had a daughter!" They said this in the nicest voice, as if it were a wonderful surprise—cake with candles, on no one's birthday. Sometimes they even patted me on the head.

I smiled. I admired their babies. Then I went upstairs and stared at the crack in my bedroom wall that squiggled down from the window to the start of the carpet. Dad had sat me down the first week of summer to explain a few things: He was trying to make some positive changes in his life. He was trying to be less angry, to talk more. He was seeing a therapist. The new friends had something to do with this. Still, he could have told them that I existed.

Maybe I didn't come up in the course of conversation. And I could see why I wouldn't, not just in professional chitchat but in Dad's head. I was the last thing left over from before all his positive changes. Everything else negative and old was gone: our house, our dogs, our blue plane, even wrinkled, red-haired Pam, our housekeeper, who had come over in secret once after Dad and Abbie had "let her go." She'd brought me the Christmas candies she used to make, the ones that looked like pieces of broken colored glass dusted with sugar. I went out to the porch to cram them in my mouth and whisper that I loved her. Then she hugged me—and went away.

Unfortunately, I was unable to blame all these events on Daniel. I tried really hard. I blamed him just fine as long as I was in my room alone. But then he'd barge in and touch my face, sticking his fat baby fingers in my ears or up my nose with such experimentation, as if he were deeply curious, both about the sinus cavity in general and the depth of my nostril in particular. Love rolled in, in huge gulping waves that compelled me to spin him by his feet, around and around until he staggered over to the dog bed, laughed, and puked out whole tortellini.

Great Alaskan Babies, apparently, took a lot of work—just to keep them from not eating shot powder in the garage or toddling through the backyard and into the lake. Dad didn't have much time for hunting or hiking or fishing. This should have been liberating. I was thirteen. I was supposed to spend my time shoplifting eye shadow at Longs Drugs or trying to meet boys who went to nearby Dimond Junior High. I, however, had a humiliating outdoor secret. I was the only Alaskan I knew who hadn't caught a king.

Kings are the salmon that made the state famous, the fish that embody exactly what their name implies. They are the great, the glorious, the royal inheritors of the kingdom of all fish, gleaming with a scaled, green-speckled brilliance, soaring up from the water with grace and authority that makes you hear trumpets and bugles in the rush of rapids.

And yet it is not that difficult to catch one. Tourists do it all the time, plunked by their thousand-dollar-a-day fishing guides into rivers rife with other tourists. Even my mother did it, a woman who first waved "hello!" to a grizzly bear before it roared into her face on the Kodiak River, then and only then remembering to jump back in the raft and escape.

Dad had caught hundreds of kings. But then he could catch anything. Back in town, that's all the adults ever had to say about him.

When I met a friend's parents or a neighbor, they never mentioned that my dad was a doctor or a pilot. They said, "Your father's Jim Newman? Why, he's a pretty good fisherman." Or, "Your dad sure can fish." Which is the most fawning compliment that any Alaskan fisherman can give another, fish praise being perhaps the only exception to the statewide love of overstatement.

Dad wasn't the first in our family to become so obsessed. The Newmans had moved west from Kentucky after the Civil War (where they had been spies for the Confederacy), eventually giving birth to Walter Martin Sterling, my great-great-great-uncle, who, according to my nana, was "an ardent outdoorsman, trout fisherman, hunter, skier, and picnicker," and my great-great-great-grandfather the Reverend Abiathar Newman, a Presbyterian minister, who begot four grim, starched-looking children and took off into the wilderness to catch rainbows, and "was never heard from again." All this I knew from a little homemade book that Nana wrote for me about Newman outdoor lore.

I, on the other hand, had yet to live up to my fishing potential. While supposedly casting, I spent a lot of time on the bank flicking water off my line to watch it sparkle in the sun or building mermaid houses out of yellow froth from the stream. And ever since Mom and I had left for Baltimore, I no longer ice fished or spent the winters with Dad tying flies to get ready for the summer ahead.

That July, I realized I needed help. Actually, I needed everybody's undivided attention. In particular, my dad's attention. All of it. Right now. Even if that particular morning, Daniel was sitting in his high chair, throwing lumps of scrambled egg at the dining room window—*thunk, thunk, thunk.*

"Is this formula?" Dad said bleakly, looking down at his mug. "Did I just pour formula into my coffee?"

"You ate dog food once," said Abbie. "Don't worry about it."

"Dad?" I said, kicking his chair. "I want to catch a king."

The kitchen went silent. Dad sat up and casually sipped at whatever it was in his mug. "That sounds like fun, Leifer. We'll try Deep Creek this weekend." Which was exactly what we did. Abbie packed up Daniel and a garbage bag full of his spit-up-coated toys. Dad threw the car seat into the back of the plane. And we were off.

The whole weekend, Daniel gurgled in the playpen while I worked the bank. Dad stood a few yards downriver, flinging over suggestions, lures, roars of approval. All of which resulted in . . . no king. On Monday morning, we moved on to Theodore Creek, then Bear Creek, Lake Creek, the weeks and weekends completely dedicated to king catching. We fished on logs and on beaches and in the water, up to our armpits. We fished with Pixies, teaspoons, Mepps No. 4 spinners, No. 5 spinners, rooster tails, and tadpole plugs. We fished with canned salmon eggs, fresh salmon eggs, fresh salmon eggs on a hot-pink yarn fly that Dad designed and tied for spin rods.

No king. The season was ending. With Dad's help, I began hitting the river at 4 A.M., when the water was still and the bugs were hatching and fish were supposedly starving. No king. I stayed until the midnight sunset, when the water was still, the bugs hatching, the fish also supposedly starving. No king. I watched Dad catch kings and approximated happiness for him. I watched Abbie catch kings and tried not to openly cry. I fished with lead weights, dragging my lure along the bottom of the river, then fished off the edge of our inflatable raft, trolling through deep fast water. I even fished on the banks of the village of King Salmon, right off the dock like some jerky tourist. No king.

And still, I didn't give up. But standing up to my waist in fifty-degree water, casting and casting and casting, I suspected why I wasn't succeeding, despite my slavish obedience to Dad's philosophy that fishing has to be an obsession for it to work. My hook was in the water. I was now obsessed.

But obsessed with what? I didn't know—or couldn't say. But I knew it wasn't kings. And deep in the water, rushing by my lures and flies and wader boots, the great and mighty kings must have known that it wasn't them, either. They were punishing me, in fact, for going through the motions, for being an imposter, for doing everything that my dad said to do to catch them, just so that nobody could say I hadn't done my best.

"You'll get one," Dad kept saying, bringing me hot chocolate on the bank or a new glob of fish eggs. "It just depends on when."

Or: "I never liked kings all that much. They're overrated as a species."

Or: "You know, sometimes I don't catch fish, either. Then I just knock off and relax and come back in a few days."

Did he suspect the truth? I worked the river harder. I stayed on the bank longer. And finally, one fateful day in deep July, on the banks of Theodore Creek, I hooked a king—and leaped off my spot on the sunken driftwood log, reeling and crashing downstream, fighting that heavy, headstrong liquid cannonball of a fish and trying not to lose him, praying my God please don't let me lose him, pulling him in at long last, holding him up, showing the world my thirty pounds of gasping, silver victory. But I wasn't ecstatic. I wasn't joyous. I was relieved. My father snapped a picture, then framed it and placed it right where I'd always dreamed of having it placed: the Wall of Outdoor Honor.

The Wall of Outdoor Honor was a small blank patch of Sheetrock directly above Dad's fly-tying desk. On it hung the stuffed thirty-two-inch rainbow trout that he caught on a dry fly, a trout the size of a salmon (the average size of rainbow being eight pounds), as well as the framed, ripped tails of Abbie's blue oxford shirt, cut off by her flight instructor after her first solo flight.

And then there was the photograph of me. I was squatting on the gravel, holding on to my just-caught, thirty-pound Theodore Creek king like a real Alaskan. Save for the fact that even a smallish trophy of the species weighs in at sixty or seventy pounds. Save for the fact that I had caught mine on an amateur lure with a treble hook instead of an expert, hard-to-set fly.

Any real Alaskan who saw that picture up on the wall would know exactly what it was—and so would any real Newman, like my brother and like any other babies that were going to come after him. Because they were going to grow up and learn to hike and learn to hunt and learn to catch the kind of fish that actually belonged here—difficult-to-catch, record-sized, legitimate fish. They were going to spend a lifetime with my dad in the bush, not just the summers. They were going to see all the desperate chasing-after in what I had done, which is all I could see looking at the photograph—in my smile, in my averted eyes, in my fresh, incandescent, hard-won king. I would have taken it off the wall, but Abbie or Dad might have noticed. And I couldn't think of a lie believable enough to serve as an excuse.

Moving from place to place, you develop routines to ease any confusion. Like never opening your suitcase your first day home. An open suitcase only leads to long hours doing load after load of tedious laundry, which, in turn, only leads to your leaving for somewhere, anywhere else because you feel too overwhelmed about everything that needs to be done to get your life in that particular location started up again.

I've been back from the Galapagos for three days and my still-packed duffel is lumped in the corner of my apartment, saggy and abandoned, looking at me as if to say, *You know there are swimsuits in here, right? The ones you didn't bother to dry? Not to mention that seashell you insisted on taking, with those potent bits of recently deceased sea creature spackled onto the mother-of-pearl?*

I ignore it, in favor of a long acclimating walk in the dark. I do this almost everywhere I go, but in New York I have a specific route, which takes me in a long, slanted rectangle around the island of Manhattan. Light spills out of the matzo factory across the street. A pit bull barks, left loose on the fire escape to guard his owner's window.

I walk and walk, up from the Lower East Side to Midtown then to the Upper East Side then back down Fifth Avenue to the West Village. The city at night is never as loud as it seems in movies, or as urban. Under the lights and smoke and bar talk dribbling through the open doors, the smell of ocean floats through the alleys of downtown; the smell of trees lingers up by the park. I lean into the wind, my hands clenched into a fist with my house key poking out between my fingers so that if somebody jumps me, I'll be ready to jab him in the eye. It's a trick a chatty homeless lady on my block taught me, though I don't see her tonight as I wind through the East Village, past the empty park and after-hours gambling club.

At moments like these, strangely enough, this loud, overrun island reminds me of Alaska. It's cold here in New York. It's hard to survive: to secure food and a warm place to sleep, to not get killed by a random bullet or a thoughtless mistake on your part, such as wandering into the path of a bus or subway, which is not unlike wandering into a grizzly or moose, in that these are all encounters with things that don't have a lot of empathy about your life or death, things much larger and faster than yourself.

And then there are the people. Somebody somewhere with a PhD and an interest in human paradoxes has got to be charting the official relationship between danger and dreamers. Alaska is full of dreamers, and so is New York. Here, they're going to be Broadway stars or Wall Street titans. They're finally going to be rich and famous and happy. There, they're going to discover gold in a collapsed Arctic mine, or buy a boat and haul in million-dollar catches of Alaskan king crab. They're finally going to be rich and famous and happy.

For the past five years—my on-and-off tenure in New York—I've noticed these similarities. I'd like to think that I choose to stay here because of them. But when it comes right down to it, I'm not really living in this city. I'm not really living anywhere.

Instead I've moved around the world in decadent, short-term stretches: two weeks in Oslo, three weeks in New York, three weeks in Bora-Bora, two weeks in New York. I've flown down the Loire in a farmer's crop duster, studying the formal gardens of French châteaux. I've studied art restoration in Florence and flower arranging in Japan. I've danced with a band of transvestite Indian boys in the desert near Pakistan and gone just over the heavily armed border to buy smuggled cigarettes from a guy with a camel. Often it feels as if these trips are daydreams—thick, rich fantasies with sound and smell and color, snow and roses, saffron and castles.

New York, however, feels even less real. It's true that *Travel Time* pays me next to nothing (a lot of people want to be travel writers; there's no real incentive to pay me a reasonable wage). But my so-called home base used to be an experimental theater. It still sort of looks like one—a vast, filthy linoleum space, with a couch and a mattress left by the previous tenant. For a table, I nailed together some scrap wood and a Formica counter that I found on the street. I haven't bought curtains or a toothbrush caddy. Everything I own fits in the two duffel bags that I keep in the closet, including my one appliance: my answering machine.

Snow is falling in St. Petersburg—feathering the cobblestones, the dusty, unpaved sidewalks. The sky is wide and white, the breeze warm and smelling of the sea. People nod as they pass, as if the snow is a secret that everyone shares but will not ruin by acknowledging out loud. Even the Mafia men guarding the entrance of my hotel have to struggle not to smile behind their machine guns.

The city spreads out—twisting boulevards, sunset-colored palaces, long gray canals crossed by bridges like fluttery, stone parades. I hurry on to the Mariinsky Theatre, a French fountain of a building, beruffled with nineteenth-century plaster moldings. The entrance, however, is nothing more than a few bare benches lit by jaundice-colored 1960s fluorescents. The guard is still smoking, as he has been for the past week. The turnstile remains locked.

"Maybe today?" I ask.

He grunts and turns a page of his newspaper.

I sit down on a bench. It's been five years since the Communists cleared out of Russia. But the mentality remains rigidly in place. I faxed the ballet director every day for weeks before coming. He never responded—a detail that I failed to tell my editor, having been too overcome by my lifelong desire to get here, too busy hustling the article idea: How was the world's most prestigious ballet troupe faring in the new Russia, a land of capitalism, democracy, and zero state funding?

Eight hours sludge by. Dancers exit and enter—not in tutus or sweaty ripped leg warmers. They wear miniskirts and thick nude-colored hose and blue eye shadow, slathers of it, as if they're actresses or very thin, graceful hookers with foot deformities that cause them to waddle. The guard never so much as glances up from his ashtray at their passage. He has a phone in his booth, in addition to that ashtray. Rotary.

I have to do something, or I'll go back to New York without a story. Without a story, there will be no job. Without a job, there will be no more traveling. And I can't function in everyday professional adult society. My one and only full-time job was with a New York book publisher, for eight long, anxious, ego-crippling months, after which my boss, an editor, sat me down and said, "You're the worst assistant I've ever had. You can't xerox. You can't take phone messages. You need to do something that doesn't require team playing."

Like what? I thought. Violin?

Now I wish I had asked him that question—sincerely. Because he was right. I'm not a team player. I would like to change this, but how? Growing up in the wilderness, packing in your own drinking water, trained not to trust your own father when he says your safety is on does not make for great team playing. And in Baltimore, where the girls knew all about teams—how to sling a lacrosse ball from pouch to pouch, how to knock a polo ball from galloping pony to galloping pony, how to drunkenly but accurately whack your best friend's croquet ball into the poison ivy—I never made the team, which by the way came with a white blazer, a deb party, and a wedding to a boy from the boys' school across the street.

Instead, at age fourteen, I went to Japan, for the most part, on my own. Roland Park Country offered all kinds of overseas exchange programs to Russia, Paris, Istanbul. I happened to score the only free one—a trip to Japan, where my job was to represent the United States as a "youth ambassador." What I did was appear on television (talking about how much Americans loved Japan), tour steel factories (admiring molten metals and bowing to plant managers), and visit schools (attempting calligraphy with preapproved student hosts). At night, I ate five-course French dinners in luxury hotels, the table stocked with local dignitaries wearing Italian suits.

There were five or six other kids my age on this trip, living with host families. But I had been separated from the group in order to perform many of these official functions, mostly, I suspect, because when it came to fermented bean curd, I was open to the idea. I liked eating all that salty, raw, unidentifiable food, some of which may or may not have been still alive. I liked approximating the seventeen intricate steps of a four-hundred-year-old tea ceremony and disassembling a robotic toilet in an attempt to get it to flush. I liked driving around in minivans with drunk grown-ups, doing backseat karaoke, and hiking through sweltering Japanese jungles, fighting off greedy monkeys and sampling pickled radishes from a bent, wrinkled master briner in his rickety hut. Most of all, I loved my hotel. I could have lived there forever in my room on the sixty-fifth floor, accessed by a talking, translucent elevator that whooshed you up so fast it was as if you were being vacuumed straight to heaven on a chip of glass.

Back in America, I had to fly five thousand miles to see either of

my parents, and yet it had never occurred to me that I could go anywhere else. The world was a tiny, fixed planet consisting of a handful of familiar, comforting airports (Sea-Tac and O'Hare) and two
distant hometowns, neither of which, at this point, felt much like
home.

Japan rebuilt the map, down to the key and directions. I had a
new place to go—not south, not north—just out. At age eighteen, I
moved to California, then to France, then back to California, then
to Boston, then to New York, then to France (Paris, plus three other
cities), then back to New York. During this period, I attended four
colleges—the longest stretch spent, to my high school counselor's
completely unchecked surprise, at Stanford. I couldn't really settle
on any one subject, so I double-majored (English? economics?) and
almost completed a third (drama?). After graduation, I couldn't really
settle on a job or geography or lease. I worked as a temp. I rented
rooms. Finally, I landed a two-month-long gig fact-checking at a
retirement magazine. My office was the company supply closet. I sat
at a desk surrounded by shelves filled with boxes of ballpoint pens.

There, in the inky-smelling quiet, I knew in a dim way—the idea
would flash on and off—that other people who had gone to Stanford had moved on to things like the Olympics and Harvard Law
School and the House of Representatives. My own trajectory to the
supply closet didn't bother me very much. But what I was envious of
was the internal clarity these former schoolmates seemed to have—
and, in most cases, had always had, which had resulted in their current lives. These were people who had refused to let anyone take
their picture with a keg cup during frat parties, for fear of where it
might pop up later in their political life, people who had written
poems and sent them to one of the seventeen Nobel Prize winners on
the faculty, along with a note saying "I'm going to be a poet. Could
you help me get an internship at the *Paris Review* this summer?"

Not only did I not know what the internationally famous, award-
winning *Paris Review* was, but saying you wanted to be a poet for

even a part-time Great Alaskan twenty-one-year-old was like saying you wanted to be a mermaid. I could predict the outcome of that scenario.

Me: *I want to be a mermaid, Dad.*

Dad: *Okay. Be the one who drinks the potion and grows legs and gets a job.*

The supply closet did, however, come with the perk of a paycheck—though no health care or retirement plan. One day, on the way to the bathroom, I ran into an editor who worked at a new magazine next door. We started talking about our rogue communal copier, which morphed into a discussion about Faulkner and the art of writing short stories. Out of nowhere, she offered me a job at her new shop, *Travel Time.*

"I'm not the right fit, probably," I said. "I'm on my way to Indonesia. Then Vietnam. And maybe Laos?"

She gave me a look, the kind that makes you look at yourself and see that you're a total idiot. "Well," she said. "You can work in a closet and travel on your dime. Or you can work for me at my *travel* magazine. With a *travel* budget."

Which is why I'm here, staring holes into the head of a post-Soviet guard. A man who is *not* going to cause me to lose the only job I may ever be capable of doing, a job that is the greatest job on the planet, thank you very much. I get up off the bench and stomp out the front door to the street. There are no real stores in St. Petersburg, unfortunately, except for oddball, Mafia-run basement places selling cherry juice, zippers, and ninety-dollar jars of knockoff caviar. A girl hustles by me on the sidewalk—eye shadow, miniskirt, bare legs, cheesy gold-painted heels.

"I'll give you forty dollars for your clothes," I say.

She looks at me. Maybe I guessed wrong; she doesn't speak English.

"Okay, fifty, plus the shoes and pantyhose."

She goes on looking, looking, looking. Maybe she thinks I'm

some kind of female American pervert. There are a lot of loose, confusing perverts in the new and improved Russia.

"Fine. A hundred. And I'll give you my clothes. Okay?"

Her face lights up. The average non-Mafia salary is about seventy dollars a month. She starts stripping down behind a corner.

At the theater, I pause before entering in my borrowed clothes. I'm a dancer, I remind myself, I belongIbelongIbelongIbelong. This is a pod of human beings this time, not dolphins—people who speak a language I don't speak and walk funny and wear too much gloppy, off-color foundation. On the desk, the rotary phone rings. A man with a suit and briefcase whisks by through the turnstile. I straighten up, apply a busy, tired, artistic look, and waddle past the guard, who does not look up, not even to register my attempt at cleavage.

Which was a lucky break, I realize later that night, in my palatial pink grande-dame hotel, after a full day of successful interviews with dancers and teachers. Cleavage would have been a serious error. My boobs are fat American boobs. Only my borrowed clothes and imitation waddle saved me. And, just possibly, my busy artistic face—a face that somehow came naturally to me, assumed without any thought or planning; I simply looked at the girls and slid their features and attitude onto my own, down to the raised eyebrow.

Looking in the bathroom mirror, I try the face again. *Hello.* Then drop it. *Good-bye.*

It's not unfathomable why I can pull off this unsettling but evidently useful trick. There was a long, embarrassing period in Baltimore, of course, when I did try to fit in. I was a teenager. I worshipped the ease of the girls in my class, their passing laughter, their station wagons slathered with beach permits and stickers of schools named like English dukes (Sir Bates, Lord Groton).

Thus began my campaign. Luckily for me, anything new in Baltimore was considered showy. That included clothes. I filched ratty ragg-wool sweaters and exquisitely ripped T-shirts extolling bars in Martha's Vineyard from the school's lost and found. I stole money from my mother's wallet. I dumped the one or two old friends I had and insinuated myself into any group that would tolerate a girl who didn't really talk but was always somehow awkwardly present, even if she had been elegantly and, at times, even kindly dismissed. Most of all, I trained my face to hold very still, or curve into a careless smile, when that entire group would spot me approaching, then jump in a car and drive away, leaving me standing in the parking lot, holding on to my backpack as if its pocket and zippers held the secrets to the universe.

This was not unlike the training for Dad and Abbie's wedding—a training that once started I couldn't really deactivate. By this time, seven years had passed and I'd still said nothing about what had happened during the divorce. I might cry about having to pump the plane floats or pluck the ducks for dinner, but that was safe crying, I told myself, that just looked like a spoiled eastern prep-school fifteen-year-old crying about having to do her chores.

Any time I couldn't disguise my expression, I left the house. The Bardells—the family of four older, savvier kids who used to babysit me—still lived next door. I fled to their house of teenage wonders, complete with ZZ Top videos, unsupervised three-wheelers, and the occasional handed-down very berry wine cooler.

That is, until Dad trapped me one night with a dinner at the Black Angus. I knew something was in the works. Dad preferred much more subtle, adult places to eat, places that served minuscule black coffees, with assorted bricks of European sugar. He had sophisticated tastes when it came to eating raw shellfish, playing Bach on the piano (every day), and collecting rare French wines (which he called Château Blow Your Dough and stored in the crawl-space cellar he built under the gun closet). A lot of Great Alaskan Dads and Moms were this way. They had passed through a lot of urban capitals before coming up north, gathering higher degrees and home libraries full of obscure novels—as well as an intense dislike of people who talked too much about these things or who made others feel badly for not having these things.

I, however, like a lot of Great Alaskan kids, had been going to the Black Angus since age six. I loved it. It was tucked into a strip mall in downtown Anchorage. The wallpaper was saloon-style velvet, the chairs branded with cattle irons, and, to order, you got to pick your own cut from a platter of raw fatty steaks, displayed tableside on a cart by the waiter.

Mostly Dad and I talked about fishing, as if we still did it together, or we talked about what dessert we were going to have: chocolate sundae versus key lime pie. Right before leaving, though, Dad announced he was worried: I was distant. I was moody. I was never home. "Are you a pot smoker?" he said, in a grim but tender voice. "If you are, you can tell me."

"Pot?" I said, laughing.

"I'm serious. It's natural, you know, to want to try drugs and so on. What I mean is . . . I'm your father. I don't want you running around Anchorage, stoned out of your gourd. This is a rough town. Girls get raped here. They get killed! They get . . . you get the idea. What we could do is . . . I could get you some dope or some acid, what have you. You could invite your friends over and have a sleepover in the family room and do drugs—in a safe, controlled environment."

All I could picture was me and a few of the younger Bardells in nightgowns and pajamas, sitting cross-legged on down bags on the carpet, watching *Flashdance* on the VCR and tripping our eyeballs off while Dad patrolled the perimeter with a tranquilizer gun slung over his shoulder, in case any of us tried to jump out the window.

It was so kind what he was doing, trying to help me. But it also gave me prickles all over. I didn't know how to respond, other than to say, in a wooden, cheerful, completely nonbelievable voice, "Dad. I don't get stoned."

Dad nodded, with a curt expression that let me know he knew I was lying. Everything would have been so much better if I could have just said, *Dad, I've tried weed, but that's not why I'm moody and never home. And by the way, why I'm moody and never home is—*

I couldn't afford to name the thought, not even with myself. I knew I wouldn't cry if I did. But I knew I'd sink, right there at the table—fast.

Moody, on the other hand, was doable. Dad thought I was moody. I had to stop being moody. I smiled and slapped on my Alaska face—one that said *It's all okay, Dad, I love you and you love me, let's just go shoot something and stop talking.* But the Alaska face was different from the Baltimore one. The Alaska face was openly happy. It was not at all careless or blasé. And it was a lot harder, it took a lot more effort, because it used to belong to me. It used to be my real face.

Now, in this Russian bathroom, so faraway and grown-up, it seems so clear what I've been doing. For the past decade, no matter where I've traveled or lived, when people ask where I'm from, the first thing I do is ask them where *they're* from. If they say a city or town in the East Coast or Europe, I say, "I'm from Baltimore," leading us to talk about history, museums, and people we might know via familiar schools and friends. If they're from the Midwest or the West or another outdoorsy place like Chile or Tibet, I say Alaska, leading us to talk about sled dogs and fly-fishing. Dividing the world like this ensures that we'll have things in common to discuss, that they'll be more comfortable, which means I'll also be more comfortable. There is, however, an added bonus: I don't have to explain about me or my family.

Your strength is your weakness, my editor in chief likes to say (usually referring to my ability to eat three hamburgers without getting ill). Leaning over the hotel sink, looking in that gilded, imitation Peter the Great–style mirror, I have to wonder if all my malleability has resulted in an upside as well as a down. I *can* fit in. I can move my face around. I can move my whole personality around.

For the next two days, I chat about Nebraska with a pimply Russian teenager in charge of the spotlights who dreams of moving to Minneapolis. I trade knock-knock jokes with two ten-year-old girls auditioning for the Kirov, and discuss with adult corps members how to survive nine-hour rehearsals—and life in general—on one bowl of meatless borscht per day. I'm invited to parties in squats in dark, boarded-up, unheated palaces, and drink sixty-dollar-a-glass champagne in a dark, terrifying Mafia bar filled solely with men and exceptionally threatened hookers—many of whom, it turns out, love ballet. I have enough material to fill an entire magazine.

On my last night, I walk into the opening performance of *Gisele* with the head of the company, a beautiful panther of a man. He's in all black; I'm in all gold, finally having landed the chance to wear the one evening dress I always bring in my duffel, just in case. Every eye in the gallery swerves our way, and a murmur ripples through the crowd. It's like something out of a fin de siècle Parisian opera, down to the actual opera glasses. He and I are not lovers. But we look it. I stand by his side like a part of the tsarist architecture—a haughty gold column with a strand of pearls around her neck. People keep stopping by and inviting "us" to gallery openings and drinks at their apartment.

I'm standoffish about these invitations but gracious—the way I imagine one should be, if I were the kind of person who used *one* as a pronoun—cool but kind, in a vague, distant way. The head of the ballet guides me around by my elbow. He smiles and whispers introductions in my ear as if he finds the whole confusion a charming and possibly interesting avenue to pursue. At the end of the after party, I give him a fast good-bye and hop an illegal taxi back to my hotel.

I tell myself that what I should really do is take this act back to New York. I need to be a haughty gold column at the office, and get my editor to fawn over me and give me a raise. I need to be a haughty gold column at a powerful media party and get somebody to give me a job at a magazine that people have actually heard of, a magazine that pays a livable salary, a magazine with a pirate chest of free Jimmy Choos and magical elves that bring you designer coffees. But as soon as I step off the plane and immediately apologize to my driver for being a half an hour late, I realize that the haughty gold column will remain in Russia, along with all her powers of glamour and intimidation.

A dim, clunky idea occurs to me, quickly, like a rumbling of the mind: Was that gold-column girl merely a grown-up, Russian version of the girl I tried to be in Baltimore? And if she was, who is this New York person I'm playing now? Some Manhattan version of the girl I used to be in Alaska? The can-do girl? The girl who can build a fire out of wet sticks or an apartment out of a few stained white walls?

It's one thing to switch faces. And another to transform any two different places into the same two different places where you grew up. As if your life, even inside where you think and dream, is only some kind of cheesy historical reenactment of where you've been.

CHAPTER 8

The Mystery of Beautiful Things

I go to Finland. I go to Denmark. Then, one night, just back from Switzerland, I wake up in the middle of my living room. It's midnight or after. The moon glows sootily through the window, the floor tiles are pearled with cool New York light. All around me stand neat stacks of jeans and shirts, plus a folded bedsheet, three folded paper towels, a tube of toothpaste, and a jar of Dijon mustard.

I'm in my underwear. I'm cold and sweaty. The apartment feels huge and dark and empty, which is the scariest part of sleepwalking. When you wake up, you feel like you're still dreaming. Except that I haven't been walking in my sleep, apparently. I've been packing in it.

This is something I used to do as a teenager in Baltimore. I once woke up with the entire linen closet folded into neat piles on the Oriental carpet beside Mom's bed. Sometimes I made it to the top of the stairs and would come to, feeling something holding me back, holding on: Mom's hand. Another time, I got all the way to the front door before she stopped me. It was horrible, waking up, realizing that my mother had had to watch me try my best to leave her.

Awake, I'd never let myself consider the idea. Mom had no other kids or family save for Maybelle, not even a boyfriend. I was her only child. I was her only everything, and yet, in my sleep, I walked out. Just like Dad.

Now that I'm an adult, I wonder what I'm not admitting to myself this time. Am I trying to leave myself, which is impossible? Or leave my life, which is ridiculous? In two weeks, I'm headed to Nepal to a luxury safari camp, and, after that, it's off to Lisbon, and then Milan. Sleepwalking, however, hasn't been my only unconscious gesture. In the past year, I've lost my passport four times, leaving it on a table in Prague and a bus seat in Madrid and a hotel room in Delhi, as if my mind had made the decision for me: No more going back home.

Which is maybe not such a bad conclusion for my mind to make without me. What's really here for me in this blank, dingy apartment, where the electricity shorts if you turn on more than three lights? At this stage, aren't I supposed to have had a real boyfriend, the kind that says he loves you and to whom you say I love you, too—and feel it? This guy doesn't even have to be the marrying variety. I just want to join the legions of women who have had college sweethearts, prom dates, nights at the movies, Chinese noodles in bed.

When it comes down to it, I'd even skip the man part and settle for a friend, regardless of the gender. For a few years, I was lucky. Stanford happened to be full of the nicest people on the planet—most of them Californians or Midwesterners, the rest New Yorkers who had decided not to go to schools with ancient secret drinking societies and mahogany-paneled cafeterias. Everybody greeted one another, not with nods or witticisms, but side hugs, during which people swoop an arm around your shoulders, squeeze hard, then—

openly and unmistakably—invite you to go eat frozen yogurt or go mountain biking.

I was flabbergasted by these West Coast rituals—and grateful. I made a lot of friends. These friends invited me to come home with them for Thanksgivings, seders, Easters. A few months later, when their parents visited campus, they would take me along with their child to dinner at an Italian restaurant or drive to Target to buy me, along with their child, toiletries for my room. These parents would redo the locks on my door, just in case, and give me lectures about the free credit cards sent to college students. I would often explain that my own father lived in Alaska and had two young kids, so he couldn't exactly whisk right down to California and put in a dead bolt. Or that my mother had three jobs and couldn't afford to come. But these explanations were usually in my head, because I was too busy reading the Mexican novel that these parents had mentioned to me or thanking them for guaranteeing my lease or basking in the glow of the nickname they had given me: HJ (Honorary Jew) or Second Daughter We Never Had. Until that day would come when those parents would buy four tickets to a musical, and leave mine taped to my door with a reminder to: *Bring a sweater! The theater will be cold!*

And I would have to break up with that friend. I would have to distance myself physically by attending another college for a bit, or changing my living situation, or just find another friend who ran in a philosophy-studying circle instead of a volleyball-playing one. I was acutely aware of one of life's ugliest paradoxes: Getting a taste of what you long for is usually more painful than just going hungry.

My friends didn't understand these abrupt dismissals. Ten years later, however, men seem less perturbed. I cheat on them before they can cheat on me, and then they go away. There is one guy in particular whom I do this with over and over. Tonight, I think of calling him, but he's with his new love, a Brazilian who understandably loathes even the idea of me.

I think of calling Dad. But it's midnight in Alaska and he's got two kids who wake up at 6 A.M. Not to mention, we just don't have the kind of relationship where we talk about our loneliness, sleep habits, and possible mental instability. We haven't even talked about what happened when he and Mom broke up twenty years ago—or why I think about the whole story as him walking out on us, when I know, factually, that it was Mom and me who jumped in a car and drove away. Instead we talk about his new dog, my total lack of retirement savings, and snowblowers. About these subjects, we agree on everything. There is no need to get upset.

On the other hand, Mom and I still can't get along for ten minutes. She, more than anyone, though, is the person I should call. She's a social worker. She's lived alone for long periods of time. She can tell if I'm upset just by the way I eat potato chips (me: stuffing them in by the handful, crunching away as if to make a sound barrier around my soul and person), just the way I can tell if she's upset by the way she eats potato chips (Mom: in a corner, nibbling like a rabbit with a secret dirty bag of carrots).

We've been through so much together, and survived. We've buried her mother at a funeral where we were the only attendees, surrounded by two hundred white folding chairs and a huge, completely empty peppermint-striped tent. We've looked up her birth parents, only to find out that they'd given up my mother but kept their three other kids. We've braved it through Father–Daughter Dinners where I went with my physics teacher because he was the only adult male I knew, and Mother–Daughter Picnics scheduled at noon, when my poor, exhausted mom rushed in for fifteen minutes, bearing a couple of tuna sandwiches in a paper bag, both of us too worried to eat for fear that she would get fired. We've run—as fast as we could—in the bullet-torn dark, from our car to the entrance of various Head Start centers in crack-infested downtown Baltimore neighborhoods, Mom working with the parents while I babysat the preschoolers, eating collard greens from a cafeteria tray and doing my homework with

four- or five-years-olds piled all over my books and painting my al-
gebra sets with ketchup and begging me to play hide-and-seek.

And yet we fight over the hand mirror I broke in 1986 and still
deny breaking. We fight over the one time she drank too much and
couldn't engage the stick shift, forcing me to drive home at age fourteen. We fight about why I don't call her on Sunday nights the way
she patiently asks me to and why she relentlessly fills up my answering machine with nagging messages to drink orange juice or invest
in cloth napkins.

She is not unaware, either, that underneath these trivial subjects
lurk old, volcanic hurts. "Do you think," she asked the last time we
saw each other in New York, "it would have been different if we
stayed in Alaska?"

And I went silent. Because I still don't know what she means.
Different as in better? *Stayed* as in if we'd stayed with Dad or as in
if we'd stayed in some discount condo down the street from him and
Abbie?

Without Baltimore, would I have found out about Tolstoy or the
causes of the Iranian revolution? Would I have learned what a horse-
country steeplechase was or how to play a mediocre but functional
game of squash? Because it took a while, but eventually I found my
place at Roland Park Country—at least, academically. I turned into
a hand-raiser, a homework-doer, the kind of girl who reads non-
required Greek epic poems and wanders down to the boiler room to
find the loving but exhausted English teacher who thought she was
going to grab a few meditative puffs off a low-tar menthol but was
now going to spend her one break of the day talking with me about
"Hills Like White Elephants."

Saltcellars, aspic, bread-and-butter notes (with city and state and
street names all spelled out, no abbreviations), all those Old Balti-
morean graces—don't laugh—have proven pretty useful in my life.
For example, in France, where people judge you over whether you
spear your bread with a fork before soaking up the sauce on your

plate, or just smear your bread around with your fingers. (Correct answer: the former.)

Then again, living in Alaska, would I have learned how to fly a plane? Would I have brought down my own moose? Would I have been president of the school, or a happy, well-adjusted hockey cheerleader with an adoring boyfriend who owned a king crew cab pickup?

And Dad?

This is where I left Mom at the too-expensive restaurant where she'd brought up the subject in the first place and took the train back to my apartment. Because I can't bear to leaf through the family scrapbook of what might have been. I can't even talk to Mom about what actually is. She doesn't know where I live in New York. We meet in the dining rooms of luxurious uptown department stores, where we split the lobster club sandwich and never order the seven-dollar iced tea. I don't want her to see my blank, empty apartment or my drug-bustling neighborhood, studded with heroin dealers, pit bulls, and users who float by like limp dead balloons. I don't want to talk about my relief at owning nothing, or at least nothing that costs money.

This conversation, unfortunately, will lead to only one thing—the mystery of lovely things. The English egg coddlers with the silver tops. The porcelain tea plates painted with fairy-tale bunnies. The cut-crystal goblets that gild the walls with butterflies of colored light.

By age fourteen, I spent a good chunk of my time rolling my eyes every time Mom asked me to admire how the sunlight rippled off the golden jungle stripes in the tiger-maple lowboy—beginning with her use of the phrase *tiger-maple lowboy*. Mom loved to say the full names of furniture, drawing out each syllable, polishing the music in the words—camelback sofa, Queen Anne table, Windsor chair.

The truth was, though, I did like to stare at the tiger maple, in the quiet of the afternoon after school. Just as I liked to stare at the little Chinese dockworkers scurrying along the painted interior of the Hong Kong punch bowl—their hair tied back in long braided ponytails, their backs bent over by packages. A whole world was painted on the inside of that bowl, filled with junks and tea and intrigue, nightingales in cages, crates of opium and porcelain.

One afternoon, I ran my fingers over the faint bumpy brushstrokes of the wooden wharf buildings. The bowl was from the 1800s, and had just appeared one day on the sideboard—no deliveryman, no box. Mom had bought it at an estate sale, she told me, for a song.

Rounding the billowed sails of a ship, my finger hit a sticker. I backtracked, figuring out why I'd never seen it before, because it blended in with the rigging. The sticker was a price tag. And the smudged number on that price tag was $1,500. I looked at it for a long time. Then I looked one mahogany table over, at the silver tea service that had just appeared one day, too—a gleaming, curvaceous, three-piece set with lion-footed legs and swooping cherrywood handles. I turned over the sugar bowl. MADE IN WILLIAMSBURG.

Mom kept all the Williamsburg catalogs stacked on the kitchen bookshelf. I leafed through the stiff, heavy pages: $985. I was too afraid to look up the prices for the new antique cedar hope chest that showed up last week.

I sat down on the steps and waited for my mother to come home from her second job. I thought of all the horrible things I was going to say to her, about where my child support had gone, about the real reason she had so many jobs, and why I'd been sitting alone in a basement since age seven, because we couldn't afford babysitting. I thought about all the times I'd asked for field-trip money or name-brand cookies and she'd called me selfish, and how I'd believed her, how I'd yelled at myself not to want anything and never to ask. I didn't understand why, if this all of a sudden wasn't true, I didn't feel relieved.

I felt nothing. I felt the lurch you feel when a plane stalls and you're dropping out of the sky, waiting for the engine to catch. And then I thought of calling Dad. I'd tell him not just about the Hong Kong punch bowl, but about all the other stuff: the school shoes we supposedly couldn't afford or the dress for my fifth-grade graduation, which I finally figured out how to pay for myself (using my winnings from a basement bingo game that Maybelle had taken me to, on yet another one of our visits down south to pay off her debts). He'd tell me that all that stuff about the IRS and him blackballing Mom from the banks wasn't true, but it wasn't that Mom wanted to hurt me. Mom had a problem. Mom got confused.

Then I thought about the custody agreement and the contract and Dad's lawyer, and what would happen. He'd take me away from Mom, and Mom had only me. Dad had Abbie and baby Daniel. If Dad knew, I'd have to go back to Alaska. I'd have to sit there at dinner, eating some fragrant, home-cooked caribou stew that Abbie had made for us, while Mom sat alone at a little table in Baltimore, eating a cold plate by herself and talking to nobody.

Except, after all those years, how could Dad not know?

Unless he did.

This was so painful, I just had to rock for a while and wait for it to be over.

On the wall above my head hung a clumsy drawing I'd done in kindergarten. Mom, who mistakenly believed I was a genius, framed it. It was full of little boxes. Above the boxes were little questions the teacher wrote out for us to fill in. What do you want to be when you grow up? A stewardess. Do you have a pet? I drew a picture of Baby, my old husky dog.

When I was sick, Mom covered my forehead in a damp cool washcloth and left me fizzy Cokes on the beside table. It was she who drove me to ballet, she who bought me tickets to *Evita* and encouraged me to perform it, complete with props and costumes, in the living room, over and over, and she who did not fall in love with somebody else and ruin everything. She was my mother. I was her copilot, "the best thing," she always said, "I ever did."

I got up off the steps. There was a sign on the window of a children's bookstore near school. HELP WANTED. There was another sign in the *Pennysaver* for a blind lady who needed someone to read her newspapers. I said responsible, clean, punctual things on both interviews.

Two part-time jobs would never be enough, I knew. But I'd find another way, without talking to Mom about what she was doing with the Hong Kong punch bowl and everything else—a confrontation that would be pointless anyway, since she didn't seem to understand what she was doing. Then again, how could she not? She knew what Maybelle did, filling up her house with cartons of ketchup-and-mustard dispensers and racks of winter coats that didn't fit, leaving us to pay the bills. Wasn't that kind of the same thing, only more obvious and identifiable to the rest of the world?

Right then, the thought occurred to me: Dad wasn't the only person who could take me away.

And with that, I cut off the internal discussion. It wasn't such a big thing to work. I had grown up loading firewood, pumping plane floats, pitching tents. Waiting tables, busing tables, holding down dogs at a vet clinic, running a grocery-store register—none of this was all that rough. All I had to do was get older, get a car, get a better-paying job, get a third or a fourth job and not get fired, not get lazy or show up late, not let my grades or my face slip, never get caught drinking or smoking or sneaking out of school, never oversleep or skip a test, never get too overweight or underweight, never let a teacher or a neighbor or a boss or a friend or Dad or Mom or anyone suspect that I was on that desert island Dad always talked about when I was little, the one that you pretend you're on when you have to do something hard and you have to do it alone. Only this time I was on an island far, far away from both Alaska and Baltimore, far, far away from everybody who might know where I was, or where I'd been.

———

Twelve years later in New York, facing down that pile of sleep-packed clothes, toiletries, and assorted kitchen condiments, I want to tell myself, *Hey, don't worry. This is just some kind of throwback habit. There's nothing you need to run away from.* The evidence supports this, doesn't it? My life—and job—are literally an escape, complete with room service and the occasional cliffside infinity pool.

But if there was one thing I learned about the day I found the price tag, it's that you have to watch yourself. Because when something starts going off inside, you probably won't realize it. Mom didn't. Maybelle didn't. And it's not like anyone will tell you that it's happening, either, especially when you've arranged things so there's never anyone there to see.

I remake my mattress on the floor with the sheet. "Don't move," I order the dream-me, wherever she is inside my brain.

She doesn't answer, the sneak.

CHAPTER 9

Homemarks

Over the next few months, I go to Nepal and sleep with an extra cot in front of my tent flaps to keep me from stumbling out the door into the jungle (home to tigers and irritable rhinos). I go to Lisbon and research a medieval castle recently taken over by a Frenchman and converted into a decadent mid-century mod hotel. Then I go to Milan. My job is to write about osso buco, the classic veal marrow dish, but my time is limited, and I have to pack in two four-course lunches a day, plus a five-course dinner.

It's a little uncomfortable, dining luxuriously in Italy, alone. Eating here is supposed to be about warmth and family—passing plates of *primo* and *secondo* and, my favorite, *contorno*. Here in the industrial north, the odd businessman will sit by himself at a nearby banquette, working his way through a saffron risotto and a carafe of wine, but I lack his newspaper and Old World confidence. The waiters try to be professional with me, but end up rushing over at every other bite—fretful, asking if the meat is tender enough, the bread fresh. Sometimes they inquire tentatively, but with great kindness, as to why I'm not finishing my food, which in Italy is social code for: *Who didn't love you? And by the way he was a fool.*

I don't have the heart to tell them I'm not heartbroken exactly— just very full and a little discouraged about my prospects for future happiness. I, too, wish I was longing for some wonderful man from my past, or some tragic but impossible love. But I haven't experienced those feelings yet. In fact, the only person I understand enough to miss is a woman who can put away as much *frutti di mare* as me, a woman who likes to fish in torn hip boots and glue rocks into bad homemade jewelry and call me a ding-dong when I'm being a ding-dong, a woman who knows more than anyone how to be happy, even when life is not turning out the way you had hoped.

This would be Nana, who still lives in her little red cottage on a peninsula outside Seattle. One of the nicest things about being an adult with several hundred thousand frequent-flier miles at my disposal is that, once I've pushed the minibar in my grand hotel room in front of my door so that if I fall asleep watching CNN, I won't wander down the gilded halls into the lobby and upset the concierge, I can call up Alitalia and alter my itinerary.

At last, I have a plan. I love Nana. I trust her. I can tell her anything. What's more, I've lived with her before, right after my parents got divorced, when Mom thought we might stay in Seattle instead of move to Baltimore. Not much has changed since then. I take the next available four flights (Milan to Rome to New York to Dallas to Seattle) and find Nana waiting for me in her living room stuffed with opera records and Indian baskets, wearing her musty silk kimono and her lipstick everywhere but on her lips. If you crossed a lumberjack with a silent 1920s movie star, you'd get her, down to her perfume-and-lighter-fluid-scented hug, which compresses your rib cage—and soul—into a small warm beating ball.

"Nana?" I say, then pause, unsure what else to say: I'm not doing so well?

She sighs, the ghost exhale of her last smoked cigarette, which she stubbed out twenty years ago. "Love," she says, suddenly. "This house is a dump." Her voice sounds so discouraged.

"I could clean," I say.

"Everything's broken."

She's right. The door springs open each time you try to close it; the kitchen linoleum is peeling; the counters are cracked and bubbled. My feet stick to the floor, which is blotched with raspberry jam from breakfast spills long, long past. Nana has never been a housekeeper. I'm still afraid of the shower in the back bedroom that has a wet gooey drain that's pretty much a Catholic home for wayward, hairy spiders. But something has tipped over into the realm of the just plain unhygienic.

"Let's get out of here," she says, marching me out to the deck. The air tastes of sap and ocean. Her rhododendrons are in bloom, hugely so, bobbing like white floral ships to the end of the lawn. She plops down on a lounger. "Nobody tells you but after a certain point it's not so much fun," she says. "All this getting old."

I sit for a minute with this. Nana is eighty-five years old. But I've seen her, at age seventy-five, dig for clams on the beach a few miles away, carrying sand-filled buckets and a heavy, awkward shovel. On a hot August day in Alaska, I've seen her haul in a forty-pound king in fast-moving, waist-deep water. Let's not forget, either, the day the two of us sat on a gravel beach on the Johnson Slough, pretending bravery to each other, inventorying the shotgun and cooler of soda that were all we had with us, counting down the nine hours that Dad didn't come back and didn't come back to pick us up in the plane—not, as it turned out, because he had crashed and died, as both of us had privately assumed after the first hour, but because the 185 had broken down and he'd been forced to get it fixed.

Nana acting sad or defeated, though, I've never witnessed. I know that she must have felt these emotions, too many times to be considered fair. Her father died when she was eight, her mother when she was twelve, her brother when she was nineteen, her husband (my grandfather) when she was forty-nine and the mother of five kids under eighteen years old. Fourteen years later, her youngest daughter (my aunt) committed suicide, and fourteen years after that her grandson Henry drowned at his own high-school graduation party. Add to this: Her youngest son, Steven, who struggled for years with drugs and drinking, recently cut all ties with the family and disappeared somewhere in the Dominican Republic.

As always, a shaker of martinis stands at attention on the picnic table. I pour her one, sloshing half of it out of the glass. "You're just a little lonely, Nana."

"This wasn't the plan."

"What plan?"

"The one where I wasn't supposed to live this long."

I take a minute. Then I say—but it's not so much speaking as warbling, because I realize not only that now is the time to bring up the reason why I've come here to see her, but also that I mean it—"What if I moved in and lived with you?"

She gives me a hug, not of joy, but pride, as in: Leigh has been a good granddaughter. Leigh has been generous and kind and full of crap.

"I mean it," I say, the warble in my voice getting almost teary. "I could fix up the house for you. We could cook. We could read."

"Leigh," she says. "There's nothing I'd like better. But I live out here in the middle of the woods. How would you ever meet anybody? That's no way for a person your age to live."

I pick at a splinter in the deck, thinking, *The middle of the woods is what I know. I make a middle of the woods out of every place I go. It would be nice, for once, to be there in dark, isolated quiet with somebody I love.*

Nana is looking at me, though, with the most unexpected of expressions: need. "I always believed," she says, "you were going to do something so . . . meaningful."

"Like?"

"I don't know." More need; need all over the place. "Run for senator?"

Hmm . . . I see what she's doing, giving me a modern, relevant, professional goal, something with power and prestige and the ability to change the lives of millions, something we both know I lack the drive, squeaky history, and charismatic handshake to do. But at least Nana avoided bringing up the supposedly outdated goal that I know gave her whole life meaning—falling in love, raising a big, short, thunderously loud family.

I hold her hand, which is difficult, due to all the boulder-sized rings. "If I am supposed to do something, I guess now is the time to do it, right?"

"No hiding!" she says, once again in the bright, commanding tone of a female general. "I forbid it."

I sip, smile, and try not to gag. Martinis taste a little like a glass of chilled disinfectant. The only thing they have going for them is Nana—and the olives.

Later, on the way to the bathroom, I stop by a picture of my dad hanging in the hall. He's in kindergarten—1950s crew cut, dopey open smile, missing tooth. My face makes a moon on the glass over his face. All those losses of Nana's were also his losses. All those missing people were his missing people: his brother, sister, father, grandparents, all gone by the time he was the age I am now.

Over the years, he had tried occasionally to talk to me about what this was like. "We moved to Mexico when my dad died," he said, when I first heard him speak Spanish—out of nowhere, fluently. "For a while. Then we came back and I started college in the fall." Or, "After my sister died, nobody in my family said anything. We all just got in our cars and went home." But his voice was broken up, as if it had cost him a supreme amount of effort to produce that sentence.

I was never sure what to say back to him, except, "I'm sorry, Dad."

Maybe I should have asked him something, something along the lines of, *What was your sister like?* Maybe I should have told him what I remembered about his sister, making sugar cookies with her. Except that memory came from a photograph, the only one I'd ever seen of her—a soft, smiling woman with curly brown hair, about twenty-five, rolling out dough on the counter. Pink Hawaiian apron. Bead necklace. Dimple. I'm in the corner of that photograph, age five, there for a Christmas visit.

"There are two reasons people come to Alaska," Dad always used to say. "You're either running to something or you're running away."

Unless, of course, you're doing both. My father went up to work as a young doctor in the Native hospital—but maybe he had to leave his old life behind as well. That's the thing about parents, I'm beginning to realize. You don't have to see them all that much to imitate them.

Hustling to make my flight back to New York, dragging my duffel bag past a Gift Mart displaying canned Copper River salmon and souvenir miniature Space Needles, I'm struck by such a wave of nostalgia that I have to sit down. There's a Starbucks in the Seattle airport now. But other than that, not much has changed since 1979—not the once-futuristic underground train shuttles, not the brown-and-orange earthy color scheme designed to inspire travelers to stop and visit the refreshing nearby forests of Washington State.

Some kids look for the church or the graffiti-covered water tank that says you're almost home. My landmark was the square-shaped Northwest terminal of Sea-Tac, where, for ten years, save for the occasionally rerouting through Chicago, I got off the flight from BWI and changed planes for ANC. Once there, I was as close to Alaska as was geographically possible from the Lower Forty-Eight. Only 2,280 more miles to go.

Even as a teenager, I could never pull off much fake blasé when it came to that last leg of the route. I annoyed the stewardesses for the entire flight with mature questions like, "Are we there yet?" and spent a lot of time trying to decide if the flight was technically three hours long (the time in the air) or four hours (due to the one-hour time difference with Seattle) or five (since the real time change between Alaska and Seattle was two hours; officials had changed the Alaska time zone in 1983).

And yet, as I got older, as much as I looked forward to landing in Anchorage, I'd proceed home with Dad and Abbie, go directly to my room, swing my leg over the windowsill, jump off the second-story roof (holding fast to a certain blue spruce), and run off into the sun-whitened night.

There was another kind of Alaska that I'd discovered, one filled with people instead of grizzlies or alders, one whose dangers came not from faulty plane engines or misfired shotguns, but from high speeds on snow machines or drunken fistfights on the shoulder of the road. This was the wildness of town, where I tried—and almost succeeded at—getting as deeply lost as if I had actually wandered off into the bush the way I'd planned as a girl.

Next door, the Bardells had grown up faster than me and far more excitingly. By fourteen, I had become their oddball younger acolyte, also known as "our neighbor up from Boston" (a geographic mistake that never felt worth correcting). At thirty-six-hour keg parties and late-night dark sawdust bars, populated almost entirely by adults who had escaped their violent-offender records down in the Lower Forty-Eight, you could find me cheerfully doing shots and playing pool and staring in unrelenting worship at the Great Alaskan twenty-one-year-olds who surrounded me.

The things my older northern idols knew: how to kiss a boy with chew tucked in his lower lip, how to water-ski on one ski, how to tell a Sammy Hagar guitar solo from a Van Halen one, how to turn doughnuts in the snow without crashing into a drift, how to tell who was a stoner or who wasn't by the placement of the eyeliner either inside or outside the base of their eyelashes, how to shoot a black bear in your outhouse, how to get a job wiping oil off individual pieces of gravel with a paper towel (courtesy of the Exxon spill), or a job on the slime line, gutting salmon for canning, or—the real bonanza—a job forklifting at a brand-new store in South Anchorage called Costco, which came with full benefits, including dental.

I soaked up all this information, usually while terrifically inebriated and leaning on some tree-trunk bar stool, my purse filled with assorted forged IDs. In response, my idols patted my head and tried to suggest we go home—a difficult task when it came to me at two or three in the morning. I never wanted to go home. I was always the last to make it into the car or onto the back of the motorcycle. Even dropped off, standing in the driveway at my house, I'd wait awhile before facing reentry, curling up with the dogs in the doghouse, the way I used to as a kid.

Sitting in the Seattle airport, I can walk those stairs in my mind, avoiding each creak and sigh of the carpet-muffled steps as if I were still fifteen. That was the summer that Dad and Abbie had had another baby, a boy named Jack. His room was just in front of the landing, and if I opened the door very, very slowly, muffling the brass hinge that rubbed on the frame, I could quietly lurch inside and watch him sleeping in his crib.

His hair was fluffy duck-blond, his ears pink. He made huffing noises when he breathed and smiled, like me, in his dreams. But that was as far as my observations—and attentions—were allowed to go. I had decided early on: I wasn't going to heat up Jack's bottles or blow into his belly button. My other brother, Daniel, needed me. He and I were each other's me for you in "Tea for Two." He and I were a team, the way Mom and I were a team down in Baltimore. So what if some cuter newer brother had showed up. I wasn't just going to forget about Daniel or replace him—no matter how soft the skin on Jack's forehead was when I stroked it, no matter how much I liked or—let's face it—loved him, in secret.

One night, I gave in and picked Jack up. We made our way, carefully yet drunkenly, over to the rocker, where he lay on my chest, half asleep, trying to nurse my chin. He was so round, so prone to random inexplicable smiles. He snuggled. He nuzzled. Daniel had been so different as a baby—wailing, furious, unless you turned him facing out from your chest so that he could see the world. Is this how life is, I wanted to ask somebody, that we are who we are from the moment we're born? And if so, who was I? Did everybody know just by looking at me—the way I knew just by looking at my brothers? Or was I too polluted and confused for anybody to see it anymore? I lowered Jack back into his crib and slunk back down to my room.

Three hours later, Dad woke me up. He was standing in the doorway in his chest waders, visibly trembling with rage—either because he'd heard me stumbling around at 3 A.M with his newborn or because I wasn't up, dressed, and ready to go fishing for reds. "Hit the deck," he said. "I'll give you seven minutes to get your gear—and the rest of you—into that plane."

If there was one thing that had not changed in my life, it was my fear of Dad. I was still acutely, dizzily terrified of him, which is why I usually chose to lie in order to get out of fishing with him or hiking or doing anything at all. He rarely called me on these mumbled, obvious excuses, and I wasn't sure why. Today, however, I sensed some kind of newfound resolve from him: He had had it, understandably, with his wasted underage daughter staggering around town.

I had had it with me, too. I wasn't even sure what I was doing or why I was doing it. I just wanted out of that house. And at the same time I wanted back in—into the family, into some mythical life where you ate dinner with your parents and talked with them about . . . what? I wasn't sure.

"Hit the deck," Dad said again.

I sat up. I looked at him. And I said, "I'm not going anywhere."

There was a long pause, when he should have been pulling me out of bed and dragging me down the stairs. Why wasn't he? I shriveled into the bedcovers. What had I done?

Finally—years later, it felt—he shrugged and said in a flat, dead voice, "Suit yourself. Go ahead and give yourself away like a birthday present. I don't care what you do."

I set my face to match his voice—flat, check; dead, check.

And out he went.

For the rest of the summer, everything was settled. I saw Abbie and the boys in the mornings, before my various assorted jobs at different restaurants. But Dad and I lived in different countries while inside that house, crossing paths only on the way to the microwave or to the closet for a rain jacket.

The weeks passed. I missed the king run, the silver run, the reds. Dad said nothing. I missed going to Homer to fish for halibut. Dad said nothing. Until, one odd day, he showed up at the Mexican restaurant where I worked as a hostess. I had my uniform on—a fabric hacienda of white polyester and black lace ruffles, with a button over the décolletage extolling, as if it were a life philosophy, CO-RONA!

Dad rocked on his heels. Waiters passed by us, bearing flaming pans of fajitas. Somewhere in the vast stucco dining room, a table of twelve was singing "Happy Birthday." "I was thinking," Dad shouted over the last chorus, "of going caribou hunting."

I nodded. I had a green crayon in my hand from the packs we gave out to kids. I drew a daisy on the waiting list. "Oh," I said, casually. "I guess I could go with you . . . if you wanted. As long as I find somebody to switch my shift."

Two hundred nautical miles away from town, it was already the

first of the two weeks of autumn. The rivers below the plane lay
lead-colored and salmon-less. The leaves on the low bushes had
turned a thin, tissue-paper yellow, while beside them whole plains
lay enflamed in raging red moss. The contrast, the speed, the violence with which the world up north changes—I'd forgotten. It'd
been such a long time since I'd seen fall from the sky. Dad lowered
the stick and we swooped down—again and again—but no caribou.

Finally, by the Naknek River, we spotted a sparse, loose, grazing
herd. We landed on the river, tying down the plane to some alders,
me pointedly using Dad's complex, semi-overwrought system of half
hitches upon half hitches. After which, the dread kicked in. Why
had I agreed to go hunting? What had I possibly been thinking?

I got busy, the best way to avoid talking. I pitched the tent. I
loaded day packs. I pumped the camp stove and boiled up spaghetti,
then served it still in the pot, the two of us forking slabs of marga-
rine into the noodles and passing the salt. The last of the season's
mosquitoes pulsed in dense clouds above the firelight, almost but
not quite stymied by the smoke.

"Dad?" I finally said, "uh, you know that I'm really excited
about tomorrow, right?"

"Me too."

"It's just. Well, I'm not so into killing a caribou."

The flames spit and crackled. Dad tossed his coffee grounds into
the dark.

"Actually, I don't want to kill anything. Ever again."

Dad stared at his knuckles.

I stared at the untied lace of my wader boot. I knew what I looked
like to him: a big liberal ding-dong from Baltimore, a hypocrite who
no longer understood the reality of the food chain. Maybe I was
that. Or maybe I was the person I'd always been, the one who had
tried to rescue mauled baby ducks as a little girl, using a lightbulb
and a shoe box. Who was also the same little girl who used to help
her dad blast healthy grown-up ducks straight out of the sky.

Or maybe I was just trying to tell him that I wasn't his daughter anymore, really sock him one in the heart. It didn't feel that way. But maybe that's what I was doing. Because that's what it looked like from the outside. Bagging a caribou is an Alaskan teenage tradition. Everybody does it. With their dad.

"That's all right," he finally muttered.

"I brought my camera!" I said, too quickly. "I'll take wildlife pictures!"

The next morning at dawn, we set out, the world wisped in fog. A light drizzle pattered off the leaves. The sky hunched low and gray and endless. We bounced along the tundra, our feet springing off the dense, spongy moss. Dark red bearberries flashed through the yellow greenery. Sometimes there were streams, and we crossed them. Sometimes there were large alder patches and we skirted them. But mostly, we walked along on the open plains, our breath misting in the wet.

I moved carefully, mindful of my thin, easy-to-tear chest waders—so much lighter and easier to walk in than hip boots. I was a grown-up, finally, at least in terms of outdoor gear. Mom's old manual thirty-five-millimeter swung awkwardly around my neck, banging every now and then against the stock of my rifle.

A few miles later, we spotted the tracks of the herd. The terrain here was slightly hilly. Dad motioned for me to follow, slow and quiet, then for me to drop flat to my stomach and crawl. We bumped along on bellies and elbows under bushes. Dad stopped to glass in, his spotting scope raised. I picked up my camera.

Not a hundred yards off stood three caribou. A cow and two bulls. They were grazing near some dwarf willows by a pool of water, fed by a stream. We set up under the same willows, protected by the drapery of fog and leaves. I snapped off a few shots, softly, no flash: The cow snuffling for a drink. The bulls rolling in the dirt, scratching their backs.

Dad settled in, focusing his scope. I kept clicking away, the heavy camera strap cutting into the back of my neck. Every once in a while, I swung the lens over and shot Dad, his cheek pressed on the dark metal of the gun.

I watched his finger, waiting for him to ease it back slowly. But suddenly the bull leapt up, as if he'd heard something. Dad's gun went off. The bull turned, the shot ripping into his front leg instead of his chest, and crumpled. The other bull bounded off into the bushes. The cow circled for a moment, confused. Dad took another shot. The cow bolted for the tundra, but the bull—by now hit twice—staggered up to standing.

Why wasn't he falling down? Dad tried again. The shots were so loud, so definitive. The buck crumpled but dragged himself forward, as if he was going to get out of there, as if nothing was going to stop him, no matter how many bullets he had in him. But he was going the wrong way, into the stream. Toward the bushes, I told him in my mind. Turn around.

He took a few stumbling steps into the water. Then sank to his knees. One more shot.

It was time for him to die. Why didn't he just die? It took a while, though. He struggled and struggled, and finally pitched forward, still shaking his antlers and legs, until he stopped, floating on the surface of the pool.

For a while, nothing moved. The smell of burnt metal hung in the air. The bull turned along in the current. I put down my camera, feeling suddenly exhausted. Blood darkened in the water, spreading out.

Dad headed down to the beach and waded in, fighting the mild current, fishing around for something on the bull to hold on to. I picked up my camera and, almost without thinking, started shooting again: Dad up to his chest, then his shoulders in water, Dad steering the bull toward the shore, Dad pulling the entire four-hundred-pound carcass by the hind leg, dragging it over the shallows to land. It didn't feel like real life, looking through the lens. I didn't think to scurry over and help. Dad was on another planet. The rain was on another planet.

"Put that down!" He was pointing to the camera. "Nobody wants to see pictures of this mess." He sounded upset, though, more than angry.

I helped him drag the bull to drier land. There he showed me how to field dress, first cutting the throat to drain the blood, then removing organs and genitals. A soft, hot cloud of musky dead rose up around us. I breathed through my mouth, and started skinning, easing the knife through the soft white tissue between the muscle and hide. We sawed off the legs, quartered the carcass in silence, and stored everything up in garbage bags.

The light was failing as we packed the meat back to camp and cached it in some semi-high trees. The rain turned heavier. We made a fire, washed our hands and arms in the river.

"I'm sorry," Dad said, unlacing his wading boots. "That was about as lousy a hunt as you could have." And then he just kept going on: He had missed the shot over and over, he had made a bad situation worse, he had ruined my first big trip. "It was my fault," he said. "It wasn't supposed to be like that."

I didn't know what to say. Dad sounded so sad, so embarrassed, so unlike Dad. "Don't worry about it," I told him. "I'll throw away the film."

Back in Baltimore, though, a few weeks later, I looked over the contact sheet in the snug red light of the school darkroom. The photos were very gray from the mist near the water. But the way I'd shot them, from the neck down, you couldn't see my father's face. In the sequence, the bull crumpled, the cow jumped frantically, then the perspective tunneled down to a close-up of a man's arm, dragging the leg of a dead animal behind him in the mud.

I mounted the photographs on poster board. I titled and captioned them. Then I hung them in a hallway, which was when I began to regret the whole idea. I never talked about Alaska in

Baltimore—not just because it might seemed uncouth and, well, slightly more innard-flecked beside the other girls' stories of summer sailing camps, but also because it hurt to talk about it. I had enough trouble keeping myself going as it was. Why add a dollop of Dad?

For days, I waited. Someone was going to say something. They had to. But nobody did. Was I that invisible? Perhaps. I asked my English teacher, Mrs. Green. Despite Roland Park Country's draconian rules, the instructors at the school were some of the most wonderful, comforting, truly original people on the earth—the kind of women who sang to their students "Ladybugs! Cross your legs, pretty please, I can see your name and address!" but spent each summer in Krakow, working on their third PhD, this time in ancient Slavic dialects.

Mrs. Green, a lanky lover of Eliot and Browning, once wrote NO FLUFF! on a piece of paper (as in: no fluffy writing), folded it into a hat, and wore it on her head for an entire class.

"What do you think?" I asked, pointing to my photos, trying to be casual.

She lowered her reading glasses, peered, peered . . . and peered some more. "It's very modern," she said. "It's geometrical? A study in forms?"

And then I understood. She couldn't actually make out the caribou or my father. The mist and drizzle—as well as my inability to focus—had turned the photographs into a fuzzy, grayish blackish blur. That is, unless you knew what was there.

I felt so relieved—and ashamed. Because even if no one at my school recognized what I had tried to show them, I was pretty sure that Dad had figured it out. He wasn't stupid. He knew what he must have looked like, dragging a dead animal around by the leg. There really wasn't any reason for me to have captured those images and shown them to strangers out of context—unless I was trying to show the world what a cruel, blood-hungry butcher I had for a father.

"We'd like to welcome Flight 4924, service to JFK International," a man's voice singsongs on the microphone. I start, jumping out of my seat—back in Sea-Tac, back in reality. I check for my bag, to make sure it's still there. It is. The great thing about a duffel is that you can mash it into an overhead compartment, allowing you to take twice as much stuff on board as in a hard roller suitcase— meaning that not only do I never check a bag but also if I want to walk up to the Northwest desk and change my flight and head up straight to Alaska, I can.

A little pastoral scene glitters through my mind: Dad and me standing by the smoking grill, slapping backs, talking and laughing everything off. Because lots of kids sneak out and drink and lie and act like self-centered, self-destructive jackasses for a while, don't they?

Then why do I still feel so guilty? Why do I feel like I've ruined something that can't ever be righted, even after all these years and, at this point, ridiculous amounts of distance? There's this huge, ugly gulf that opens up every time my father and I talk—and we just keep skittering over it, ignoring it, chatting about his new vacuum sealer for frozen fish or my latest trip to Turin. I'm not sure if he'd be hurt or relieved if he found out that I'd come this close to Alaska and chosen not to pay him a visit.

"New York," the man on the microphone says. "We'd like to welcome our first-class passengers and elite World Perks members to begin boarding." I stand up. I even reach for my wallet. But once at the counter, I feel foolish. I don't know what I'd say to Dad, and I can't just show up at his door without calling—which, I know more than anyone, just means I won't, because can't *does* live on won't street—just the way he always said.

I get in line, along with the families and "passengers requiring

extra time such as those with small children, disabilities, or unac-
companied minors." I'm no longer in the latter category, of course,
and the stewardess gives me the eyeball as I hand her my ticket. I
give her one back. She stamps my boarding pass, and lets me on that
plane.

CHAPTER 10

Street Wolves

Back in New York, late at night, tucked into my mattress on the floor but too afraid of sleep-packing to sleep, I try to think over my options. It does occur to me that, rather than leave for yet another country, why not let somebody else into my own—literally, as in let them sleep here and do practical, companionable stuff like cook with me and watch TV with me (if I had a TV) and make sure I don't stumble out the door at 3 A.M.?

Having people over, though, as friends, roommates, lovers, or anything else, makes me exceptionally stressed and just the tiniest bit inhospitable. They can come over and enjoy a glass of wine or have sex, but then it's time to go. I usually signal departure time with a lot of needless, loud dishwashing—as if this person and I have been married for thirty-five stereotypical years and one of us (not me!) has forgotten to take out the trash.

This no doubt dates back to earlier times. In Anchorage, my reason for having friends was for them to get me away from Dad and his family—as fast and destructively as possibly. They did not come over for pizza or hang out in the family room on Friday nights.

In Baltimore, the situation was similar, but for different reasons. Something had turned confusing and strange with Mom by the time I'd reached high school. I didn't know what it was and I didn't know who to ask and, even if I'd had somebody, I was too afraid to do it. Was it: Drinking? Pills? Exhaustion? Even I understood that being a single parent with three jobs will wipe a person out to the point of no return.

Or did it have something to do with the mental problems that her own mother struggled with? Some nights, Mom screamed at me in a slurred, low voice, accusing me of ruining her life, then coming in to break a radio or a jewelry box—only to completely forget about what had happened the next morning, wake me up, and hug me and tell me I was her raison d'être, the most wonderful daughter in the universe. Other nights she smiled at me blankly when I asked for help with something like an SAT class or college applications, as if I were a stranger, speaking a Cantonese dialect, then wandered off to polish the furniture. The most unexpected issues made her obsessively attentive: I absolutely had to mend those holes in my jeans that made me look "like an orphan" or I absolutely had to drink a glass of orange juice before school to boost my immune system. Meanwhile, she turned off my alarm while I slept, claiming I looked tired. I was tired. But I also needed to take my exams to graduate, exams that I missed one after another.

One night, right before all this started, I ended up in the back of a station wagon with a bunch of hugely glamorous fellow fifteen-year-olds whom I had attached myself to via various less-than-developed friendships. These high-school freshmen—some of them real, live boys—had no place to go to that guaranteed beer or even the smell of beer. I had no place to go, period. Somehow the words "We could go over to my house" came out of my mouth, and I couldn't take them back.

As soon as we arrived, I left everyone on the porch and ran into the kitchen for something to eat or drink. It was eight o'clock at night. Mom was sitting in the kitchen, wrapped in her pink flannel robe, with her hair sticking out, her eyes fixed on a lit candle on the table.

"Mom?" I said.

She jumped, startled.

"I've got some friends here, okay? We'll just hang out on the porch. Everybody will go home by ten."

"Friends?" she said. Already she sounded nervous, too fast, high-pitched.

I grabbed my guitar and a pitcher of water. (Why, God, why did we not believe in soda or even mass-produced iced tea?) Back on the porch, it was dark already, the soft, crickety dark of late spring. Everyone was slouched over chairs at the wrought-iron table. There were five total—two girls from school and three boys whose names I didn't know. The cute one with a chipped tooth took the guitar and started playing something delicate and plucked—a moth of a song from those stubborn, impossible strings.

One of the girls lit a cigarette. Maryland was a tobacco state; most parents put up with smoking. Maybe my mother would, too. Or if she didn't, maybe she would just ground me later, after everyone went home.

I sat down.

"Alec," said the boy with my guitar.

"Huh?" I said.

"My name."

"Oh, right." I sat back, slowly. Alec was just a name, I told myself. Get the dorky happy dance off your face.

The storm door opened, Mom's face peered out. "Are you youngsters all right out here? Wouldn't anyone like a blueberry muffin?" Her voice, though, sounded trembled, frightened, young, as if she were a child who had just woken up from a nightmare. She was looking at the brick wall behind us, instead of at us. And blinking very fast.

"No thanks, Mom," I said.

She let the door bang shut again. Alec picked out a Neil Young song. I knew the words. Kind of. Something about a maid. Or man.

Creak, the door opened again.

"Wouldn't any of you youngsters like a blueberry muffin?"

This time the whole porch went hushed. "No thanks, Mrs. Newman," one of the girls said.

I kept my eyes fixed on the green indoor-outdoor carpet. "We're fine, Mom. Go inside."

This time, the silence after Mom had shut the door was absolute. Finally, a cough. Alec strummed through a broken chord. His friend practiced smoke rings. But every time people began to talk—the door creaked open. It was Mom again. Then again. And again. Asking in the same bewildered, eerie, child's voice, the same blueberry question.

By the tenth or eleventh time, all conversation had stopped. Inside, I was curled up into a tiny snail inside a little snail shell, waiting for it to be over. "Let's go over to my house," said one of the girls. "It's cool actually. I don't know why I didn't say so in the first place. My parents are never around."

I didn't know whether I was invited to leave with them or not. I got very busy cleaning up glasses until, finally, they wandered off without me.

Outside in the New York darkness, a street alarm shrills on, ricocheting through the walls. I get out of bed and wander around the vast dingy blankness of my apartment. It's true that owning things sends me into a panic about the possibility of my loving things and buying more things. But at the same time it's hard to invite people over without owning a chair to sit on. Worse, the rat that lives in my oven is banging around in the walls and the last time I tried to scare him off, he chewed straight—but raggedly—through the broom handle, scaring me away from the stove in general.

I might not know how to kick-start intimacy and all that "meaningfulness" that Nana was talking about, but I do know how to find a real estate agent in Manhattan.

With her help, I get myself a new apartment, a clean, homey one-bedroom semi-dump with working electricity and heat. It differs slightly from the home I always imagined I'd have, which dates back to a collage I made in Scenic Park Elementary, circa 1976: a clumsily cut-out magazine picture of a glamorous lady (me) and a white fluffy canine (a husky dog), alongside a clumsily drawn picture of a log cabin because there were no photographs of log cabins in magazines.

And yet I can see people coming over to this apartment for bowls of nurturing beef stew and games of Scrabble. I prescribe myself some purchased furniture—purchased, yet used and very cheap, anti-lowboy, anti-highboy, anti–Hong Kong punch bowl furniture. I shove it all in there and eyeball it critically. If I were a documentary filmmaker, I would pan the camera across the sofa, the spatula, the toilet bowl scrubber and say, "Hey, there's a lady who has a life!"

Then I go out to a party, so as not to stay at home and end up throwing it all out.

Far, far uptown, the party is taking place at the Mayflower Hotel on a wraparound terrace. On one side lies Central Park. You can smell the spring trees twenty stories below us, pollinating in the wind. On the other, cars comet up Broadway in vapored streaks of horn and light.

A massive media titan is the host. He doesn't believe in caterers. He made all his money himself, and he throws his own parties. His menu has one course: Veuve Clicquot. The bathtubs of the full-floor suite are filled with champagne bottles and deli ice, as are the sinks and mini fridges and multiple, scattered Styrofoam coolers. Even the planters have been put to use as chilling vats. The actual plants have been pulled out and dumped—their roots left parched and tangled on the carpet. Here a ficus. There a fern.

I'm lingering by an assortment of popped corks when a man approaches. He is bouncy, jaunty, either married or a music producer or . . . married, married, married. "Excuse me," he says. "But—"

I look at his hand. Twinkle, twinkle little ring. He tells me his friend has been watching me all night. I respond the way I always do: a glazed, distant look over his shoulder, the equivalent of sliding an airplane bathroom OCCUPIED sign across my eyes.

But this is the new me, I remember. The meaningful one. I have a homey apartment. I'm open to love and promising futures, even if I'm not really open to them, but only faking it as genuinely as I can until the openness becomes real. I trudge over to the other side of the terrace.

"And this is my friend," says Mr. Married.

"Hello," I say.

His friend is looking down at the arches of Central Park. He's blond. He's blue-eyed. He's wearing a suit—banker? hedge fund? management consultant? He begins to talk about arches and stone and Philadelphia brick, but I'm not listening. A general nimbus of tenderness and intelligence surrounds him. Soft puffy clouds float through his eyes. Prozac? A dreamer?

What the—?

Just like that, Tender Intelligent Man is kissing me—no warning, perhaps drunk, perhaps not, but who cares? I kiss back. Now he's pulling me in, really kissing me. "I have to go," he says. "You should come with me."

An ancient, embarrassing New York fantasy goes whooshing through me, the whole Brut cologne commercial: suave guy from the city, hick girl from the tundra, a terrace, sparkling lights, love at first sight. Instead I say, "I'm going to Canada."

Tender Intelligent Man looks at me a little funny. "Okay."

"Then some island in the Caribbean. I forget which one."

"If you don't want me to call, it's fine. No pressure." He holds up a pen.

I write on his arm. But as he leaves, I call out "Wait!" and chase him down. I grab his arm and scratch out the fake number I'd written. Not that he'll call anyway. But technically, I managed to give him some real Leigh, at least in terms of seven specific digits, assuming a Manhattan area code.

One week later, I'm driving through Canada. I'm in the happy, saltwater-taffy part of Canada, doing a story on 5 Old Fashioned Seaside Inns. Canada is so big it's like a country off a McDonald's menu. Vast distances lie between seemingly close points on the map. I forge on in my rental sedan, headed for golf greens and white resorts with lemonade porches.

I talk to no one other than bellhops. I check into hotels, then wander the towns. There is no need to even interview people. Out of desperation *Travel Time* has changed its editorial direction. Instead of doing long evocative essays that examine art and culture, the magazine is now going to specialize in service-oriented list stories: The 10 Sweetest Salmon Restaurants in Scotland. 15 Romantic Irish Inns. We're going to be the *Lucky* of travel. In other words: a fun, peppy, flip-through catalog-style magazine that generates lots of ad sales. Immediately.

The last night of my trip, I arrive at an inn in Nova Scotia with an authentic whale-watching walk on the roof. It's not an inn, though. Some kind of error has been made and I'm booked into a bed-and-breakfast. I walk into my oversized bridal suite—upgraded!—and flop down on the four-poster bed next to a teddy bear dressed up like Sherlock Holmes.

Dreamy as this may sound, there are so many problems with the situation. B&Bs have no restaurant, which means no room service, which means I will have to drive to a seaside restaurant packed with happy vacationing families, and eat alone at a huge empty booth. B&Bs mean a communal breakfast table, where the minute I sit down, postcoital semi-in-love couples will suddenly begin to eat the banana bread off each other's plates and call each other pet names, because I'm the epitome of their worst fears, I'm the black fate that might befall them—single! alone at a romantic B&B!—if they don't fully, publicly fall completely in love right this minute.

B&Bs also means no night clerk to stop me should I sleepwalk out of the room and try to sleep-drive away. I pick up Sherlock Holmes. He smells as expected—chemical potpourri. I punch him in the muzzle. I hate stuffed animals dressed as people. Real animals need no trench coat. They're human in their eyes and expressions, not their wardrobe choices. This is why people own dogs; dogs stare right at you and understand.

I vault out of bed and grab the phone. I call my own number. I listen to my message, waiting for the beep, waiting to say *Get a husky dog!* so that I can't blow off this idea when I get back to New York. Because a husky dog will fix everything. I knew this at seven years old, and then at nineteen, and then somehow, over time, stupidly forgot.

But my machine is full. My machine, the computer voice says, is not accepting messages. I must have the wrong machine. I never have messages, except from myself. Everybody knows that I'm out of town. And even when I'm in town, they assume I'm out of town.

"It's me," says the first recorded message. "From the terrace."

It's been six weeks since the Brut cologne party uptown. I told Tender Intelligent Man that I was going to Canada, then the Caribbean. But apparently, he thought I was joking or playing hard to get. He has left four messages. None of them is needy or creepy or angry or refers to sexual positions. None of them was recorded after midnight. On the last one, he says, "Hey, I'm not going to call you anymore, but you should call me back. You seemed kind of different—in a good way. I had some stuff to clean up in my own life. I know I took a while. But we could go out to dinner."

I look at Sherlock Holmes.

Soon, I will have a real husky dog. Soon the husky will look up at me and say, with his big emotive eyes, *You're sad. I'm a dog, so I'm sad, too. Why do you make yourself sad, which only makes me sad?*

I'm not a total jackass. I'm not going to make my dog-to-be depressed. I'm going to do the healthy, happy thing, and call Tender Intelligent Man . . . who is not home. Perfect! I leave a message. "What a great idea! Let's go to dinner." I suggest a date two months from now, in case he thinks I'm just sitting around, waiting to be asked out on a date.

Back in New York, I do not have time to follow the humane course of action and buy from a real breeder. There are a lot of hours in the night. I need my husky dog now, who will bark at me if I get out of bed in the middle of the night. I leave the office in search of a pet shop.

Our corporate magazine tower is located in Times Square, right next to a Mars-themed restaurant, which features a life-sized spaceship that takes off and lands, over and over, on the sidewalk. There, on a nearby street pole, hangs a flyer reading in raging Magic Marker, IF YOU DON'T HELP, THIS DOG WILL BE PUT TO SLEEP. There is no picture. I write down the address. Behind me, the spaceship takes off, enflaming the flyer in a panic of blue, blastoff light.

In Queens two hours later, a lady in a snowflake-appliquéd sweater answers the door. Her name is Denise. She is clean, middle-aged, and sane looking. Then she opens her mouth. "My dad has the allergies," she says, going down the stairs to the basement. "It's the worms. He's dying of them. He went blind already. I told him not to go to Mexico."

I'm not sure about the basement. This seems like one of those moments when, in order not to be the idiot dead girl in the horror flick, you should break out your handy-dandy pocket hatchet—which, sadly, I failed to bring along with me—and announce to the hunchbacked bogeyman at the bottom of the steps, "Hey pal, I'm coming down. . . . with a *hatchet*!"

But then I hear the sound of whimpering below.

"I have the worms, too," says Denise. "In my tooth. It's not right. I like the carrots. I like the crispy food."

"What about the dog?"

She shows me a huge leathery growth on her toe. She talks about "the lettuce issue." Then finally, she pulls a very large dog out of a small wire cage. He is a brownish, blackish, shepherdish, beaglish, Labish, dachshundish, wolfish, foxish, rib-caged mutt, also known as a New York City street wolf. He is far too big to keep in my apartment. He trembles. He looks like he might throw up. Denise snaps on his leash. It's a six-inch-long dog collar extended into a leash. She drags him out of the basement onto the brown grass. He pees in a bare puddle of dust. Then she drags him back toward the cage. "Twice a day!"

"Great," I say. "I'll take him."

"He likes the cage. It's safe. From the virus."

But we're already out of there, running down the sidewalk. Except that the dog doesn't know how to run. Or how to climb the stairs to my apartment. He gets an aggrieved, worried expression on his face, right before spraying liquid diarrhea all over my living room walls and bathroom.

"Leonard," I say, the name coming to me suddenly, as I mop around with bleach. "You have to learn to be with people. I know about basements. I spent a lot of time in the basement. And let me tell you, you're out of the basement. You're in your homey apartment now."

He cocks his head.

"But so you know, I travel. I can't be here all the time."

He cocks his head again, in a way that's just so sensitive and understanding, and, quite frankly, noble. It's true, apparently—somebody can look at you, just once, in the right way and you can sign up for a lifetime with him. I make Leonard and me a nurturing beef stew for dinner. I let him sleep in my bed, even though the beef stew runs through him and comes out as . . . beef stew. For Halloween, he and I will be *Julie of the Wolves*. I will be Julie. And he the wolf. Or vice versa.

I go to Copenhagen. I go to Milan. I go to the Bahamas, and fall asleep on my stomach in the sun. Back in New York, Leonard seems to have little sympathy for me. Now that he's relaxed and developed some solid bowel movements, he's developed certain undeniable personality traits. One is the ability to trot rapidly around me and laugh as I try to blend dark orange foundation over the half of my body that did not get violently burned.

Tonight, this is not so helpful. Tonight is my date with Tender Intelligent Man. Which isn't a date, not really. It's just a dog walk with a man: a date-walk.

I try on a sweater. The sweater looks stupid. It is also hot, since it is July. But there is an actual demarcation line between my skin colors.

Leonard laughs a little harder.

I'm somewhat dreading this date-walk. It is not a good idea, not a good idea at all. If you can't be yourself with yourself, how can you be you with other people?

My dog, on the other hand, can be himself with everyone, even if they might prefer if he acted like somebody else. He is not afraid of expressing who he is and who he likes (me), not to mention what he likes (barking and whipped cream from a can sprayed directly into his mouth). The things he doesn't like, he's also extremely vocal about: brooms, garbage bags, shadows on the sidewalk, reflections in the mirror (including his own), people in wheelchairs, people who get too close to me, people or trees or streetlamps or cars that might come too close to me. After all, one of them might try to shove us into a basement.

Leonard will know what to do about Tender Intelligent Man. He will sniff him, find him either unworthy or too worthy, and drive him off via a series of terrifying barks, lunges, and growls. I pull on a coat—a corduroy coat, a snuggly fall jacket, but I'm out of ideas for skin camouflage. Off the two of us go, claws and heels clicking over the cement.

The East Village dog run is a pit of fenced-off mulch surrounded by drool-slimed benches. In the center towers a giant sculpture of a dog bone, carved out of a single log with a chain saw by a manic-depressive neighborhood artist off his meds.

Like Leonard, I love the dog run. I love the ambient cloud of humid, rotten poop. I love the dog freaks, all of whom I know by both dog-freak name and dog name, who rehash daily their animal's latest bowel movement (stringy, chance of chicken bone) and savage the innocent young children who attempt to enter the dog run to pet the dogs, screaming, "No non-dog-owners allowed! No non-dog-owners allowed!"

Today, as usual, a gleeful mass of dogs is running in clawed, homicidal circles around the surrounding fence—the pack! the pack! the pack! the hump! the hump! the hump! Like any good bully, Leonard sits on the bench, trembling in fear. Next to him sits Tender Intelligent Man, who has shown up with a bag of mini cheeseburgers. He is tossing them, like rubber balls, into Leonard's slavering maul.

"Nice dog," says Tender Intelligent Man.

I stand off to the side, with my plastic poop-scooping bag. It might look like I'm blowing off this date, but, in reality, I'm in shock. In the daylight, Tender Intelligent Man is very, very handsome. He has a jaw like the jaws of men who ride wild mustangs across the plain. And yet, he smells like a sensitive, mom-loving boy—fresh and cottony, as if he's not afraid to do his own laundry.

I'm not sure why I didn't notice all this the night we met. Maybe his outfit distracted me. Today, Tender Intelligent Man is wearing pegged, stonewashed jeans cut off at the knee, along with a striped shirt and a plaid cotton jacket, all of which is topped off by a baseball cap with a huge, vertigo-inducing spiral design on the center. A kaleidoscope of unfortunate clothing.

"Uh," says Tender Intelligent Man. "Are you hot?"

"Excuse me?"

"I mean, temperature hot."

"Why?"

"You're wearing an overcoat."

"Yes."

"It's summer."

"It was chilly. At home. By the way, I like your spiral hat."

Tender Intelligent Man looks at me, then breaks out the chocolate shakes. They are thick, towering shakes, with a fine sweat of ice on the outside of the waxed-paper cup. Leonard experiences a fit of ecstasy and falls off the bench. He sits up, looking quickly in both directions to see if anybody else saw.

"Are you a banker?" I say to Tender Intelligent Man, now to be known as Tender Machiavellian Man. "Or maybe a management consultant?"

"I work at an architecture firm."

Leonard is the whore of Babylon, the slut of Santiago. He is slurping down the chocolate shake, which Tender Intelligent Man is letting him drink straight from the oversized straw. I, too, let Leonard slurp the straw. But only at home, where it's more hygienic.

"Well this was nice," I say. "But I'm in Italy next week."

He laughs.

"No, really, I'm in Italy. Florence, then Tuscany."

"Sure."

"Sure is right."

"Who are you dating? You can tell me. It's not like I'm looking to get married."

"I'm going to Italy!"

"Okay, then I'll come, too." He laughs. I laugh. He gets up. I get up.

"I gotta go," we both say, at the same time. But I frown first. Then pull Leonard off down the street.

"About Italy," says Tender Intelligent Man. "I wasn't kidding."

This is why God invented certified-humane choke collars. For tearing your dog away from people he might end up loving more than you. As I drag Leonard down the street back to our homey apartment, I remind myself that I am not taking my first date in two years to Italy. That is ridiculous. Not to mention unsafe. I don't even know this man. He could be anybody, really. He could be a psychopath or polygamist. He could actually be tender and intelligent. Or rude and dumb. Or kind and sweaty. Or boring and good in bed. Or sad and artistic. Or silent and mean. Or loud and funny on the outside but lost and alone and confused and needy and self-sufficient and chanting *leave me alone leave me alone leave me alone* over and over on the inside. Even if, on the outside, he is already calling me up and asking about a second date.

PART III

Back in
the Water

CHAPTER 11

Love and Altitude

The morning of my wedding, I'm on a ladder, hanging Rajasthani lanterns, screaming for the garland of Japanese origami cranes and the extra-long extension cord. I'm down on my knees, slapping dance-floor tiles onto the black oozing mud. I'm deep in the pond, trying to plant tiki torches in the toxic fertilizer manure gunk on the bottom, which has sludged down into the water from the cow pastures.

"What do I do about the pump?" says my groom-to-be. "There are wasps in the pump."

"Pretend you're—"

"We're not on some stupid desert island, Leigh! We're getting married!"

I ignore him and charge on—cursing, kicking things, bossing around close friends who have come up expressly to help us, yelling at random tiny children not to throw their goddamn Popsicle sticks in the daylilies. The tractor for cutting the grass has broken; part of the porch roof on the farmhouse has collapsed due to the weight of the daisy garlands. The signs directing guests to the wedding have blown off in the wind.

There are not many weddings in this cow-rich, cash-poor, dairy-dependent valley in upstate New York. Milk is literally cheaper than water. People are born in Sullivan County; they do not move here. In fact, the locals do not understand why that young couple from Manhattan would have wanted to rent this farmhouse for so many summers when there is a perfectly acceptable faux-brick rancher right on the property. With plastic stained-glass windows.

Even for our Great Alaskan Wedding Guests, comfortable with claw marks from bears on their cabin doors, getting married at the farmhouse is a stretch. The walls are home to bats and mice and moths and raccoons and squirrels and—once—a bobcat who thumped around in the attic, screaming with dark hot fury. There are large gaping holes in the floorboards that you can fall through multiple times and still fall through again.

But Tender Intelligent Man and I have spent the past four summers here. It is the only place we ever considered getting married. For some mysterious reason neither he nor I see the falling-down part.

Then again, we are the only two people I know who would consider our fourth date—lost in the dark forested hills of Tuscany, with no water or functional map or food—to be the greatest date of our lives. Because, four years ago, Tender Intelligent Man—to be known, now and henceforth, as Lawrence—was perplexingly not at all dissuaded by a sudden trip to Italy with a woman he didn't know, a woman who had dragged her large, very odiferous dog along on their three previous dates (a dog who sat between them, eating both their food). Lawrence simply bought a ticket to Florence and flew over.

I wasn't sure about this, not sure at all. People traveling with you can make you do things. Like check your bag. Like take you to a dinner show of Tuscan folk dancing. Besides, I thought, what if I want to do something? For example go forty miles out of the way to eat wild boar? What if he resists? Somebody who isn't interested in traveling to eat wild boar isn't somebody I could fall in love with. I'd never tasted wild boar. However, common sense told me: You were either into wild boar and raw oysters and fresh sweetbreads and goose-fat drippings or you weren't. You'd either come to Alaska one day and meet my family and suck the marrow out of a caribou bone (which no man had yet done). Or you wouldn't.

At the airport in Florence, all was solved. Lawrence wasn't jet-lagged (check!). He'd brought only a carry-on (check!) and he was ready to hit the road (check!). "We should rent a car."

"Why?"

"To get to the boar" (check!).

"What about a train?" I say. "I love trains. Driving is so stress-ful."

A look crossed Lawrence's face. I knew this look. He was decid-ing something. In fact, he was deciding about me, via an interior dating rule about cars. It was true! I wasn't a driver. I could only fall in love with a man who drove a stick shift. But due to my proclivity for daydreaming, I couldn't drive the vehicle in question. While at the wheel, I'd backed into other cars; I'd sideswiped gasoline pumps. I'd hit my own house once, crumpling a canoe-sized dent across the side of Dad's Dodge king crew cab.

"I'll drive," Lawrence said. "Just don't rent us an automatic" (check!).

Speeding away from the airport—at terrifically high speeds, even for Italy—Lawrence displayed such a decisive, masculine way of changing gears. His arm was pretty much chopping wood, except he was driving a car. I was all aflutter. Not to show it, I studied the vineyards on the side of the road, the yellow, dusty, earth tones of Tuscany whizzing by.

Up we went, through twisty, narrow roads, at faster and faster speeds. The car rocked. The guardrail trembled. I was intensely car-sick. I was going to vomit. And Lawrence was not my father. He was not going to hold out the hood of his parka and tenderly motion for me to puke into it because we couldn't land the plane. "Let's pull over!" I said. "That town on the hill looks . . . historic?"

Bagno Vignoni is home to hot springs where Romans used to lounge, steaming away their ancient cares, eating grapes. The whole village reeked of faded decadence and crumbling stone. A tiny, jeweled blue stream dribbled out of the bathhouses. The sun throbbed overhead. We stuck our feet in the water. Lawrence studied a posted map. "You know what? Boar town is only two towns over. We could hike it."

The trendy style of purses at the time was a little backpack that fit a wallet and keys. I threw a toothbrush and a bottle of water in mine. "Let's go."

On the map, in fact, it showed a trail between the towns. But with an arrow pointing in the direction opposite to the one that we were headed, from the boar town to Bagno Vignoni instead of the other way around. "Hmm," Lawrence said. "Let's not rush into anything."

"Oh please," I said. "What's an arrow? We better head out, it's like ten klicks to the pass."

Lawrence looked over. "Were you ever in the army or something?"

"Airborne. Forty-Ninth Regiment of Dad."

The hill leading out of town was steeply pitched and dry. We shuffled down the powdery earth in a zigzag to slow our speed. At the bottom started the trail. Trails are one of those little non-Alaskan pleasures that I will never get over. The tidiness of a trail, the transparency, the joy of not having to brutally cut your way through the bush or just shoulder through, behind a parent who is bigger than you and faster than you and whose pushed-aside branches whip back in your face, leaving you two choices: (1) drop back and get separated in the wilderness, or (2) stay up to pace and fantasize about making that parent pay for the cosmetic surgery you will need once the scars develop from all the stinging, bleeding cuts all over your forehead and cheeks. Not to mention, the relief of not worrying about running into a bear, tucked away just ahead of you in the impenetrable greenery.

The dry, rambling wilds of Tuscany smelled of rosemary, warm and heady, massaged by sunlight. We started uphill. It was a long, grinding, relentless uphill. Out from the trees came a group of Germans marching downhill with walking sticks. And water. And hats. And sunscreen. And woodsy woolen outfits. Then came another group. And another group. All headed downhill.

"I can't stand Germans," I said. "They're always so equipped and organized."

"My dad was German."

"Oh."

The uphill went on and on. And then there was a downhill. For fourteen seconds. And there was more uphill! And more uphill. It was becoming clear why the arrow pointed the other way and the Germans were walking in an orderly line in the opposite direction. We were on a ten-klick death march straight up.

I wasn't about to admit this.

Lawrence, it appeared, wasn't either. He, I found out, as we chatted and climbed and broke through the forest to a fresh round of hills, belonged to a species of human known as the Badass Twenties Traveler. The Badass Twenties Traveler is similar to a Walk-About Australian, only American and thus on the road for a shorter time period. The Badass Twenties Traveler spends his postcollege youth sleeping in the park benches in Yugoslavia, at the start of the Balkan War. The Badass Twenties Traveler wanders Europe and the Middle East for two years, on a budget of two thousand dollars. He lives on sardines and stale bread. He speaks a little Hebrew, a little Arabic, a little German, and a few key words in Greek. He worked for a year on a kibbutz in Israel, right after which he also floated the Nile on a *falouk* with no running water or toilet, roasting tomatoes on a brazier for food. "And then," Lawrence said, "I came to New York and turned into your average working guy."

Now was not the time to brag that, due to the hard-hitting nature of my current job—a job I was doing at this very moment, writing a roundup of 10 Terrific Tuscan Inns!—I could accurately guess the number of stars that a hotel had earned with one quick sniff of the turn-down treat left on my Euro-sham pillow: mint? chocolate mint? or chocolate?

On we go—up and up and up. "This is so relaxing!" I said.

"Yeah!" he said.

Without looking at each other, we both began to laugh. We laughed and climbed and panted and laughed and took a wrong turn and went uphill for another four or five klicks and then up another wrong hill because, apparently, there were a lot of trails in the Tuscan hills (which were mountains by the way), and the one sign of civilization we found was a beautiful medieval monastery, where the monks weren't allowed to talk or even open the door. The next was a crumbled stone barn with swallows and an old rustic man sitting on the step. "Water?" we said, making all kinds of drinking gestures. "Help?"

"*Sì!*" he said, nodding, running off, coming back with two huge bottles of cold, thirst-quenching—wine.

We sipped the wine (me white, Law red) out of politeness, but we were so dehydrated and had been hiking so long, our sips turned into a long, glugging gulps. The old man clapped with approval. We smiled dopey drunk smiles at him. We headed off into the forest, holding hands, on our way to a night that I was pretty sure we were going to spend sleeping in the dirt, holding on to our stomachs, having caught Beaver Fever by drinking cold refreshing sobering water from a fetid stream.

"L'amore!" the old man said, calling out to us. *"L'amore!"*
It was official: We were in love in a foreign language.

Over the next four years, certain things were confirmed. Lawrence actually was tender and intelligent. Add to this: He swam fast and believed in cheating while racing from one end of the pool to the other. He knew how to tease you very drily and accurately, almost without your knowing it. He could speak accents from every place he had ever visited, Israel to Czechoslovakia, including a very funny, slow, ungrammatical version of Québecois based on a maple-syrup farmer whom we met one night in the woods. He drove a completely smoking hot ancient manual Jetta with little paint, and no heat or front grille. He skied fast, he snored quietly, he bought cheap antique chairs and girlie-flavored soaps, he stopped in the middle of dinner between courses to kiss me over the table, and while he didn't eat oysters on the half shell, he'd fake eating one in order to placate me, then let me eat the rest of his half dozen, as long as he got to eat my dessert.

All in all, he was the greatest, sexiest, most wonderful man on earth. But he was also not quite ready for commitment. In fact, the first night in New York after Tuscany, he looked lovingly into my eyes and said, "I'm not really ready for a relationship."

I blinked. Deep in my heart, I was making strange, wounded-kitten noises, which was a bit disconcerting, because I wasn't ready for a relationship, either. Except what if I was? Then I was sunk, because *I'm not ready* is just polite code for "I don't like you enough." I stood very still. Finally, with perfect girls'-school/ Alaskan-survival composure, I said, "Me neither. In fact, I think we should see other people. Starting now."

So we did. One year passed, then another and another and another. He lived in his apartment and I lived in mine. I didn't keep socks or CDs at his place. He didn't keep socks or CDs at mine (thank God, because he was partial to lite jazzy Brazilian numbers).

If I decided to make him a beef stew, I lugged all four of my French copper saucepans (graciously given to me by my uncle Steven before he ran off to the Dominican Republic) two miles over to Lawrence's apartment and then, in the morning, brushed my teeth with my finger and packed up those same pots and staggered home with forty pounds of semi-tarnished metal on my back. Leonard was my dog, not his. I was free to see other people. He was free to see other people.

In my dark liar's heart, of course, I knew that if I found out that Lawrence was actually seeing anybody else I would kill him. Except that I wouldn't kill him. I would just sob and watch helplessly as he stomped over me and walked off into the distance with his hotter, no doubt sweeter paramour. This meant I also actually had to date other people, as many people as possible, so that when he stomped off I wouldn't be standing alone like my mom, sobbing; I'd be standing with some guy I wasn't in love with and I'd had sushi with once—and only once, because he was too tall and not Lawrence and hated snow. (Ugh.)

However, when it came down to the really crucial issue, me getting the hell out of there, Lawrence and I were on the same page. If I had a story, he'd either come with me to Bombay or Toronto or Madrid or Portland—or he'd let me go by myself, and he didn't think it was strange if I didn't call or email for a few weeks from Kyoto or Lafayette or Marrakech. He didn't miss people, he claimed. His parents had divorced when he was nine. Then his dad died when he was twenty. Then his mom died a few years ago, suddenly, of bone cancer.

This was such a relief, to find somebody who didn't miss me the way I didn't miss him. I didn't have to summon a phony sense of despair over the phone. Or bring him some dopey Pope-on-a-Rope soap from Rome. I could just come back and love him and tell him only once every couple of weeks, not to freak him out.

Also comforting was our arrangement. We traveled together and we spent weekends upstate at his falling-down farmhouse rental, but not the weekdays when he had "stuff to do" and I "had to go." The longest time we'd been together straight was twenty unbelievable, sun-stunned days in the deserts of Tunisia, living in a silken tent on the edges of an oasis, with a valet who brought us cold mint tea on horseback, wearing an authentic "Nights of Arabia" turban.

That is, until the fall of year four, when I sublet my apartment to earn a little extra money and go on vacation. My plan was to come back from Milan for work, stay for three weeks in New York to file stories, then head out of town for another three weeks with Leonard on the road, cross-country. It was a Saturday, the day I'd gotten back from Milan. Lawrence was reading the newspaper. I was looking at AAA maps. "So I guess we'll just crash with you, and then head out really early on the fifteenth of October."

He looked up. "Huh?"

"I have a subletter. I can't stay in my place. There's a girl living in it, paying my rent."

"Three weeks."

"Well it's not like I'm a stranger. You love me and I love you. It's not like I'm moving in."

"It's just . . . that's a lot of commitment."

Nothing from me.

"Actually, I don't want to be a jerk, but it's too much commitment."

The door of horrible understanding opened, and a flood of rotten stink water washed over me. I was thirty years old. I couldn't stay at the love-of-my-life's house for three weeks—which for the record I was thinking of as nothing more than a hotel-style stay, except that I wouldn't pay or tip him. I stood up. I whistled for Leonard, who remained passed out on the sofa. I said—rapidly, with no planning or awareness—"Either we get married or this is over. You have two weeks to make up your mind. I am leaving town during this period. Don't call. Don't write. I'm taking my dog . . . and your car."

Lawrence's mouth fell open.

Mine was already open, which evidently is not just a metaphorical expression. Your jaw can drop as if a tiny but crucial screw in the joint has shot out and skittered across the floor. You could fit a toaster oven in my mouth. Or an armchair. You could fit a whole entire person, the whole entire other person who took over my soul and made me—

Propose. Or threaten a proposal at least. As if I were obsessed and professional about getting married, when, up to this moment, I'd never had one single thought about getting married, except with raw, gibbering terror. I mean, why would any intelligent person want to get married? Why not go directly to the brick factory and stand under the brick-machine and let it spit bricks down directly onto your head?

I had to go, I suddenly realized. I had to get out of there, right now, on any kind of road, at high speeds, without stopping to pee or eat. Off I ran, pulling Leonard, who also looked shocked. And kind of worried.

Three weeks later, I was staying with my welcoming if surprised mother. The phone rang. It was the age before caller ID. I picked up. "I miss you," Lawrence said.

I miss you, too, I almost said. Except the voice that had taken over my mouth the last time we talked popped out again, not unlike a magic bully in a bottle. And the voice said: "What's your verdict? In or out?"

"Well." He sighed. "It all happened so fast."

"Hah-hah," I said. Then laughed for real. He laughed, too. Then I stopped laughing, because if there was one thing Lawrence was good at, it was charming his way back in. His was an honest, vulnerable charm, the kind nine-year-old boys use (without quite knowing they're doing so) to get out of going to juvie hall after getting caught stealing baseball cards. But it was charm nonetheless—frosting on a bruised apple. I stopped laughing. "Lawrence," I said. "Four years is not fast. Four years is glacial. Entire species of Galapagos boobies have come to life via genetic aberration in four years. The Revolutionary War was won in four years." (If there was one thing *I* was good at, it was rattling off dubious factoids in an authoritative, trustworthy voice.)

"Here's what I think," Lawrence said. "And I really have tried to sort this all out." Thus began his spiel: He thought it was a good idea if he thought and I thought about getting married maybe, sometime in the near future. There was a lot of family history, for both of us. There were also some issues between us. There were some fears and some considerations and emotions and so forth. And for the record, the Revolutionary War lasted eight years, 1775 to 1783.

"Like what fears and emotions?"

"Like what if I get mad cow disease? I'm not sure you'll stay home and nurse me."

Mad cow disease. From the man whose worst fear was breaking his kneecaps. From the man who would not *walk* with scissors or a sharp-looking toothbrush. But also from the guy whose parents both died from evil sicknesses that came on and took them over and took them away. "I'll stay home and nurse you," I said. "What else?"

"If we get divorced, you'll take all my money and kick me out."

Did I mention Lawrence grew up kind of poor? He called it working class. I called it three kids and a single mom living on a teacher's aide's salary. Every now and then, he'd mention the little miracles that helped them survive, such as the time a strange man hit his mother's car (hurray?) and they were able to use the insurance money to live instead of fixing the dents. "I'm not going to take your money. If I need money, I make my own money. I have been doing it since age twelve."

Now was the time that I was supposed to share my fear: If he cheated on me casually, he must never tell me, especially not to make himself feel better. And if he cheated on me and fell in love with somebody else, he still just had to pretend to love me for at least another ten years, after which he could off me with a painless animal tranquilizer, which for me would be easier. Being dead is safe, in that you have no heart to rip out of your body. I didn't say any of this, however. I said, "Okay, fears taken care of. In or out?"

"Well, it's a big decision. It's a life change." He said this in a quizzical, pensive voice, completely devoid of any joking, as if he were puzzling something out. "All those feelings involved."

"I'm not interested in feelings. I'm interested in action. I'm not losing any more altitude with a romantic dibble-dabbler. You have to do something."

Thus, one week later, Lawrence moved out of his giant rambling loft apartment into my tiny homey dump—citing problems with his landlord, who wouldn't allow him to have a roommate. He didn't bring any furniture or books. He brought a toothbrush and a few shirts. But he slept there every night. It occurred to me that other people who lived together owned blenders in common and opened joint checking accounts, and applied for—I don't know—communal Blockbuster cards?

But, quite frankly, the living together was already a little difficult for me. I hadn't thought about what it meant when another person moved into your five hundred square feet of previously total privacy. Lawrence came with a lot of periodicals. He read four newspapers a day and subscribed to over ten magazines, all of which he refused to throw out until they'd been read cover to cover and the choicest articles clipped for future reference. Not unexpectedly, he couldn't keep up, and had solved the problem with a Byzantine system of piling that was not so much a system as a bunch of dirty mixed-up piles of paper and bills and clippings that aged and yellowed and tottered in every corner. In his huge, rambling apartment, these towers made him look like a cute, absentminded English librarian. Here in my tiny homey dump, it was a little difficult to get to the refrigerator.

Not to mention that when he slept, he took the soft pillow.

Often, staring up at the ceiling, my head on the hard, lumpy, neck-cramping pillow, I thought, *What was I doing when I rammed the marriage idea down Lawrence's throat?* Maybe I was just hurt about not being allowed to stay with him for a few weeks and wanted to really get him back (it's not unlike me to go all the way to getting married in order to win an argument). Or maybe there's some humiliating, needy person inside me who just wants to get married. Is this humiliating, needy person also the dream-me? Ever since Lawrence moved in, I'd stopped packing in my sleep.

So here we are, one year later, at the falling-down farmhouse, about to get married. One hour before the ceremony, I'm still in a tube top and cutoff jeans, both flecked with black mud from my efforts to build a small silk lounge tent beside the large main wedding tent—all on ground that's just a little too close to the pond to be dry or stable.

My original wedding idea had been for us to run away to Greece and say our vows on a volcanic caldera. That is, until Lawrence brought up his idea: inviting his entire Irish extended family, plus everyone he'd ever liked ever, dating back to nursery school in Buffalo. I was slightly taken aback, considering our dating history. But I took to the brute labor of ordering gold-painted plastic forks and wiring icicle lights, as if I were building a sauna out of river rocks dragged from the bottom of a glacial lake by hand (something Dad, Abbie, and I did once during a family fun week in the bush).

Lawrence, on the other hand, didn't exactly take to a year of prep and slavery. His contribution to the planning was tablecloths, as in, "Leigh, relax. We'll just invite everybody and get some tablecloths and, you know, put them on some tables."

Holding a shovel and a punch list, staring at the cold, empty chafing dishes that have not been filled with lamb vindaloo and paneer paleek because the couple who owns the one Indian restaurant within a two-hundred-mile radius of Jeffersonville has not yet found their way through twisty, unmarked roads to the farmhouse, I begin to sink into a bleak, glazed silence.

My friend Lewis orders me to leave the wedding site. I pretend to head out, but really go start weeding an abandoned tomato patch filled with dead vines. Lewis finds me one more time, and shoves me gently into my mother's car. Then he runs off to find my mother, who's supposed to drive me to the hotel to get dressed.

The wedding, after all, is in one hour.

I sit there on the hot passenger seat, alone with my hedgehog of panic—that bristling, clawed little ball that I can manage in front of other people, as long as I'm yelling at them to fluff the daisies in each and every mason jar. Here in the quiet of the car, though, the hedgehog unrolls; the hedgehog begins to scrabble around, looking for a way out of the newspaper-lined cage and back to the happy forest burrow, stabbing me with its exquisitely sharp quills. Because I have some idea—in a textbook way—what you're supposed to feel at your wedding: joy (lots of joy) as well as maybe some nerves or even fear, if not a few upset old feelings about relatives or confusing friends, in addition to a sense of import about the life-changing nature of the occasion.

But slice me open with a Ginsu knife and what you have is Styrofoam. I have no feelings, save for a frantic desire for somebody to look straight at me and say, in a deep, godlike voice, infused with ceremony, YOU ARE DOING THE RIGHT THING. That somebody, who is all-knowing, then needs to patiently explain how much in love you need to be in order to spend the rest of your life with someone, as well as explain the differences between loving somebody; being in love with somebody; love that's really just lust or passion; and love that's really just a thick, white plaster cast over a broken hole of loneliness. That somebody will also know where Lawrence and I fit within the panoply of scientifically proven love rubrics—and explain in a dismissive, patronizing, high-skilled-doctoral manner that I do not, under any circumstances, fit in the last loneliness category—after which she or he will stamp our foreheads: APPROVED.

This is a stamp I have wanted for quite a while, in all kind of situations. It's a ridiculous ambition, clearly, and I long ago found my way around it by confronting the fact that, when it comes down to knowing what you want to do: I don't know what I want to do; I don't have anybody to ask; the people I could ask, I won't believe; and so to get over the hedgehog balling and stabbing and prickling me all over, I just do the nearest, fastest, most difficult thing and live with repercussions.

A wedding, however, has some pretty serious repercussions.

My mother slides into the driver's seat. Her door thunks shut. She gives the steering wheel a little nurturing tap, the way she always does, as if it to encourage Baby, which is the car's name. Baby is a seventeen-year-old white BMW sedan, with a streak of green glitter paint across the side made by enraged ghetto sixth-graders on Halloween, when Mom left Baby at a Head Start center overnight. "That's my girl," says Mom to the car as we rev out of the valley.

I haven't seen her in about five hours. This morning, she left the farmhouse in search of scissors at nine o'clock and came back four hours later—with thirteen pairs of scissors and ten rolls of tape that were no longer needed, plus a surprise she purchased for me at a country antiques shop: a lovely vintage sugar bowl. The sugar bowl is, indeed, lovely. I could probably spend the rest of my life looking at the whorls of my fingertip through the frosted, translucent blue of the glass. She hands it to me now, mentioning I'd forgotten it in the kitchen.

"Thanks?" I say, holding it carefully as we speed up the twisty road that leads over the mountain and out of the valley. I'm tempted to ask, *Mom? Do you think I should marry Lawrence?* Last year, however, I asked her this very question and she looked at me, then said in a kind but distant voice, like the one you use with a hard-working, overqualified waitress whom you'll never see again, "Dear, that's none of my business."

Meanwhile, right now, I have a sugar bowl in my lap. I need to let it in. I need to thank her. She is trying to love me with this sugar bowl—down to the little silver cover on the bowl, embossed with wildflowers. This kind of love has been going on since I left home for college, when all of a sudden she began sending me gifts, exquisite, inexplicable ones: luxury umbrellas, a strand of pearls, decorative crystal rocks inscribed with the word COURAGE. I was never sure if these were apologies for the confusions of my childhood, or if she had simply gotten happier since I'd left home. Raising a child on your own is a lot of work, especially if your child happened to be me.

After the blueberry-muffin episode, I started behaving in Baltimore the way I did in Alaska—only with a big, fat splash of attitude. Mom didn't have other kids or a husband she might love more than me—which, sadly for us both, meant I just wasn't afraid enough of losing her, the way I was with Dad. I sneered and savaged and stormed out, coming back only occasionally, and only to change clothes. Maybe I was confused and upset on the inside, but that was way, way, way deep on the inside. The rest of me was livid, even when she was behaving normally or even trying to help me by offering to wash my shirts for school.

Then the call came, a few weeks into my junior year of high school. I found Mom sobbing in her bedroom. Maybelle had snapped and gone catatonic. She'd been committed to a state asylum. I tried to study for the SATs as we drove to Alabama overnight—too broke for a flight as always, trading off at the wheel during the twenty-five-hour-long straight shot down I-95, stopping once and only once, at a Waffle House on the beltway outside Atlanta.

We found Maybelle strapped to a wheelchair. She still looked like the kind of person who should be talking about her past as a dancer at the Copacabana, wearing pancake makeup and a faded orchid behind her ear, which only made it all the more upsetting— her in a diaper and not much else, her staring at the air, as if she could see through reality into the combinations and recombinations of invisible oxygen molecules.

I sat there patting her hand, trying to think of some possible way we could get her out of there. Nobody deserved this, nobody.

"Baby girl," she crooned, suddenly coming to. "Baby girl."

I patted her hand. "It's okay, Grandma."

Mom was standing across the room. "Leigh," she said. "Go get the nighties we brought her, will you?"

Maybelle suddenly cocked her head. She sat up ramrod-straight and said in a sharp, clear voice, as if she had fully recovered, "Dolly girl! You git over here right now, you selfish little shit."

My mother froze, the way squirrels do, as if not moving might blend her into the surrounding linoleum.

"You git over here," Maybelle said.

I took a step, moving in between the two them. But I didn't need to. Mom wasn't going anywhere near her mother. She was trembling, violently so, enough for her purse to jitter along with her. She seemed to kind of fade away from us. She was there, but she wasn't there. Behind her eyes, the lights were off.

Maybelle grunted and shook her head.

The flat, vicious tone of her voice, the sight of my mother at age forty-five sinking into what amounted to a standing coma—I suddenly understood, the way that I couldn't at age seven when I'd first seen it, that cruel and irrevocable things had happened to her as a little girl, things that she hadn't gotten over and would probably never get over. For example, her crooked, broken teeth, which she'd always claimed were hurt in a fall off her tricycle.

I was seventeen years old. But even then I understood that my mother wasn't going to be able to explicate in tidy, revelatory detail what had happened all those years ago, and that I had to stop blaming her for not knowing about thermometers or dentist's visits or how to take care of somebody. Nobody had taken care of her, I realized. Nobody had bought her a winter coat or given her advice on her wedding day.

All of which I remind myself of—loudly, in capital letters—as Mom pulls us into the lot of the hotel where all the guests are staying. We park the car. We unload Baby and head into the hotel, which had looked cozy and rustic when I'd seen it buried in snow six months ago, but now looks like what it is: a dump, complete with a blinking VACANCY sign.

Our room is a dark, dismal extravaganza of wood paneling and airborne mold. With forty-five minutes left to go before getting married, I sit on the bed, on the nubbed, discolored comforter, still holding the sugar bowl. Mom fusses with her bags, pulling things in and out of them: sweaters, toiletries, sandals, slippers. "What do you think of these?" she says holding up—

Pajamas. She has bought herself pink Ralph Lauren mother-of-the-bride pajamas.

If I were a better person, I would tell her how much I love the sugar bowl. If I were a better person, I would tell myself to be glad she disappeared for five hours, because that meant she didn't have to watch Dad and Abbie and Daniel and Jack, the whole Newman clan doing what Alaskans do best, from commandeering a neighbor's tractor to mow the field to setting up the electric piano. Four against one is just not fair. I'm not unacquainted with that feeling.

But I can't help it. I'm desperate for my stamp of approval. I want her to tell me what to do, and—this is the hardest part—for me to believe her. How do you stop longing for what you absolutely know you can't get? Which really means: How do you absolutely know you can't—and won't—get it, not ever? How do you pinch out that wisp of feeble, ruthless hope?

Mom, I suspect, struggles with the same exact question. She no doubt longs for a daughter who hugs her and drinks champagne with her on her wedding day, giggling and snapping pictures—instead of some silent lump sitting on a motel bed. This is a loss we both express by arguing vigorously about shower gel. Then we bicker about the dress I made her wear (just for the record: It matches her eyes).

"Put on your own dress!" says Mom. "I don't want to talk anymore."

"Me neither," I say. I pick through the suitcases, the bags, that great cashmere heap of Mom's accessories. No dress. We search the closet, the bathroom. No dress. And it's not in the back of the car, either. I have nothing to wear to my wedding, which, according to the digital bedside clock, is due to take place in thirty-two minutes.

Something in me cracks—and gives. I slump down on the carpet. I'm out of panic. I'm out of rage. For the first time in my life I just can't race out of the room and find that dress, right goddamn now. I'm too tired. I've ruined my wedding day being crazed and rude and unfeeling. And now I just want to shut the door to the room and stay here for the next twenty years. I rest my head in my hands.

Mom, however, is suddenly karate-chopping down doors, interrogating housekeepers, while I sit on the floor, blank and useless. One hundred and twenty-five people are waiting on the lawn. Plus the other ten who didn't RSVP and whom we have no chairs for.

"Stay here," she announces. "Don't move!"

And off she commandos in her car, her progress identifiable by the clouds of dust rolling on either side of the wheels as she tears up and over the mountain between the hotel and farmhouse. All this speed and violence is so immediately reassuring. It hits me, with absolute, total conviction, that Mom knows what to do; she will find that dress.

Because there *are* people out there in this world who might not know how to do regular life so well, but in a crisis will leap over small country mountains and break land-speed barriers. Maybe because they grew up knowing only that.

It occurs to me that for the rest of my life, I need to remember this moment—waiting for my mother, infused with the kind of deep, old faith that goes back to who we used to be together, who we could be once again maybe—me at the sink on tiptoe, her combing my hair in long, slow, uneven strokes, the smell of her skin like the world's original perfume. This is what my mother can give me if I let her, love in the form of rescue.

When she returns twenty minutes later, having ransacked the falling-down farmhouse until she found the friend who had "tidied" up the wedding dress by storing it in a hallway closet, I'm still sitting filthy and useless on the motel floor. She spreads the dress gently across the bed. Part of the train swoops down to the carpet.

I stare upward at the gauzy hem. It's like looking at a swan from the bottom of a weed-choked pond. Mom runs the hot water. She puts me in the shower. She washes my hair. And she takes care of me, my mother.

By the time my baby brother Jack—now age sixteen—begins playing the wedding march on the piano, Lawrence is waiting in a shockingly suave suit on the farmhouse porch. The minister stands beside him, adorned in casual interfaith raiments. Daisy garlands and twinkle lights distract from the broken boards and gutters. A bug-bomb jammed down the pump has wiped out the wasps.

Dad and I wait at the top of the hill by the barn. It's a long country march to the farmhouse. All the people down below look like little pastel flowers in the grass. This is happening, I realize. I'm getting married. I wobble a little, visibly.

Dad, too, is in a shockingly suave suit. He hugs me. He hugs me again. All that bitter, rusty, unsaid stuff may still stand between us. We may not see each other that often, and when we do see each other, we might both simultaneously revere and dread it. But the fact remains, whatever differences we've had, I will never lose faith in the law of Great Alaskan Dads and Daughters: Whatever he says to do, I will do. And whatever he doesn't say to do, I will also do, because if he's not saying it then he's just assuming that I know enough to imitate his actions (crawl on the ground, save your water, walk down the aisle) and keep myself from dying senselessly in a patch of alders due to some danger I don't yet have the wisdom to comprehend.

In other words, for me, my father is about as all-knowing as it gets. He could give me that red stamp of APPROVAL right this second. He is a doctor; he may just have some kind of authoritative, diagnostic pen in his pocket with which to scribble the word on my forehead. I almost ask, *Dad, tell me the truth, should I get married?*

But he hugs me one more time. He's floating, the Cinderella of fathers. I've never seen him like this. The median age of a Great Alaskan Bride is 22.5. I am thirty-one. It's been a long, anxious wait for him, a wait that is now officially over. Why ruin his big, beautiful moment—one of the few I've ever been able to give him?

Besides, Dad already tried to address this question. He invited Lawrence up to Alaska and put him through a series of grueling tests: a thirteen-kilometer cross-country ski in ten-below weather (check!), a trip to the shooting range to see if a guy from New York City could blast two clay pigeons out of the sky with two shells (check!), and a dinner to make sure that, despite any dopey phobia about broken teeth, that same guy could eat a whole roasted mallard, whose meat contains various molar-cracking bits of shot (check!). Then he took me aside and said, "I tell you what, honey. That Lawrence might make a pretty good Newman."

I didn't have the heart to tell him that Lawrence wasn't the one who was supposed to change his name. Besides, what Dad was really saying was: I like Lawrence. I approve. Which made me feel ecstatic at the time. I ran around telling everyone. Now, all of a sudden, the logic flutters and curls. Dad was approving of him and Lawrence and the possibility of all of us getting together for semi-annual fly-fishing trips, not me and Lawrence getting together and staying together for the rest of our natural lives.

A butterfly whisks by. In the distance, the sound of a tractor.

Dad and I start down the hill, toward the apple tree, where all those people wait, all those Alaskans, Baltimoreans, New Yorkers, Californians, Parisians, Russians, Pakistanis, New Zealanders, assorted family, old friends, new co-workers, dairy farmers from down the road, all clumped down there. It's amazing, the love that vibrates off people during weddings, as if the ancient god of ceremonies has ignited a fresh glow stick through the inner being of everyone present.

Wow. That's a lot of people. And wow. They're all looking at me. I'm not sure what I'm supposed to do with my face. Am I supposed to look like I'm filled with love or just sacred, solemn convictions? Dad gives my arm a squeeze. I'm a little afraid we won't make it to the minister without him stopping to hug a fence post.

Mom smiles at me, equally euphoric. With Dad in his suave suit, they still look like they could be married. They have that matchy-matchy quality (in their case: small, loud, inexhaustible) that couples have, which makes strangers occasionally mistake them for siblings. You'd never know that inside they were so emphatically—and geographically—different.

Lawrence and I also have this matchy-matchy quality. We, too, look similar, except for our eye color (him blue, me brown) and volume (him soft, me loud). Not to mention that we both love to swim and ski and laugh and travel and play Scrabble and eat too much food and draw without any talent or training in the art form whatsoever. In short, we have all the things in common that make for a life in common—something Dad and Abbie have always had, and they've been married for twenty-three years.

It would be convenient if I could convince myself that this is what marriage is about: compatible choices. But isn't there supposed to be something more than that, something twinkled and holy? If only my dad wasn't my father, because then I could ask him—without feeling as if I were intensely and irrevocably betraying my mother—how the hell you know if you and another human being share this. Because Abbie and my dad must have something happening on a higher, less earthly plane. They don't burn down the kitchen or long for other people or storm out of the house, sobbing, and drive straight to a Holiday Inn in East Anchorage where they ask their six-year-old daughter to go get ice from the ice machine every ten minutes so they can scream some more on the phone, without her hearing.

It's generally easier to articulate the disastrous than the miraculous. But I would like some hint at least, about the latter. After over two decades together, do Dad and Abbie still dream of each other or whatever it is that defines the reason why you need to—and should—spend the rest of your life with another person?

Fifty yards from the minister and daisy arch, I start drifting off the aisle, into the vague, non-wedding grass. Dad follows my lead. The piano music stutters, then restarts. When out of nowhere, Leonard suddenly rips away from his snarling and muttering laps around the guests, and bounds joyfully toward me. He drops into step by my side. He is heeling. He is marching along like Lassie—my dog, the dog who ate my portable phone trying to defend me from a caller inside it, the dog who will not "sit!" unless you pull out a chair for him at the dinner table.

I start bawling. Because here is my all-knowing person, here is the one who can actually yea or nay what I'm about to do, the one whom I can trust. Because Leonard likes no one and he likes Lawrence (save for one regrettable confrontation involving a slab of smoked salmon). And because Leonard is right here, stepping on my floor-length train, causing my head to yank painfully back.

Dad eyeballs my dog. It's clear he has a short-term plan, which is to toss Leonard on an iceberg and push him off to sea for the good of society. There's a long pause, not unlike a gunslinging moment in a cowboy movie, where we all consider one another's strengths and weaknesses. After which, to my surprise, Dad simply waits for Leonard to step off my veil, then adjusts the veil for me and leads us on—with great tenderness and grace. This goes on every three or four steps: yank, wait, adjust, walk on. It's a long procession. He is the most patient father of the bride ever.

At the pump, the minister-for-hire—a kind, slow-spoken woman with hair the color of a forest fire at sunset in Tahiti—begins the ceremony. Lawrence is holding my hands. He's looking into my eyes. He's been glow-sticked also. He's beaming, but in his low-key, understated way—opalescent happiness.

And it hits me, deeply, deep as the summer thunder that will roll through this valley in two hours and unleash torrential rain all over our tents and tiki torches and gifts, all of which we will have left out on the grass. Law is very, very, very sure about what we are doing.

Where did he get that kind of confidence?

I look at his face and suddenly understand—in gorgeous, full-color, slow motion—that when he told me he wasn't ready for commitment, he really wasn't. And when he told me he was ready, he *was*. Because he is one of those people who know what they are feeling.

I'd realized this before—but only sloppily. I'd admired his calm and his ability to remain genuine in times of what should have been intimidation and duress. This happened frequently at loud, kissy-kissy New York parties, where very exceptional people (example: a nuclear physicist who developed the H-bomb) found him sitting alone in the corner, happily eating peanuts, and blew off their award-winning friends to spend the whole night talking with him, wading through hefty heated arguments about the Gaza Strip, followed by a discussion about their fears over having a mole removed from their chin. Because Lawrence might be intelligent and tender and funny but, mostly, people feel they can trust him. And this is because he trusts himself.

The minister begins talking about meeting us for the first time (correction: the only time) and our mutual love of scuba diving. Lawrence takes my hand. He does realize, right? That I do *not* trust myself at all—not when it comes to people.

A hideous, cold trickle of sweat begins to slink down my armpit and into the white netted silk of my dress. A moth lands on the pump. The wind picks up, smelling of pond and citrus. The minister's mouth keeps moving slower and slower—a long, rolling O of lipstick and words and teeth. On she goes—saying things, lighting candles.

"I will," Lawrence finally says. He squeezes my hands.

I look at him. I give myself a minute. Because as long as I'm looking at him, I have that feeling, the one I get when he and I are alone (without all these daisies and faces and candles and pomp and tiny, invisible, circling gnats), as if a cool creek were burbling up and down the length of my body.

"I will," I say.

There is the sound of applause. There are stars, even when I know they are camera flashes. As long as I keep looking at Lawrence, I tell myself, it'll all go quiet. It'll go still and sunset-colored, just him and me. The years will pass, and eventually all that trusting-of-himself will rub off on my self, and I will stop staggering around and just know, with inner conviction, what I need to do and what I feel. We'll sit together, old, gray, and rumpled, on some bench in rural Italy, full of twinkled and holy advice for similar not-so-young people, in similar confusions about love and life and the need for bug spray at a country wedding at dusk. That will be our life. Just as soon as everyone stops hugging us and crying on us and touching my dress as if it were made out of butterfly wings and finely woven, never-realized dreams.

CHAPTER 12

Riding Out the Updraft

Here we go, a memory: Dad and I are flying back from Lake Iliamna in the 185. He's in the pilot's seat, I'm next to him, playing with my set of identical controls. It's early evening. The plane is loaded with reds. The sky is silver and bright. All of a sudden the altimeter begins to spin in crazy circles. We're at four thousand feet, then six thousand, then eight, ten, twelve, fourteen.

"Well, that's kind of funny," Dad crackles over the headset microphone.

"What?" I say.

"A single-prop plane isn't supposed to be able to fly at seventeen thousand feet."

I laugh and laugh. "Are we in trouble?"

Dad laughs and laughs, too. "If your lips turn blue, then we're in trouble."

I look at his lips. His lips are blue. I laugh and laugh. I'm eleven years old. I never laugh with my dad anymore. I don't let myself, especially when he tries dumb old tricks like stealing my nose or tickling my collarbone. I laugh some more. The altimeter hits eighteen thousand feet, twenty thousand. The height of Denali at the peak.

"Boy," Dad says, giggling. "If I pass out, you just turn off the power and we'll drift down eventually. Got it?"

"I feel great!" I say, holding out my hands, marveling at the blue of each finger, my skin the color of the veins on the dictionary map of the human body. It's cold. The updraft doesn't make one sound. It's so silent, invisible, lifting us up and up like a tiny, dry snowflake.

"We're not going down," says Dad. He reaches over and turns off the power. Then he pushes the stick all the way forward and points the plane directly at the ground. I've never seen him do this before. In general, in flying, you don't want to see things you've never seen before. But nothing, not even this, upsets me. I feel great.

"The bad thing about this is," Dad says, "we'll probably drop off this updraft, then have to stop our fall pretty quick."

I laugh.

"If we can stop it."

I laugh.

He laughs and laughs until it turns into a stream of giggles. "Lack of oxygen makes you laugh!"

The altimeter is spinning again, but down this time, from twenty to eighteen to fifteen to twelve. It's a gentle sinking—as silent on the way down as on the way up.

"Wow," Dad says. "We really should be falling right out of the sky."

"But we're not!"

"Nope."

I look out the windshield at the world getting closer and closer to us, slower and slower—trees, stream, ocean. There all of it is. There we are, flying above it, upright.

"Leifer," he says, "let's not tell your mother about this . . . I mean . . . your stepmother."

Three months after the wedding, I'm thinking of this incident while lying on a futon in Massachusetts. I'm wondering why I wasn't scared, even afterward when I had enough oxygen to understand that we almost died up there. The whole experience felt very drifty to me, natural and unreal at the same time. Because really, there was nothing we could do—no switch to flip, no choice, no struggle. We just had to ride it out. Everything—living, dying—it all was going to be decided for us.

There's such odd comfort in that.

I've been looking, I think, for that same feeling all my life. I'm not sure how you get there without almost fatally crashing. And I'm pretty sure you can't get there if you don't get out of bed. But the futon where I've been lying for the past month is not some place that you just want to rush away from. It's like sleeping on a silken down cloud. There's a layer of thick luxury fluff strapped to it, known among bedding aficionados as a pillow top.

The pillow top, the quilt, the sheets, the two soft pillows (one for me, one for Leonard) all came from the landlord who rented me the garage, which also came with pastoral French doors with a view of the woods. The garage is not called a garage, either. This is Massachusetts, where poetry grows on the trees, along with apples known as Ambrosias and Earliegolds and Royal Empires. In this state, a garage is called a carriage house.

I'm here on a fellowship to grad school—an opportunity that presented itself a few weeks before Lawrence and I got married in the form of an acceptance letter. I'd always wanted to write fiction and I'd been thinking that, due the impending nuptials, I should probably stop traveling so much and spend some time with Lawrence. I applied to nine schools for creative writing (three of them in New York) and got into exactly one—in Amherst, three hours outside the city.

"Well," I said. "It's closer than Switzerland."

"You'll come down on weekends," Lawrence said. "I'll come up."

Neither of us brought up the subject of him coming with me. First of all, he has a job that makes a livable amount of income. Secondly, this was a schedule like our old schedule. Me away for a few days, then the two of us in our tiny homey dump for a few days, and so on . . . This arrangement, at least, would keep us in the same time zone.

From the futon, the garage looks not unlike my childhood dream cabin in the woods. If I squint, Leonard is, roughly—although with a muskier, more violent body odor—a husky dog. Plus there's a woodstove, crackling with propane flames—which means no Great Alaskan Chopping and Hauling and Stacking of Logs! It's perfect, a fantasy come to life.

Except that I'm here all by myself.

The one pesky, unfixable flaw of the garage is that it has no plumbing. In other words: no toilet. To relieve myself, I have to get out of the futon, exit the French doors, walk across the backyard, enter the landlord's farmhouse, and climb the stairs to the one dinky bathroom. By week six on the pillow top, this is too much exertion. I can't get out of the futon and go all the way over there. Fifty yards across the hard, stubbled grass is too far.

In a single, Herculean effort, I get myself upright, drive to the store, and purchase an attractive, rustic-looking pail. It's like an outhouse. But it's inside the garage, right next to the futon. I make a rule—and this, too, takes effort—that I can only use the pail for a number one. I pull up the quilt. I snuggle in with Leonard. I can now lie on the pillow top in peace, admiring the backyard—the assorted high, overgrown boxwood hedges, the cardinals flashing by, the occasional suburban child's birthday balloon.

A note about garages: They are so dusty and silent and wonder-ful. Mine in particular comes with the advantage of emptiness. I own nothing here except for clothes and books. There are no boxes of wedding-present wineglasses. There are no piles of rotting peri-odicals. Nobody is watching me or photographing me or telling me, "It's all about people," as Lawrence did during the reception when I cried about the cold samosas and the missing trash can of cham-pagne.

He was laughing when he said this. He was trying to comfort me, to show me the light and truth in the universe beyond our tower of two hundred just-slightly melted cupcakes, and he was right. It was all about people . . . and yet what I couldn't bear to tell him was what he already knew: People go away. They don't mean to go away, they don't want to, but they end up doing so, even if you build In-dian silk tents for them and set off bottle rockets for them and bake a chocolate cake you don't know how to bake for them, even if you make sure they catch a nineteen-inch rainbow on their first day fish-ing ever, and do all the rest of the heavy lifting, those expressions of love that are also lurching attempts to either distract or dissuade them from what is going to happen anyway—a good-bye, honey, said with great tenderness.

Now that I'm alone, all that work seems like too much work. Because this is the first time in a long, long time that I'm not anxious or scurrying around with a shovel, passport, or a bunch of copper saucepans. I'm just lying here, drenched in cool, silent relief.

A swift little river of logic whisks through me: People get mar-ried because they don't want to be alone. But I've been alone for most of my life. I'm used to it. It's not comfortable, but it is comfort-ing. And it's not exhausting, either. It's like taking off your ski boots or climbing boots (which are really just ski boots but for climbing mountains) and easing your foot out of that toe-to-top-shin, plastic-and-buckle-prison. Your feet swell and breathe—and become feet again, blistered raw ones, but feet nonetheless, instead of two numb, dead stumps at the bottom of your body used for getting up shale slides or down a run of iced-over moguls.

Lying here on the pillow top, when I shut my eyes, I can't see Lawrence's face. I can't smell his smell or remember the color of his eyes, even though I know in a clinical way, as if reading off his driver's license, that they are blue. Clearly, this is what happened every time I left my dad for my mom or my mom for my dad. But shouldn't I have outgrown it? Because there's nothing to stop me from standing up, packing my duffel, shoving Leonard in a crate, and grabbing a plane for somewhere else—say, Seoul, where my friend from college has a job teaching English. I've always wanted to see South Korea—and North Korea for that matter.

The same goes for Lawrence. He's back in New York, not missing me, either, free to jet off to Brazil, the way he's always talking about. And if I really think about it, this is our real problem—the problem curled up inside the hedgehog of fear during the wedding, a hedgehog I should have forced out of its hole long before getting married. Missing is longing. And longing is love. Which, according to this logic, I don't know how to feel. And which he doesn't, either.

This is when it hits me, a kind of sweeping, inner updraft—ten thousand feet, twelve thousand feet, sixteen thousand. I look out the garage window, feeling a little panicked. But it's a quiet, dull, familiar panic. All I have to do is not move. Twenty thousand feet. I hover there. I wait. I don't have to decide. I just have to breathe. I know what comes next.

Three hours south, there's still some summer left in the fall. The leaves are yellowing on the linden trees. People rush down Clinton Street, wearing thick, complicated scarves, but with sunglasses on and shoes without socks. Manhattan.

Lawrence and I are sitting on the steps outside my old apartment. We've been married for three months. But I'm not changing my mind. I don't want to go upstairs. I don't want to go talk. I just want to sit here and say it fast: Lawrence can have my apartment. He can have the Le Creuset casserole and lobster-claw crackers. He can have the geranium I planted in a coffee can. He can have everything. He *should* have everything. Including Leonard. All this is my fault. I'm the one who shouldn't have gotten married from the beginning. I should have known this, but I never know what I feel, which is the number one reason why I can't be married. And quite frankly, since he is the one who brought up "fears and considerations and feelings and so forth" before we got married, he should have realized the failure-to-feel problems on my end. "You never wanted to get married in the first place," I say. "I forced you into it. And now I'm letting you out of it. I'm sorry."

"But," says Lawrence, his voice sounding oddly calm, almost puzzled, as if he doesn't understand what's being said.

I can't look at him. I just have to be clear and not get distracted. This is the down part, after the up of a decision. Consequences are always scary and rough. "I'm leaving. I have to go."

"But Leonard is your dog."

"But you should keep him."

"But he's your dog."

"But you should keep him."

"But he's your dog."

"But I'm leaving you and you're going to need somebody so, please, just fucking keep the dog." I start walking quickly down the street. Unfortunately, Leonard was abandoned at birth. He is basically my shadow with fur. He trots along behind me. I walk him back to the bench.

"Sit, Leonard," I say. "Stay!"

Leonard sits on my shoe. Lawrence looks down at his hands, maybe to keep from looking at me. I wonder if he's thinking of the dog trainer we hired from Slovenia last year, who kept confusing our names and screaming, "Stay, Leigh! Stay, Lawrence! Sit, Lawrence! Leonard, you must follow through with the treat!"

We never talked about alliteration and the reality of having that many L's in one house before getting married. We never followed through, either—not with treats or leases or electric bills in both our names. I throw the car in gear. Leonard tears down the sidewalk and jumps through my open window, clawing across my lap to the passenger seat. Lawrence looks up. He lifts his hand, looking so lost. "See you next weekend?"

I don't know what to say to that. I drive away.

CHAPTER 13

Boulder, Boulder, Paddle

I know exactly no one in Massachusetts. Driving up there, this feels like a wonderful thing. I'm safe from caring, inquisitive friends in common. I'm pastless, open to new futures, speeding in my sturdy, all-wheel-drive vehicle through the college town of Amherst, which is a snug, steepled, brick-and-clapboard village for about one square mile. After that, it turns into mass-market America—a long, traffic-snarled highway lined with Jiffy Lubes and Dunkin' Donuts.

The grocery store, Super Stop & Shop, is larger than my whole New York apartment building. I push a cart down the endless, glittering aisles. All the choices, all the possibilities, all the applesauce and laundry detergent and fried fish sticks lie before me, flashily packaged. I'm not used to laden, appetizing shelves like this. I'm used to a dusty can of Pringles and a browning pile of plantains from the corner bodega. The air at the Stop & Shop smells so fresh, so chilled, not unlike waxed florist flowers.

At a pyramid of juicy, fresh, symmetrical oranges, my newfound euphoria pops. There are too many oranges, too many kinds of soy sauce; there is too much choice—in the supermarket and in the rest of my life, the huge, looming rest of my life.

Somehow I make it to the meat section. In the refrigerated case is a package of thirty-two chicken wings—all with pimpled, puckered, yellowed skin. Who on this planet could possibly eat that many chicken wings? Orphans. Sitting at a long sad wood table, with empty tin plates.

The star-shaped sticker on the package, however, reads FAMILY SIZE!

I have to dump the cart and run out of the store and get away. Lawrence and I were not a family. We were two people who got married. And we never talked about having children, the way we never talked about anything. How could I possibly ever raise a child—me who thinks of orphans, when the rest of the world apparently thinks of moms and dads and brothers and sisters, sitting together, eating chicken wings?

It was my mom who was adopted—not me.

But somehow, even the basic family stuff escapes me. While in college, I went up for summers to Alaska, just to make sure my brothers would know me, even if I was away for most of their day-to-day lives. The summer Daniel was six—and Jack three—their babysitter quit. Overnight, at age nineteen, I was in charge of child care. I had a lot of love for the boys, but not a lot of ideas. Much of our time was spent playing "Eat Froot Loops" or "Dance to *Abbey Road*" or "Nap." By five o'clock we were all collapsed on the carpet, stupefied by sugar and praying intensely that Abbie would walk through the door.

I didn't understand my stepmother at all. She felt no need to bellow at us, even when Dad tracked most of the red, clam-digging clay in the state of Alaska all over the kitchen floor, which she'd just swept. Did this make her a wimp? Or did this make her some kind of mind-control warrior? I wasn't sure. But hers was a different way of doing things, especially with my brothers. When they mouthed off, she reacted in a strange and wondrous way: She sent them up-stairs to their rooms to sit by themselves for two minutes.

Even more astonishingly, my dad began doing this, too. In the evenings, I watched him in the backyard, either working with his bow and arrow, shooting bales of hay, or practicing C-casts with one of his new fly rods. One night Daniel was out there with him, throwing rocks into the lake. He picked up a rod. "Careful," said Dad, continuing to cast.

Daniel starting using a rod as a sword, jabbing it at the bushes, then looking over to see if Dad saw he was jabbing.

"That's a delicate rod," said Dad.

"I know," said Daniel—jab, jab.

"That's Daddy's. It was a gift from a friend and very, very expen-sive."

Jab, jab.

"The rod, son." Dad put his own rod down and started over, but Daniel smiled tauntingly and jabbed one last time, at the alder bushes. The rod bent. Snap went the tip. Dad grabbed him by the shoulders.

Twenty feet away, I flinched.

But Dad only knelt down and said very calmly, "You were not listening to me, son. Now the rod is broken. You'll have to have a time-out."

I backed away, confused, furious. Why hadn't Daniel gotten whapped? That rod was bamboo, custom-made. If it had been me, I would have been flat on my back, my head reeling and the world gone tilted. I grabbed my jacket from off the deck chair—but stopped by the path at the edge of the yard. What kind of person was I, that I could wish that on my brother? I loved Daniel. I should be glad that Dad was being different with him. I should be glad that Dad was being different overall. I knew he was trying, and I knew how hard it was to change yourself. It was pretty much impossible, but he was doing it—while look at me, running off again.

The differences in the house struck me so much that I began taking field notes in an old spiral notebook. Like: *hitting kids, not effective. bribe them with stickers?*

Then came the incident with *Star Wars* cards. Abbie, Daniel, Jack, and I were strapped into the minivan, headed for home from a late playdate. Daniel was in the way-way back. His arms were crossed. He did *not* want to play with his friend Ronny ever again. "Why not?" said Abbie.

"Ronny did *not* share his Boba Fett."

Abbie pulled the car over—right there on the shoulder, on busy Jewel Lake Road, despite the fact that we were late for swimming class. (Newmans are *not* late for things.) "How did that make you feel?" she said, turning around.

"Mad," Daniel said.

"Well . . . are you sure you were mad? I usually feel something else when my friend isn't being a good friend."

I stared at Daniel. Then at Abbie. What was she thinking? Daniel was six years old. He thought you could find dinosaur fossils among the frosted detritus of his breakfast cereal.

"Actually," he said (his favorite word, pronounced *act-chooo-ally*), "I am sad. I love Ronny and he doesn't like me."

Holy crap. I went home and wrote this in my notebook. *Ask kids about feelings. Specific ones. Mad. Sad. Broken Heart.*

Back at the garage, without groceries or Lawrence or the children we didn't have, my daily vitamins now come from cigarettes. I smoke all night and day. I'm turning into smoke, free and light and drifty. You're okay. You're okay, I say to myself over and over, wandering around, picking things up: sock, dog nail clippers, glass of water, phone.

Leonard lifts his head off the bed and looks me over. I put the phone down.

A week later, though, I pick it back up. I call my mother. She answers in one ring. "No time to talk, honey. The taxi's waiting!"

Mom is on her way to a mock hurricane in Texas. The mock hurricane only takes place once every three years, with actors playing the victims and real firemen playing real firemen, erecting tents and aid stations. If you don't make the mock hurricane, you can't volunteer for the Red Cross during real hurricanes, which my mother has always wanted to do in order to make up for the fact that she did not do the Peace Corps and, instead, at age twenty-two, got engaged to my dad.

I tell her my news.

She says, "I'll skip the training. I'll hop in the car. I'll be right there. Don't move!"

I slump immediately. Here it is, the moral showdown: Leigh versus hurricane victims. How can I ask Mom to race away, at high speed, from one of her lifelong dreams? She is made for the Red Cross. She is made for helping people who need help, and I don't need help—at least not in that way. Nothing was done to me by the hand of God or a freak act of nature. I did all the devastation myself. "I'm in the car," says Mom on the phone. "I'll be right there!"

I lie down on the bed and stare up at the rafters of the garage. In nine hours, Mom will be here, bearing a Polo shopping bag stuffed with soothing Wedgwood plates for my new garage (which also lacks a kitchen). And it will be as comforting as our constant arguments or the bag of chips that we'll eat while watching black-and-white horror movies in silence. This is what my mother can do for me—and it's not a small thing—she can brush my hair and love me with DVDs. But I need to figure out the rest of my life. And that will take something different, something she can't give me, something I need to find by myself.

"Mom?" I say. "I'm okay. Go to Texas."

Next call: Dad. This will be easy. This makes sense. Dad walked out of a marriage, a marriage with a child even. He'll forgive me. He'll tell me what to do. That's his job, besides saving my life, over and over.

"Leifer," he says.

"I'm okay!" I say, then hang up.

I throw the phone on the bed, under the covers, where the rings are muffled when he calls back ten minutes later. I can't talk to Dad. What if he tells me to go back to Lawrence, now, for Christ's sake! What if he doesn't? What if he says, *I knew it all along, Leifer. That was a FUBAR relationship from day one.*

What I'd really like is a paddle to the head.

This goes back to the canyon, when I was eleven, maybe twelve. We were floating the Talachulitna River with Abbie's sister and brother, up from Ohio for the summer. They were looking for a family fun trip in the wilderness. They took our small Avon raft, and we took our big one. Rafting isn't exactly a hard-core adventure. Basically, you sit in the raft, letting the current pull you along, plunking lures into the water. Every four hours or so, you pull over to a gravel bar and fish the hole, hopefully procuring a silver for dinner. Then you pitch camp and, the next morning, do it all over again.

The day of the canyon, the sun was out, warming the thick gray rubber of the raft, inspiring me to doze between casts with one foot hanging off the side. We had heard from other rafters about the canyon: It was a box canyon with a tricky, pretty drastic left turn at the exit. There we were, noodling along, tanning, chatting about country-music singers, when the rapids started. They were a little rougher than expected. "Gosh," said Abbie, her face getting a little white.

In about three seconds they weren't rapids at all, they were ocean waves in an angry river with lots of huge rocks. "The rain," shouted Dad. "Last month!"

And suddenly there was the canyon—a black stone throat,

vomiting boulders and waterfalls. We had no helmets, no water-proof bags, no straps tying down anything, and no experience in serious water. We were normal Alaskan fishermen, not semi-suicidal adrenaline addicts from Colorado who kayak out of flying helicopters.

But there we were, in the water, too fast for any of us to plan. Abbie's sister and brother-in-law led the way in. They bounced through the first set of falls, then shot up onto a massive boulder at the turn. Here, their raft stuck—half underwater, half out of water. Abbie's sister, Joanne, in back was submerged, and the boat was filling up, their gear whisking off in the current and froth.

All I saw was Joanne. She was a rag doll, wet and blond and breathing. And then wet and under and not there. And then she was up, yelling at her husband to push with his paddle.

"Leverage off the rock!" Dad was screaming. "God bless—! The paddle! Leverage! Shove!"

I crouched down. Our raft was spinning. There was no place to pull over and plan a route. Down we went. "Paddle," said Dad. "DON'T HIT THAT ROCK!"

Screaming from Leigh Newman. High-pitched, frozen screaming.

"Paddle," Dad said.

More screaming.

Down came his wood paddle, bam, on the top of my head. I sat up. My brains wobbled.

"You're okay!"

I picked up my paddle.

"You're okay!"

Uh?

"Now paddle. Goddamnit!"

I got to work; we made it around the rock; we snagged the other raft and pulled it off the rock with us; we got slammed by water, all of us, a wall of water; we lost most of our gear. "You're okay," Dad said, over and over, as we bumped off boulders and down waterfalls and finally came to a beach where we could pull over, take a minute, laugh from the adrenaline, and plan out how to keep going with little food and wet tents and clothes. "You're okay!"

"I'm okay," I tell myself now. The futon trembles again—the ring of the phone muffled by the pillow top. I don't pick up.

My new life in Massachusetts is disturbingly easy to kick-start. As per my curt request, Lawrence doesn't come up to visit. And I don't go down to New York, not even to file the separation papers. Oddly, this new life is more like my old life in assorted overseas countries than I want to admit. I stay in my garage with the lights off, as if I were holed up in a dark train-station hotel, with a view of a subway bridge (a common occurrence at the end of my *Travel Time* tenure, when expense budgets were slashed). My fellowship means that I don't have to teach or work at a restaurant like the other grad students, who are bonding over training sessions and pairing up for drinks. I see them only once a week, for two hours during our one class.

For the most part, these students are twenty-two or twenty-three. And yet, not only do they seem older than me, they're also far more intellectually focused and profoundly educated. Schools did not have official writing majors back in my day. And if they had, no doubt, I would have felt it too confining to study only one area of interest.

After class one night, some of them invite me along to a bar with bicycles hanging on the ceiling. There, over two-dollar beers, the table begins to argue about novels and poets and installation artists and experimental films that I think I might have heard of, maybe, once. Or maybe what I think is a poet is a band. Or maybe a literary critic.

I put my head on the table, while everybody keeps talking about edgy, artistic things that I'm too confused even to contemplate. Maybe my head on the table will go over as quirky and eccentric, instead of crazy and inappropriate. I'm so grateful for their voices and laughter. This is the first human contact I've had in weeks.

Now, though, everybody is getting up. We're going to a show, which, as it turns out, means a concert in the indie-music world, of which tiny Amherst is evidently a major capital. The show is in a big wooden bar with a stage. A band goes up there and plays. But no one dances. Our group, like the rest of the audience, just stands there, listening to the lyrics and quietly, drunkenly swaying in the dark.

I do this, too. It's not so bad. I like moody, depressing music. I like that nobody holds up flaming lighters or jerks their heads back and forth in time to the pounding deep bass and schizophrenic lights so inevitably requisite to massive European discotheques.

For a minute I think: This is what I'll do from now on, on weekends when I'm alone. I'll go to shows. I'll listen to indie music and pick up an obscure instrument like the Dobro.

Then I look around. I'm wearing black leather pants and a fluffy pink sweater. I'm also wearing my mother's horrible veins that pop up along your hand and show the world that you are no longer in your twenties. The rest of the crowd is wearing shrunken vintage shirts and library glasses and skin that makes me think of Copenhagen and the thick bowls of cream they pour on herring there. Because I spent my twenties missing all this counterculture in favor of places like Denmark, where I drove around the flat, bleak countryside, spending the night at eighteenth-century manor-house hotels, dining with power couples playing Lord and Lady for the weekend by drinking obscure Romanian wines and getting hot-rock massages.

For the first time in my life, I realize I can't buy an outfit and sway in the dark and fit in. My age—and bewilderment—won't let me. This should be discouraging, and it is. But it's also consoling. If

I can't change myself for the people I love, then at least I'm not going to change myself for people I don't love and I don't even know—people who refuse, despite all the music and space and anonymity, to dance, even badly.

Before I can figure anything else out about my new single life, the phone rings. *Travel Time* has finally gone bankrupt. One of my laid-off old colleagues has found a new job at *Bride-to-Be* magazine. *Bride-to-Be* is a handy guide to life down the aisle, from shoes to honeymoons. As it turns out, she needs some travel writers. "This gig is perfect for you," she says. "You're like the voice of our readers!"

"I am?"

"You're an actual newlywed!"

Even though a tiny, know-it-all voice is saying to me, *This seems a little masochistic,* a louder, more desperate voice is saying, *You know how to do this. And doing it will make you feel better. And if you feel better, you'll look better and act better and go out and meet some other funny, tender, intelligent, badly dressed, wonderful guy and this time not ever, ever marry him.*

All I have to do is make my one graduate class during the week, then take off for honeymoons by myself during long weekends. "All right," I say. "I'm in. But does my newlywed husband have to come on all the stories?"

"We don't have the budget. But write as if he were there. Make us feel the romance! The poetry!"

"Romance," I say. "Poetry. Got it."

I'm sitting on the tin pail, holding the cell phone, trying to keep my sizzling pee noise to a minimum. Pee noise undermines my argument. And I need my passport. I try again: "We need to talk to someone about a formal separation. We need to take legal steps."

Nothing from Lawrence. A long, long pause. Then he says, in a casual tone, "Why don't you come down for the weekend? Or I could come up."

Is he ignoring me? Or just distracted by the noise at his office? "We need to talk to a lawyer."

"Okay. Let's talk about it over the weekend. I'll come up—with some kind of papers. I'll stop by city hall and see what we need." His voice remains calm, unruffled, as if we're talking about buying fabric softener.

He arrives on a bus. He has my passport, but no separation papers. I do not yell at him for not doing what he said he would do (one of our classic arguments). Instead we drive around in the car, taking scenic byways through the woods of Massachusetts.

I hate scenic byways. I get motion-sick two minutes in. But I rest my head on the window and say nothing. We drive over twisty Route 2, past waterfalls and the state line and south to the bombed-out river town of Newburgh, New York. We drive over to Beacon. We drive past it. We drive back up the Hudson, crisscrossing bridges.

Outside the boarded-up methadone-clinic town we're circling, Lawrence tries to hit the brakes. The pedal gets stuck. He reaches down. He fumbles. He comes back up with a smashed Taco Bell bag. Oozing through the paper is an ancient Burrito Supreme that I didn't quite manage to finish.

"I can't believe this," he says. He isn't yelling, but he never yells. His whole being slows during stress, his volume decreases. He can't stand garbage in the car. Not that I can, either. Both of us grew up with what we refer to as the Single Mom Mobile, a dented hatchback filled with office papers, apple cores, extra sweaters, the occasional broken umbrella. There was no room in the Single Mom Mobile to give friends a ride. And even if there had been, we would have been too embarrassed—in the deeply painful, completely out-of-proportion seventh-grade meaning of the word—to offer those friends a ride.

"It costs fifty cents to vacuum," he says, speeding the car faster and faster, off the road and into the lot of a weedy, dead gas station. He yanks open the door. Leonard leaps to the back and hides by the pile of jumper cables.

There is the sound of plastic, glass. I turn around. Lawrence is hurling garbage across the parking lot—a Filet-O-Fish wrapper, an empty bottle of antifreeze, then the snow scraper, the first-aid kit. "Have you ever heard of a garbage can?" His voice is compressed, cold, terrifying.

I shrink down, and an unfortunate thing happens. I begin to smile hugely, unmistakably, in the style of me at age eight when my dad bawled and refused to stop hugging me good-bye in the aisle of a 727. This is not good. I try to dig below my seat, to show him that I'm helping, that I'm taking his feelings seriously and find—a milk shake cup half filled with dried vanilla cement.

"Don't touch it," he says. "Don't *you* touch anything in my car."

And then he finds the tub of Kentucky Fried. It is half eaten. It is a few weeks old. He rattles the tub near my face. "You disgust me," he says. "Do you hear me? You. Disgust. Me."

Nothing from me.

"Look at yourself. When was the last time you showered?"

Nothing.

"You're not even eating this crap." He kicks the chicken tub across the lot. "You just buy it, take one bite, and throw it out."

I sit up, right in his face. "I'm not going to the grocery store, either! I'm not playing the guitar! I'm not skiing! I'm not planning us trips to the beach! Or baking you oatmeal cookies! Or cooking goat cheese tarts! Or throwing you surprise birthday parties! Or taking you for picnics! Or diving! Or reading! Or dancing! Or doing anything I like doing!"

We both go really quiet. There are windy highway sounds all of a sudden. There are bird chirps and branch rustlings.

"Well that's a stupid fucking way to live," says Lawrence, his voice his again—human. He kicks the tub of rotten chicken across the lot. "Clean up my car," he says. "Now."

I pick up the wrappers. I throw them away. He doesn't look at me. He drives and drives and drives, the muscles on his arms flexing as he hurls the car up to ninety. We are still fighting, apparently, about the car garbage. But not about my high-speed marital exit. And this, I tell myself, is yet another reason we should not be married: We don't know how to fight, either, not with real words and feelings.

At the bus stop by the Amherst common, Lawrence pulls the car over. Something strange washes through his face—an exhausted calm. He gets out of the car. He knocks on the window. "I'll call you later," he says quietly, "about next weekend."

I nod, confused but too tired to correct him. What is his problem? Why won't he just let us cut this off fast? Pain only seems scary while you're waiting for it to happen. After it does, it's just hurt and recovery.

The day before class, I write a short story. The discussion at the table is brief: My teacher, classmates, and I all agree. The story is simplistic and hysterical and just plain bad. It's about a woman married to a man who fills up their house with gadgets designed to protect them: an air purifier, a bug zapper, an electric fence to keep out deer and thus Lyme-disease-ridden ticks. One weekend, he slathers all their windows in several hundred black plastic bird stickers to prevent live birds from flying into the glass.

Smothered, the woman asks her husband to leave, only to cower in the living room in fear that night. Alone, in the dark, without him, the bird stickers seem to come alive, turning into bird-looking bats that swoop down, trying to peck at her.

I'm not the woman in the story, of course. I'm not going crazy without my husband. I'm just getting thin. I have lost 17 of my 117 pounds. My hair is falling out and my skin is gray. I look like me after my parents' divorce. Minus the boils.

A week before I'm scheduled to go to Bermuda to write about quaint limestone cottages where honeymooners can spend the week, drinking high tea and playing croquet, I get a call. It's Nana. "How are the newlyweds?" she says.

"Great," I say. "We're doing great!"

There's a long, inexplicable pause. "I feel a little funny," she says. "I'll call back."

But she doesn't call back. I try to call her back, no answer. Dad calls. Nana has had a stroke. He tells me not to come; we don't know anything yet. Besides, it's almost Christmas. I can go see her over the holidays.

"Okay," I say. Then I get in the car and drive to the airport. By the time I get to the hospital in some distant strip-mall town outside Seattle, Dad is there, too. Nana is puffy, swollen, paralyzed on one half of her body. Her eye droops, her hair is plastered to her head, and she is moaning. I pick up a cup, then a box of tissues. I want to hold her hand, but there are tubes all over—thick, hefty, upsetting ones.

There is a window in the room, with a view of the parking lot. Seagulls wheel over the rows of cars. Bright, impossible sunshine slants across Nana's bed. She has no pillow.

"Take me home," she says, her lips sludging to one side.

Instantly everything in the bleak, silent room restarts. Dad and I have something to do besides stand there stunned and gaping. He runs downstairs and pulls around the car. Then he runs back into the room. "Get a wheelchair," he says. "Let's go. Hop to!"

Hop to is an all-purpose hunting-dog command for "get in the kennel!" or "get in the car!" or "find the goddamn duck!" It works very well on me, too. I grab a wheelchair from the hall, plus some sheets from a closet. Nana tries to sit up, but her arm won't work. She almost slumps out of bed. I can't hold her, either. A nurse bustles in. "What are you doing?" she says. Then she spots the wheelchair. "This woman can't travel. This woman has had a stroke."

"Take me home," says Nana. "Please."

My dad is looking at the floor, blinking and confused. I'm confused too. By him. My dad is my dad. He's a doctor, a surgeon. He's supposed to be telling this nurse to shut the hell up and help us get his mother into the wheelchair. Instead he looks at Nana. Her leg has flopped out from under the sheet, the skin torn up with welts.

"Correct," he says to the nurse. "Correct. The wheelchair is not an option."

"Take me home," says Nana.

"What we need is an ambulance. Can you get us an ambulance?"

"It won't be covered," says the nurse.

"Just get us the ambulance, will you? For Christ's sake!"

From here on out, all there is is action. And this is a relief. Dad and I don't have to discuss or catch up or not argue or decide or plan anything. Talking of any kind—including marriage talk—is off the table. We just have to get to Nana's little red cottage before the ambulance.

Inside, the house smells of mildew and cat litter and the cold, dark Pacific Ocean, which is the view from the living room windows—dark green water to the horizon, broken up by the occasional barge. Everywhere there are Indian baskets and beach glass and Mexican pottery. There are Greek prayer beads and seashells and a whole shelf of cookbooks just on pasta. But there is, of course, no hospital bed or wheelchair or bedpan.

Nana's bedroom is right off the living room. We help the EMT guy roll her into her big, soft regular bed. She moans. The sheets hurt her. The fabric is too rough. I run to the closet to look for new sheets. There are stacks and stacks of towels and pillowcases in there—a lifetime of linens. I grab what I can and run back. She begins to scream. I drop the stuff in my arms and try to figure out how to prop her body off the bed.

But she's too heavy for me to lift. I can only manage one limb at a time. Dad runs for couch pillows. I try the bed pillows, one under her arms, one in between her legs, one under her head. She quiets. For about three minutes, she doesn't hurt; she is so grateful, she holds on to my arm, saying thank you, thank you.

Then she begins to scream again. It's a deep, low scream—a sound from inside the body, a sound that has everything to do with pain, not fear. All I want is that sound to stop. I move the pillows, from under her elbow to under her hip, from under her hips to under her neck, unsure if it's better to move them as fast as possible and hurt her in short, excruciating bursts or move them slowly and hurt her less but for long, extended periods. She screams again. I move the pillow back under her hips. This seems to work; she is quiet, dozing off. And then she screams. I move the pillows again, from under her hips to under her back. This goes on, over and over, for eight hours. I pass out on the floor. Dad takes over. Then he passes out on the floor. I take over.

The next morning, the doorbell rings. It's the hospital bed. We roll her onto it and break down all the other furniture in the room, leaning her old bed frame and mattress against the wall. The house is littered with Kleenex and receipts and bits of abandoned, uneaten toast. The lights are off, to keep the brightness from bothering her. It is so quiet, no Pavarotti or the Three Tenors, no TV, no talking. None of us has the energy to move our lips.

Nana curls on her side, trying not to scream. She cries. I want to punch somebody; the hospital bed was supposed to fix everything, and it so clearly doesn't. Dad is still wearing his coat. I think he slept in it. He jams that under Nana's knees. "She's got to drink," he says. "We have to keep her hydrated."

I bring water in a small jelly glass, but she can't sip. I tear though kitchen drawers and find a takeout straw. She tries to suck on it, but she can't; she doesn't have the strength. I cut the straw into a three-inch section. Dad holds her up and she pulls some water in her mouth, swallows. She goes quiet. It is wonderful, the most wonderful thing in the world when we get to the moment, for however long it lasts, when she doesn't hurt.

Only then do I realize about her nightgown. It's bunched around her chest, almost to her neck—a classic Nana bed garment: creamy JCPenney satin with a froth of French lace at the neck. She has drawers and drawers of them; they're her trademark, along with the kimonos and martinis and hot-silver hair. Many years ago, she'd gone to Paris with her friend and bought tickets to opening night at the opera. She didn't have a formal couture dress—and so she strode into the Palais Garnier in elbow-length gloves and a silky full-length nightgown, heavy on the ruffles.

Nana catches me looking at it. We both know what has to happen. The fabric is like fire on her skin. I get the scissors out. I look her in the eyes and start at the hem, cutting slowly over the folds, the scissors suddenly so loud in the room—so final.

Somehow, she moves her one working hand onto mine. "You make me so happy," she says. "You make everybody happy. That's your gift, Leigh. You fill people with joy and life."

I stop, scissors still mid-cut. What she's saying—it's impossible for me to think this way about myself. It is so alien, so at odds with the sadness and cruelty I have been inflicting on Lawrence for the past three months, so at odds with the person I think of myself as, which is some kind of distant, invited but not really invited guest—not unlike a plus-one at a glittering grown-up party who hangs out over by the cold buffet, picking at the shrimp and looking down at her watch as if she were really, really late for someone or something instead of just hovering hopelessly, waiting for anyone at all to come over and save her, even when no one will because everyone thinks (due to the watch-checking) she is about to leave.

At times, I know, I can fake confidence and even fabulousness at least enough to make people laugh—but that isn't filling them with joy, that's filling them with ease. At times, I can listen to people and make them feel better, but that's not filling them with life, that's understanding their lives, even though I don't know how to share my own.

On the other hand, there are so many, many times Nana filled my life with solid, unstoppable joy: dressing up with me in wigs and sunglasses from the 1960s and going out for dinner in these outfits, teaching me how to roast a chicken and how to pry limpets off the beach rocks, slathering my hot dogs with her secret condiment (butter). And I wonder why she's bothered to waste her strength on saying such a beautiful thing to me, something I will think about for the rest of my life, when what she really needs to be is quiet, to save her energy, because—

Everything in my mind, in the room goes still and quiet. It's so suddenly and absolutely clear: Nana is dying. I'm here to help her die. We sit together for a while, without saying anything, holding hands. It is the most intimate silence of my life.

Dad comes in. He's brought washcloths, a heating pad. He's made calls. I pull the nightgown slowly off Nana, inch by inch. It's so good to be with him, just working and watching, each of us knowing that the other is there. Nothing between us has changed in the old, important ways. We work together. We do together. And I've missed it.

Soon my father's brothers and sister will arrive, and there will be decisions to make and a chicken that I'll decide that I can cook for everybody but forget to turn the oven on. I'll try to repair this mistake by sticking the whole bird in the microwave, where it explodes, leaving us with a few shreds of dry chicken shrapnel to eat, which we wash down with Scotch. The next morning, Nana will ask me to go home. I'll refuse. She'll pass out and wake up and no longer know who I am. I'll finally leave the house in a taxi wishing I'd left when she asked me to. A few hours later, while sitting in the old familiar molded plastic chairs of Sea-Tac, where Nana used to meet me and walk me from the Alaska gate to the Baltimore one or the Baltimore one to the Alaska one, it will hit me like a club to the head: She's gone. And then my uncle Mark will call me and tell me she really did die; she died forty-five minutes after I left the house.

But right now, lying on the floor of Nana's room, waiting for the next round of screaming, I think back to when I was a child, staying with her for a few months, right after my mother left my father. This was when my boils first broke out. Most of them were on what Nana called my derriere, making it very hard to sit. I think about how she used to pull off the bandages stuck to the open sores—slowly, with tiny, soft, delicate lifting motions, working the gauze off the skin, as I begged and begged her to go even slower—which she did. This indulgence was not at all like Nana. She'd lost her whole family before the age of twenty. She doesn't do good-bye; when she leaves your house, she just walks out. When she feeds her dog, she tosses him a chunk of hamburger wrapped in plastic, forcing the poor guy to figure out how to get to his food, often by choking down the wrapping along with the meat. By all rights, she should have pulled my bandages off with a sudden, fast, excruciating rip.

Instead, against all common sense, she used tenderness.

I'm no expert, but maybe we all can be different with different people. I would like, more than anything, to be the person she described—the joy-giving person, the life-giving person, which must have been the person I was to her. How will I ever be that person with myself? She was the one person I might have asked.

By the time I land at Bradley Airport in northern Connecticut, I have one hour before class. It doesn't occur to me to blow off grad school. In Amherst I leave my luggage in the car and go directly into the classroom, where everyone is discussing my story. It's a meandering tale about a girl whose parents get into an ugly screaming fight, which causes her father to drive off and her mother to go on a crazed, manic shopping spree in the grocery store, during which this mother urges her daughter to live it up, to be free, to do whatever she's ever wanted, filling up cart after cart with wheels of Brie and hunks of roast beef and pricey triple-crème ice creams from Sweden.

The story is sappy and boring and far too long. "The characters aren't believable at all," says a guy at the table. I estimate his age: twenty-three. "That woman sounds like a character from a Lifetime movie." Which is unfortunate. Because, this time, of course, I realize the story is about me. I could be any one of the three of them: the girl blinking between her parents or the mom longing to escape or the dad driving off. In fact, I am all three characters as they chow down on Swedish ice cream at the end until they're sick, not unlike Dad and I did during the summer of the all-the-humpy-you-can-eat grief buffet.

Now, of course, I'm at my own grief buffet. I buy Double Whopper value meals (with bacon and cheese) and can't get down more than the first two bites because as soon as the food hits my mouth, I'm not hungry, which is karmic payback. I don't deserve to eat anyway, I tossed my life—and Lawrence's and Leonard's—into the garbage disposal and hit the switch. And, as of today, the one person I could confide in is dead. I almost climb over the classroom table and punch out the guy, with his industrial intelligentsia glasses and smug asswipe smile.

But the whole experience has a quivering, unreal quality—bubble voices, bubble people, bubble table and chairs and brick bubble collegiate buildings, pop. I drive back to the garage. I drag out my duffel. I repack my duffel. I have four hours to make my flight to Bermuda.

And I'm not going to pee in a goddamn pail. I march into the main house, which used to be a farmhouse in the days before suburbs and fences. My landlord has rented a room on the second floor to a beefy guy with a baseball hat. The guy has a rottweiler, also beefy and far larger than me, which usually lives in a wire cage from where he looks at me through the door, swinging his heavy head to check where I am in the hallway.

But not tonight. The dog is in the living room, curled up on the sofa. I head for the stairs—casually, because if you're calm with dogs, they're calm. One time, in the remote hills of Umbria, an entire pack of feral dogs descended on me as I walked down the trail. With no time to move, what I did was stand very, very still, as if I were a tree, and what they did was flow around me—a stream of heat and musk and teeth—then flow on, continuing toward the unsuspecting chickens and lambs that lay ahead.

The rottweiler, though, pads after me, stopping on the landing to nuzzle my leg. I stop. I bend down and pet him, just so we both know that I'm a friendly, kind human, not at all scared, not at all aggressive or bothersome. On I go, petting him slowly and evenly, even though I'd prefer to get just the tiniest bit away from him, because, to be honest, he has always made me a touch uncomfortable. Living in a cage—dog or no—is never good for your head.

He nuzzles my leg again and then out of nowhere, almost lazily, as if he wasn't really committed to the plan—he noses up and bites deeply into my arm just above my wrist. I hold up my arm; blood is leaking out a hole, a tooth hole. The rottweiler cocks his head, as if he, too, is surprised. Then something hardens in his eyes. The decision has been made. He jumps. I put my hands out to stop him, but he lands on my chest, and whap, knocks me on my back.

For a second, all I see is the bottom of the bathroom door, the flaked green paint, the nailed brass strip that separates the end of the hallway carpet and start of the tile floor. The dog isn't barking or growling. He's not making any sound at all. He's just going for my throat and he's too heavy and my hands don't move fast enough, I'm screaming, trying to kick him off me. When somebody finally rips him away.

"What the fuck! What the fuck!" this somebody is saying. It's beefy baseball guy. I think he's asking me if I provoked the dog, if I did something. But I can't be sure exactly and I can't move. The cool air, the ease of breathing, the removal of the crushing weight and heat of the dog from my chest is too overwhelming. I lie there for a few minutes and just endure it—the understanding that I'm still alive. Then I stand up. I go downstairs, careful not to fall, holding on to the banister. The kitchen is warm and white. There's a bucket of cleaning rags by the stove. I bend down and take one. Blood splats on the smudged linoleum. My head goes fuzzy. I hang there, ordering myself to remain vertical; there's nobody to catch me if I fall.

Then I swing upright and move onto the porch. I rip up the rag; it's an old sheet, the fabric gives in soft, limp strips. I tie up my arm. There's a break in the bushes between our yard and the next, where I see a neighbor standing on her own porch. She's watching me— and my arm. "Are you okay?" she calls out.

"Uh," I say. "A rottweiler attacked me. I left my husband. And my grandmother just died." My own voice sounds like it's coming through one of the pneumatic tubes at banks, the words sucking off into wind and vapor.

"I think you're in shock. Wait there. I'll come right over." Now the woman is coming up the porch steps. She has a housecoat on, glasses. "I think you're in shock."

A bolt of hard, screeching rage goes through me: I'm not in shock! I'm fine! Because, as I tell this neighbor, in a very loud, angry voice, "I helped my grandmother die, that's all. It was a beautiful experience. It was a privilege. It was how anybody would want to die, surrounded by people who love you—not looking up at some bathroom door, lying by yourself in some hall in Massachusetts."

The neighbor's eyes are big and blinky. She's looking at my arm. I look down at my arm, too. Blood is seeping through the rag fabric. "Sorry," I say. "I have to go to Bermuda now."

She nods, perhaps in shock, too. I get in my car and go—not to the hospital—but to the airport. Though I've never had stitches or a broken bone, it seems to me if you keep a tight seal on an open wound, it will close.

This isn't completely faulty logic. I spend the week alone writing about honeymoon cottages, pink-sand beaches, and Dark and Stormys. I keep the hole in my arm dry and covered (no swimming) and swallow handfuls of the broad-spectrum antibiotics that I never travel without—not since my first trip to the Galapagos during which the entire boat got an overachieving stomach bug on the very day that the one onboard bathroom ceased to work.

At this particular junction in my life, there is something tremendously comforting about staying on an island where everyone wears madras shorts without irony and pulls their socks up to their armpits as if their shins are too personal to display to the general public. Nobody in Bermuda asks about my bandage and I certainly don't offer any witty, revealing backstory. I sit on the terrace of my rental cottage and type up my story before I even leave.

My breakdown on the porch in Massachusetts has left me with one thought: Even hysterical, I was correct, my grandmother did leave the world surrounded by people who loved her. The way I'm headed, though, it seems unlikely that will happen to me.

Back in Massachusetts, a few months later, Lawrence invites himself up for the weekend. This time, he promises, we will talk about lawyers. I'm ninety-seven pounds at this point. I have a thick, round, tooth-hole scar on my forearm. We drive around and around and around. As we do, I have time, lots of time, to think about why Lawrence may be putting up with me. He grew up with a father who used to get beer-drunk every night, tell a few wry jokes, then pass out in his saurekraut at the table—and that was before his parents got divorced and his father had to have both his legs amputated due to diabetes.

Lawrence grew up with catastrophe. I am now the cherry on that catastrophe. He will keep on driving us around the highways of New England, just the way he kept drinking all of his milk and clearing all of the dinner plates except the one that his dad was sleeping in. Until I stop him. Now.

I ask him to take the next exit. He does. Neither of us knows where we are: There is snow, then trees, a valley, a bookshop. A sign for hot dogs—our favorite kind, in the shape of a giant 1950s hot dog—juts up from the trees.

Lawrence pulls into the lot. He goes to the stand and comes back with a cardboard tray in his hand. The hot dogs are covered with every needless condiment known to man: cheese and relish and on-ions and barbecue sauce and chili, all of which I love and he does not, believing that such lavish toppings pollute the purity of the dog-ness. Worse, there are two small root beers. And he hates when I get two small root beers instead of one large root beer, which we could split, getting the same amount of drink for substantially less money.

I'm not sure how to react to this. Because Lawrence has a lot of wonderful qualities, but one thing he isn't great at is taking care of people. He's skipped my birthday so many times I've stopped ex-pecting a present or even a card. He made me dinner once (tuna casserole, five years ago) and that was the end of that. We used to fight about this all the time, but maybe I liked that kind of oversight somehow. Maybe I would have been smothered by somebody shov-ing roses and homemade pasta into my life at the end of the day. Or maybe that's what I need and have always needed. The point is: I still don't know.

And yet here he is with a hot dog that bespeaks me and every-thing I am, holding it out as if to show me how it could have been if I had just hung in there with him. I start to cry all over the food and the cardboard box it comes in. He is crying, too, I think, but I can't see really, I just hear some deep racking sounds from the driver's side. When I look up, he's hunched over the wheel, his face wrecked by tears. The heater clicks on. He wipes his face with the back of his hands. "It was the wedding," he says. "I didn't help with the wedding."

"No," I say. "You didn't." Not that I helped with the wedding, either. Charging into battle with a veil isn't getting married.

He turns on the car. He lets it sit for a while, idling. "You're not coming back, are you?" he says.

I shake my head. Then frantically begin to eat everything in front of me, which is a little like bolting out of the car in that my mouth is full; there will be no more talking. Lawrence does the same thing. Then Leonard moans for fries. I crawl in the backseat of the car with him and curl up in a fetal position. I feel a little ill. The hot dogs were my first real meal in weeks.

Lawrence drives us back to the bus stop. He gets out. I get in the driver's seat. "See you next weekend," he says.

I'm going to Baja for *Bride-to-Be* next weekend. I don't have the heart to remind him.

Three days later, with no warning, Lawrence shows up at my garage. It's unexpected, considering our last conversation. Plus, he's wearing some very disorienting, unflattering clothing: plaid pants, striped shirt, a jacket with shoulder pads that dates back to glory days of David Hasselhoff. "I'm going with you," he says. "To Baja."

"But we're separated. And you could have called."

"I'm coming."

"But we're separated."

He has a grim, determined look on his face—a look I have not seen since I left him, but that I recognize. This is the same look he uses when he tries to make a fire, which is a long, baroque process for him, but which he sticks to silently, furiously—him versus wet, green wood—for hours, until it catches. "You owe me," he says.

I look down at my slippers. There's a tear in the cork sole that I examine extensively, because, considering my behavior, of course, Lawrence deserves an all-expenses-paid nature cruise. "We are not sharing a bed," I say. "And do not tell people we're newlyweds. Or separated. Or . . . anything at all."

Off we go, on different flights. I prepare myself on the airplane: The kind of honeymooners who will be on this particular cruise are not the kind who go to a remote village in Mexico. They will not wish to sleep in a hut on the beach and clamber over jungle-covered ruins, swatting malarial mosquitoes off each other. These honeymooners will be sunburned, gelled, and slightly smashed at all times. Late at night, after many Jell-O shots, they will tell kind, patient, understanding Lawrence their stories—how Tim showed up at the sorority house with a ring floating in a box of Lucky Charms (the bride loves cereal), how Jenny bawled her face off when Richard's blimp saying MARRY ME floated over the college football stadium— while I sit in the corner, rolling my eyes, trying to disguise my longing for their dumb young bliss with a safe, prickly coating of disdain.

This was a terrible idea. I shouldn't be going on this trip. And neither should Lawrence. And it's my fault because I didn't have the courage to say no, good-bye, let's just end it, the way you're supposed to during a breakup, if you actually care about the other person.

And yet, there Lawrence and I stand on the vast, broiling, cement quay, both of us toting our separate duffel bags all the way to the ship. Where we stop. A long, long line of passengers is waiting to go very, very slowly up the gangplank. Because they're having trouble managing their walkers and wheelchairs and giant plastic sacks of low-priced Mexican pharmaceuticals.

There's evidently been some kind of mix-up. We're on a cruise for people aged seventy-five and up.

In the olden days of endlessly dating, we might have laughed at this. Now we stare glumly up at the boat. We sit glumly through the group dinner, where the buffet is Mexican, minus the spices, salt,

and peppers that might give anyone heartburn. It's like eating pu-
reed death. On a tortilla.

I can't get it down. Neither can Lawrence. We go glumly up to
the top deck, doing anything not to face our stateroom, which is not
a stateroom so much as a vacation jail cell with two narrow iron
bunks bolted to opposite sides of the room, no TV, no room service,
no turn-down mints.

We flop down on deck chairs. We say nothing, both perhaps
aware that this is neither the romantic trip where Lawrence is going
to win me back, nor the ship of fools, brides-gone-wild adventure
where I will prove to him that marriage is ridiculous. This is something else: a tub of despair.

"Don't they even have an ice sculpture of a dolphin?" says Lawrence. "All I want is an ice sculpture of a dolphin."

"All I want is a towel folded into a swan."

"All I want is Isaac." Then he does Isaac's cheesy smile and double finger point, straight from the open bar on *The Love Boat,* circa
1978.

From over by the lifeboats comes a waft of laughter. A sharp-
faced, cackling woman is pulling a bottle of tequila out of her bag.
And bottles of mango juice. And a lime. So are the rest of the ladies
at her table. Now come the snacks: tortilla chips, mixed nuts, canned
Frito-Lay bean dip of the kind, tragically, you will find in any Mexican 7-Eleven.

"Little ones," a woman calls over. "Come have cocktails."

"I'm not paying sixteen dollars for a drink," another says. "I
pack my own bar." She is not kidding. She has a plastic thermos of
pre-mixed margaritas, which, as it turns out, are refreshing and
light and just what we needed. We sit and play gin rummy (everyone
also has brought decks of cards). During margarita one, the conversation revolves around what a wise, tough leader George Bush is.
During margarita two, the conversation revolves around why the
staterooms have separate beds. All the elderly ladies are very

bummed out about this. Even though their husbands are sitting at a different table, playing poker.

"Who cares?" says Lawrence, quietly.

"Yeah," I say. "It's just a place to sleep."

Looks ricochet around the table. From then on, we're officially adopted. We're not left alone for one minute. We're invited to nature talks, water-safety demonstrations, coffee hours. We're given sleeping pills and hard candies dug out of the bottoms of purses. These are people who have been married for fifty years—or were married for fifty years before one of them passed away. They pretend not to notice Lawrence and I slumping through the mariachi band or sitting on separate sides of the dining room. And for this, we're grateful. We don't have to talk very much. We fill our days with helping people read the paper and listening to stories about the Korean War.

Until the day trip off the ship. We're all supposed to hop in little rubber rafts to putter over to a beach. This is hard for a lot of our new friends. Ray, a ninety-two-year-old with arthritis, needs me to sit with her, in case she slips off the seat. Lawrence is helping Amos, who has Parkinson's.

We all watch as Marion climbs into a raft. She's on oxygen and has to take the tank with her. Ten stewards hover over her every breath. Her husband, Jerry, tries to climb in. The steward stops him. "It's against company policy."

"I'm going with my wife."

"Sir, I cannot allow you to do that."

"She's not feeling well and she's afraid and I'm going with her."

"Sir, I can't allow you to do that. You'll have to get back on the boat."

Jerry flexes with rage. He is tall and stooped and elegant and spectacularly polite in a low-key way that doesn't exist anymore. He used to be a postman. He has seven grandkids. He is not going to punch anybody but it's heartbreaking, watching him control this impulse and give in and finally climb in another raft. That is, until he whispers to the driver. His raft suddenly slows down, motoring alongside his wife's at the same reduced speed, so that the two rafts are, in effect, holding hands.

All that open tenderness: It's too deep, beautiful, and acute. Lawrence and I look at each other then look immediately away.

The next day, we hug good-bye and fly home on our separate flights. I tell myself that that cruise was the perfect last trip of our marriage. It was depressing and miserable, and it showed us that all the real, wonderful couples of the world know how to be together. But us? We're not in the same raft. We're not in the same plane. And this is okay. I get the window seat for once without bickering. I love the window seat.

Except for the black seizing pain in my chest.

Is this what missing is, finally? Wishing for somebody to bicker with? Wishing for somebody to shake you awake from your nap and remind you that windows are not for resting your head against but for looking out of? Lawrence loves a vista. It can be the patchwork of hills outside Sienna or the crags of Atlas Mountains in Tunisia or the smogscape of a row of New Jersey factories. He'll notice it and force me to stop daydreaming and notice it with him until I see what he is seeing, which in this instance would be the rolling grandeur in an expanse of clouds—that opera of altitude and sky, fat, puffy ladies strutting across the blue. It's so easy to forget when you're all by yourself—how being with someone isn't always about the effort it takes not to leave them and not let them leave you, either. There are those moments you sit astonished—the secret, almost-impossible ones where your two imaginations meet.

Back in Massachusetts, I get a call. It's Lawrence. He's going to stop bothering me. All he wants is for me to come to New York for the summer. We will have three last months together, months like we used to have, just hanging out, no pressure. And then we can call it quits—in a kind, caring way, as friends.

CHAPTER 14

Cinq de Plus

June looms ahead of me. I drop Leonard off in New York and take one last job. Soon to be legally single, I'll need a lawyer and any income I can get. The job is in Spain, for a new client who wants me to write stories of my old ilk, a thoughtful essay on vibrant new Spanish architecture as it relates to the vibrant new Spanish politics. I visit Bilbao and Barcelona and Santiago de Compostela all by creaking bus, since the old Spanish politics were fascist and required that all trains go through Franco's capital of Madrid, meaning there are no rail lines between small hip provincial cities.

Valencia is my last stop. Some kind of conference is taking place, and every hotel in town is booked. My taxi driver finally finds me a pension outside the city limits at the shut-down seaside. It is midnight. Still, I resist. No matter the country, the city, the state, the time zone, there is nothing lonelier than the shut-down seaside. We make laps around the suburbs and downtown and port. I finally surrender.

The pension is empty save for the junkies who have spent the winter there, apparently unable to understand that last summer ended eight months prior. They linger on the steps, gray and dazed. The ocean roars by in the darkness. I lie in bed with all my clothes on and my wallet clutched to my chest, shivering under a thin cotton shaving of a blanket. All I have to do is make it to the morning and wrap up my article.

Studio laughter, honking horns, wild applause ricochets up the tile steps from the front-desk TV. I sit up. I'm not going to make it. I can't survive a night like this—the kind of night when you realize you are so alone you might do something unthinkable just to stop the feeling and there is nobody you love even to find you the next morning. Which means you can go ahead and do the unthinkable without the guilt of directly traumatizing anyone. This is not a good thought to have, considering my family history. And yet it's not the first time I've had it. It's just the first time I've had it so insistently—a whisper like the air leaking out of a tire.

The truth is, I don't deserve to be around other people—and life is full of other people.

I put my shoes on. I go straight into town and buy a ticket for Madrid. In Madrid, I buy a ticket to Paris. The Basque country clicks by, the Pyrenees, flat yellow fields and red-tile villages, then Lyon. Then Paris, which roars up like a wave of stucco, marble, and soot.

For a long time, I've suspected I am not that original of a person. Sunshine makes me happy. It makes me really happy. So do all the other usuals: bicycles with shiny bells, double scoops, black Labs, killing a mosquito in the middle of the night with one slap, and, of course, Paris in the spring.

There are ducks in the parks and little wooden sailboats. There are Rodins and restaurants that serve only melted cheese. There are handfuls of cheap Arab street candy. There's a free swimming pool on a riverboat and a secret Swiss mountain garden hidden behind the zoo. There's also an unofficial system in the subway: If you look poor or even just a little sad, people will offer to let you pass through the turnstiles with them, in effect giving you a free ride on the train.

Some people seem to think Parisians are rude. These people have never lived in New York or shopped at a mega home improvement store in the rest of America. Here even the taxi driver asks how you are before clicking on the meter.

My trip is unplanned and not exactly feasible. I find a dumpy sausage-smelling hotel by the Gare du Nord train station. I make some rules: (1) no spending any time in the hotel other than sleeping during the night (for a maximum of eight hours); (2) no calling Parisian friends and pretending to be blasé and carefree about your upcoming divorce over chilled glasses of Lillet; (3) no planning any farther than three hours ahead. In other words, when I'm having a coffee for breakfast I can think about going to the Arab art museum at 11 A.M., but not about spending the summer in New York.

I'm doing something I haven't done in years. I'm not working or writing or traveling between families or schools or jobs. I'm on vacation. I can do whatever I want.

I head to the twisty, romantic Saint-Germain-des-Prés. I walk into the fanciest flower shop I can find. It's a dazzle of glass inside, as though the counter ought to be covered with emeralds tossed casually, by the handful, on swaths of black velvet.

Like so many people in the world, I love flowers. I love walking down the street with them, the bouquet in my arm transforming my posture and entire being into somebody who dresses in haute couture and fights off admirers, laughing photogenically. I love that they come and go, down to their cheap glass vases, which you can always recycle or give to a neighbor. Actually one of the things I always loved about Lawrence was that he was macho enough to like flowers, too. He bought himself white tulips every April.

A saleswoman approaches. She is wearing a yellow block cotton print from India, specifically the city of Jaipur. I have bought the same fabric at the same market. But she's had hers made into a tunic with intricate, body-hugging tucks and folds. It is very sexy for a tunic, a cross between an apron and a corset. Meanwhile, she's not young and has done nothing about her many wrinkles, save to apply a pair of green cat-glasses that make her look artsy and smart. You can practically smell the sculptors and poets who have fallen in love with her over the years, and thrown themselves off moonlit bridges.

"Good evening."

"Good evening." The saleswoman smiles at me. I'm unnervingly close to asking if I can smell her—or work for her for no money, just for a few months. I can sleep on the floor. But she wants to know if I'm looking for something for a dinner party, perhaps? Or a friend?

"No." I blush. "Just for me." I point to some tall, elegant cut lilies. Swans, essentially with petals.

She shakes her head. *"Pas pour vous, mademoiselle."*

I like lilies. I would like to be one, in fact, cool and mysterious. Then again, I also like being corrected. Especially by her. Her face seems to say, in the kindest way, *Why don't you try again? I know that you know the answer.*

I've forgotten this about France. The shopkeepers want you to stay and discuss and consider and admire in order to reach the absolutely perfect selection for you, specifically. For all the obvious reasons, this process makes me anxious. I study the buckets, each so artfully arranged. The roses are the little tea ones, romantic but too young. There are some lovely mixed bunches, but I have never been a mixed-bunch person. I'm a one-flower lady, hold the baby's breath. The Gerber daisies are too dyed-looking and spiky. The orchids are too expensive and manly. Then along come the irises.

They are a little wan and lonely, cool and bluish purple. But also a happy yellow at the center. I point, very tentatively, at them.

She beams. *"Excellent choix!"* Out come the ribbons and plastic and tissue and gilt stickers. Her hands flurry around with clippers— this stem is too long, that leaf too chunky. She wraps on the paper, then the plastic, then the ribbons. It's a graceful minuet of endless, microscopic folds and tucks and snips. I'm so grateful. This is the nicest thing to happen to me in months. In fact, I can't bear for it to end. So I do something horrible. I ask for another flower.

The saleswoman undoes the whole bouquet. Then adds another iris. Then repackages the paper, the plastic. Then reaches for a sticker.

"*Peut-être encore une de plus,*" I say. "*Ou cinq de plus?*"

Not a blink from the saleswoman. Off comes the plastic and paper. In go five more irises. On goes the paper. On goes the plastic. "*Ca c'est mieux,*" I say. "*Mais.*"

She pauses.

"*Cinq de plus?*" I say.

She dismantles the whole bouquet yet another time. On goes the plastic, the paper. In go five more irises. I'm not quite sure why she's not yelling at me. "But where did you learn French?" she says.

"I used to live here" is my standard answer—a simple, easy answer that's not exactly true. I learned French in Alaska, from my babysitter, a Frenchwoman who had married a commercial fisherman. But only toddler French. The grammar I learned in Baltimore, where I'd been too petrified to actually speak French in French class. In the suburbs of Paris, at seventeen, at yet another sister school of my girls' school, I learned that *héro* had nothing to do with Superman or heroes of any kind, but that my host sister had a serious heroin problem and that was why we were spending our nights skulking around the deserted streets of the *banlieue*.

At nineteen, after leaving Alaska and then Stanford, I learned *ancien français* by enrolling at the University of Paris–Jussieu, where I spent my days in the library, reading *Lancelot du Lac,* the only one in my class to do so, because as, it turned out, French students don't study, they spend their time making out with Americans at Tex-Mex bars near Les Halles. Besides, nobody speaks *ancien français*. It's medieval, for God's sake.

Modern French I learned in New York at twenty-one, from a group of French banking interns who spent their nights clubbing and their days at work kissing one another hello and going for lunch. Slang French, argot, I learned from the same group at age twenty-three, while living at their summer houses in France, once I got fired from my New York editorial job for being what can only be described in retrospect as a hopeless employee.

So really, all in all, I learned French in Alaska, Baltimore, New York, Paris, Montpellier, Bretagne, and Mayenne. All in all I've never lived in France for more than eight months at any one stretch, which brings up an old confusion for me yet again at age thirty-two, a confusion that even I must understand has something to do with the reason why I can't stay in any one place or with any one person: How long do you have to live somewhere for it to be home?

"I moved around a lot," I say. "I had a babysitter . . . in Alaska?"

The saleswoman looks up, one exquisite eyebrow raised.

For the first time in my life, I flop into the whole, long story, which can't be told, apparently, without going into my parents' breakup. Then my breakup. Luckily, it's in the middle of the afternoon. The shop is empty. People buy flowers in Paris after work, on the way to dinner parties, where, by the way, it's impolite to bring wine. The saleswoman adds more ribbons, more plastic, more gold stickers as I blab and blab and blab, occasionally interjecting and asking me questions that force me to blab some more. *"Comme c'est intéressant,"* she says, when at last I've stopped talking. "And what are you here to learn now?"

"I don't know," I say. "I just feel at home here. I feel safe for some reason."

She smiles. She's going to laugh. She is going to say, *But this is not your home, dear. You are just another silly American with a mediocre accent and certain, exceptionally affected cultural pretensions.* After which, a loud, ugly gong will go off and she will point dramatically to the door and I will be forced to slink out.

But she continues to smile—pleasantly, charmingly. Then she reaches into a bucket and presents me with one of the stately lilies that she had the good sense not to let me buy.

Instead of a gong, a lightbulb goes off—not unlike the one that went off when I figured out, in third grade, that all those crisp letters on the page, when shoved together, made words. Why shouldn't this woman let me feel that I belong here? I'm not bothering anybody. I'm just being happy. I have the right to be at home in Paris, struggling down the sidewalk with a bloated bouquet of irises the size and height of a sixty-pound king salmon. Even if—let's face it—I do have another home. And, sometimes, I still miss it.

CHAPTER 15

A Tablecloth in the Wilderness

Anchorage is the only place I know better from the air than from the ground. This was due to the loran, a prehistoric instrument on Dad's cockpit panel, part compass and part odometer, that looked, essentially, like a Radio Shack digital clock—a flat panel with a series of knobs and flickering backlit orange numbers and letters. My job as the Great Alaskan Copilot was to monitor the loran for our direction and position, then affirm its accuracy by looking out the windshield. In this way, I—and I alone, at age eight—would keep us on course.

Now that I'm an adult, I understand that while flying, you should never rely on the actual landscape or the surrounding sky. Clouds lie. Especially during storms, when the plane can flip upside down and plummet toward the ground without your being able to see or feel it. Dad invented my little job, both as a way to keep me from vomiting all over him due to airsickness and to teach me how to map the terrain where we lived.

My impromptu flight from Paris has taken three long, soul-shredding days (Paris to New York to Milwaukee to Seattle to Anchorage). As the jet finally gets in range, I look out the window. First comes the cold, gray, chopped expanse of Cook Inlet. Then the pine trees of Fire Island. Then the long, sandy tidal flats, which end at Campbell Lake, our lake, a narrow curved water-runway that feeds into the sea. New arrivals to Alaska often walk out on the tidal flats, not realizing how easy it is to get stuck in the heavy, silt-rich mud, or how fast—and unforgivably—the tide rolls in.

To the west lies the brackish stink-marsh for duck hunting, to the east the downhill slopes of Alyeska. Directly ahead lies Anchorage, the light and glass and haze of the city rising up from a low valley set between five massive snow-slashed mountain ranges. The reflection of these mountains, plus a wisp of cirrus cloud and pink sunset light, races over the windows of the skyscrapers and hotels—gilding the façade of downtown with a frosting of wilderness.

On the family deck, Dad has the barbecue smoking with welcome. Abbie is mixing a bowl of my favorite lemon rice. Jack swoops down for a hug, impossibly tall. I'm a little bewildered. My younger brother is supposed to come up to my waist, just barely, on tiptoe, and pee in any available houseplant if he can't make it to the potty (a trick I taught him). Instead he is talking about SATs and duck hunting and high-school girls and our other brother, Daniel, who is now at UCLA in California.

We sit down at the picnic table. The sky is white. The wind flickers through the aspens. This early in June, the lake is flat and glassy mineral-colored, as if the ice were still there, holding the water in place. A duck bustles by with a line of fresh chicks—a short line. A weasel has set up house by our shed and is eating most of her eggs.

Dad passes the platter and smiles.

Abbie offers me the lemon rice and smiles.

Jack cracks open a Fresca and smiles.

All this beaming, loving attention makes me feel so acutely huge and ugly and failed. Even if my family doesn't know yet that I'm getting divorced, it feels like they do. Why else would I be here? I only come up at Christmas. Maybe they think I'm upset about Nana. Maybe Dad figured everything out at her house, while she was dying. I'm such a jackass. I'm the Great Alaskan Jackass.

"Wow," I say. "I didn't even know you could buy Fresca anymore."

Dad is looking at me—correction, studying me. He's even squinting. "It's a quality soda. For the calories."

Abbie says, "Somebody's watching their weight."

Jack says, "I like root beer. Why can't we buy root beer?"

Do they understand how many times we've had this conversation? Which is actually a conversation about Dad's wacko yet obsessive fear of getting fat. As well as Abbie's rapidly dwindling patience over the last few months as Dad has, no doubt, stomped around, dieting and muttering and accusing people of making intentional crunching noises while eating pretzels just to taunt him. Jack's request for root beer is never going to happen; unlike Daniel and me, he has never committed to truly harassing other people.

In short, nothing has changed since Jack was in diapers and Daniel was in pull-ups and I was in an ambitious yet ill-fitting teenage bikini, spraying them with a hose from the deck. Worse, all of it reminds me of Lawrence and me eating at the hot dog stand in Amherst, able to discuss our dying marriage with words that referred to ketchup and chili toppings.

I've forgotten the under-conversation that goes on during family dinners. All that knowing. All that unverbalized past and understanding. My skin prickles. I cringe in my deck chair, plotting the quickest way out—such as jumping up and saying, *I'm on a story, I have to cover big Anchorage hotels. So I need to go check into one right now!*

Before I can say anything, though, Dad reaches over and slaps my back. "I tell you what, how about you and me go fishing?"

The Naknek is a thirty-five-mile-long river. And yet somehow Dad brings the plane down on the same spot where we went caribou hunting seventeen years ago. Is he thinking of that sad, blood-soaked trip—and my part in it? Thankfully, I don't have time to ask. The sky is murky, the tundra leaden underfoot, the mosquitoes a black rage around the plane. It's been a rainy summer, apparently. We set up our rods and packs, and start moving fast.

We walk the tundra at a solid pace, collapsing every once in a while into sinkholes up to our thighs and crawling back out of the muck. This is not nearly as hard as I remember. We hit a patch of dense, green alders. Dad passes through the branches, holding them for an extra beat to keep them from whipping back into my face. It's a strange thing, being tall in the alders, and being able—so effortlessly—to keep up. Was I too busy daydreaming when I was young? Or was I just too little to keep up the pace?

I remember slowing down a lot to see if Dad noticed that I wasn't right behind him. Then, if he didn't notice, slowing down some more and some more until he was very far ahead, too far ahead, the lure on his rod clinking as it hit the top branches of the bushes. At which point I'd think, furiously, *It'll be his fault if I get eaten by bear. He left me behind.* Which seems a little like a setup, in retrospect.

At the end of the brush, we come out at a shallow wisp of a stream. A fish breaks the surface just as the clouds open up and the world goes dazzled with sunlight. To the east, the mountains slope up, purple with afternoon light, peaked in late snow. To the west, the tundra flushes into the distance, blending into the wide, rolling sky.

I've forgotten how freeing it feels to be surrounded by all this vast, open hugeness. It's a physical sensation, as if there were suddenly extra room in your lungs, a gush of undiscovered oxygen.

We step into the stream and walk up it like a sidewalk, casting to the right and left. A rainbow jumps on my line. Not more than six inches. I release her. Dad catches a Dolly, the same size, and releases her. On we slosh. It's quiet, except for the hiss of line, the riffles of current. I've forgotten how quiet it gets out in the bush. I've forgotten the sharp, cranberry smell of the tundra and the way the water over the rocks looks like what it actually is, liquid ice.

Lawrence so artfully called it gin-and-tonic water when he came up to meet Dad four years ago. I wish he were here now, mentioning casually how many rainbows he's caught, then adding, "Not that it's a contest." Then laughing behind my back as I charge around, double-counting his fish and tallying up our respective totals, "not to be winning the contest we're not having."

But—even if it's a new feeling for me—so what? Missing him is selfish. Look what I've put him through. Look what I'm about to put my dad and Abbie and my brothers through. They love Lawrence. They love him so much that, the first time he visited, they offered him the legs off the barbecued mallard—a succulent morsel that we all usually bicker over, and not in a charming, just-kidding way. How do I tell them that they won't see him again?

Upriver, Dad works his way over some boulders. I catch another rainbow, then a Dolly, and another Dolly. The stream widens into a river. Dad has something on the line ahead. His rod is bent. He fights the fish toward the bank. The river gets a little wider. He keeps fighting, moving not to lose the fish on a boulder. The current starts to pick up, the water to deepen.

Ding goes the little wilderness buzzer in my head. But I slosh on, keeping an eye on Dad and his fish. The riverbed is rocky, not muddy, making it easier to find purchase with the toe of my boot. I feel out each step before taking it, leaning forward against the current—when, just like that, the bottom drops out and the water licks up around my waist, where it turns with such force it's hard to keep upright. I'm a little worried about it snapping my rod tip; water does this, when moving fast enough. I sling the rod over my head and stumble on.

Dad pulls himself up on a tiny island in the middle of the river and lands his rainbow, waving to me. I can't hear him over the roar of water, but I drag myself up onto the island. It's more of a gravel bar, really, with some bushes and dead logs.

Dad tosses the fish back in the river. "Why didn't you move over to the bank?"

"You were waving. I thought you were waving at me to come over."

But he's already pacing. We examine the crossing on the nearest side. The island has forced the water into a narrower channel, creating a deep, raging torrent of current, swollen by rain. We examine the other side. Ditto.

We're stuck. We stand around for a while, discussing what an almost funny situation this is. We can't go back the way we came—we were moving with the current then; now we'd have to move against it. Night is falling. The water is not going to die down in the morning or in a week or in a month. And nobody knows where we are. The only solution is to try leaping over to the bank of the river, somehow, now, before we think too much. Acting in some situations—okay, not in a marriage maybe, but situations involving windchill and shelter and long-term food sources—at least changes the game before the game gets to your head.

About halfway down the island is a fallen birch, drowning in the current. It's a young, slender tree, just barely clinging by its roots to the island, but unattached to the bank. Dad backs up. "Once I'm across, I'll rig up something sturdier," he says. "Just don't do anything dumb."

He takes a running start, jumping off the island, trying to use the birch as a narrow, sinking support that he can very, very quickly hop across. Except that it sinks the minute his foot touches down, and he slides into the water, rolling to the center of the tree, where he's too far for me to reach.

He holds on to the trunk, his body submerged, his head above the surface. The current ravages around his shoulders. His face goes red and set and grim. I stand there, not doing anything dumb. His head slips under, his hands still holding on to the branch. But I stand there, not doing anything dumb. He's flailing underwater, his waders ballooning, pulling him in deeper.

Dad lets one hand go. If he inflates his life jacket, he's going to float up into the branches of the tree and trap himself and drown. And if he doesn't, he'll stay underwater and drown. And if I jump in now and try to save him, we're going to drown together. Which is exactly the dumb thing he ordered me not to do. Which I understood from the minute we spotted the fallen birch and swollen water. Because Dad and me, we've spent a lot of my life not dying together.

"Dad?" I say. He can't hear me. He can't breathe. He's drowning, while I stand there on an island, not doing anything dumb. I rip off my jacket then back up, to get some speed, because speed is what I need to jump and dive and reach Dad without being pulled immediately downstream. And I run—

Just as Dad does the impossible. In one concerted burst of will, he heaves himself down deeper in the current and then back up and over the trunk. After which he jumps, swims, gropes, leaps through the river onto the opposite bank, where he is now lying, puking water out of his nose and mouth. He stays there awhile, panting. I act casual, as if I'd just been lounging around here on this log, the whole time, not directly disobeying his orders. He sits up. "Come on now," he says, and holds out his hand.

I throw my pack over. It lands in the branches of the drowning birch. Dad gets a stick and fishes it out. And then I back up as far as the island will let me and run and dive, hands first, crashing into the river where my father is lying like a piece of human rope, his feet braced between alder roots, ready to catch me by the wrists. He grabs me. He pulls me out. We sit for a minute, exhausted, marinating in the feeling of being safe and alive—if drenched.

Night is falling. The temperature drops. On cue, the first icy splat of rain. We move into the alders out of the wind, where we make a fire. Dad pulls a collapsible camp chair out of his pack.

A collapsible camp chair? It unfolds like an umbrella, into a seat and four legs. It's the kind of thing that old men sit on at college bowl tailgaters or on the sidelines of a lacrosse game, the kind of thing that perhaps you might consider leaving on an island before jumping into a lethal swollen stream. Dad sits down, dripping, leaning his elbows on his knees. Then he gives me an injured look. "My hips hurt, okay?"

I rummage through my gear. I have a tent, bug dope, granola bars, and one package of Mountain House chili mac, dehydrated into a solid foil brick. I pull the rain cover of the tent over my head and start fumbling with poles and pockets, trying to keep the tent dry and off the ground, trying not to think about the sleeping bags that we left in the plane because this was supposed to be a quick day trip. It is terrifically cold. Tonight is going to be like sleeping on winter concrete. Except wetter.

"This is no fun," Dad says, all of a sudden. "This is just surviving."

This time, unfortunately, I have no idea what he's thinking. His is a general statement, maybe, about the rain and cold and almost dying but not actually dying, which as an Alaskan you can't afford to talk about or you'll never go back out in the bush. Or if you do go out, you'll go out weak and the all-knowing mojo of nature will somehow sense it, and you will be picked out by a grizzly or wolverine or snowstorm and never make it back.

But under the rain cover, which stinks of plastic and mildew that dates back to the 1970s, I'm thinking in broad, inappropriately thematic ways. I've been looking for a Chinese fortune cookie. And there it is. What we're doing is just surviving. And Dad and I have been doing it for a very long time. All of a sudden I'm too tired to do it anymore. I want my dad back. I'm not doing so well without him.

"I love you," I say, still under the rain cover.

"I love you, too." Long pause. "Never stopped."

I crinkle around in the rain cover. Then crinkle a little more. Then finally I pull the rain cover off my head. "Are you cold?"

Dad hunkers down in his camp chair. He looks cold. He looks gray. And he even looks a little old, or at least older than I want to acknowledge. "What do you say," he mutters, "if we hike it the hell out of here?"

It's too late to hike, though. We break camp. We load up. And we run the five miles back to the plane, with full packs. The side benefit of running in full-body rubber chest waders being that we are now very, very warm.

It's 2003. Lattes, microbreweries, and a single Banana Republic—though not a Whole Foods or Macy's or H&M—have finally arrived in Anchorage. Even more miraculously, a motel has been built in the bush, or, rather, moved from someplace in the Midwest, floated out in pieces on a barge and reassembled.

From the plane, the motel appears as a long narrow shoe box along the fat, wide Naknek, the gray silted river now thundering down the tundra like some great six-lane interstate. Inside, the rooms are replete with hot water and fragrant, decadent, only mildly used bars of soap. The restaurant has whiskey. And food on plates.

But not too much food.

The waitress thunks down a bread basket. "We're out of salmon."

"In the village of King Salmon?" I say.

"Don't you go New York," says my dad, but only with his eyes.

"No buffalo, either."

"What have you got?" says Dad.

"The T-bone. And the risotto."

"One T-bone, one risotto. And just slosh gin all over the whole dinner. It's been a long day." Our table stands beside a giant picture window, framing the river and the motel dock where our plane is tied down for the night.

"I left Lawrence," I say.

Dad takes a sip of his gin. "Well," he says. He takes another sip of gin. "I'm sorry to hear that. I really am."

"I'm not sure what to do."

"Me neither, Leifer." Enormous sip of gin. Correction: the whole glass in one gulp.

"I think we're getting divorced. I think that's what's happening."

"I'll tell you one thing." He looks at his ice, then at the bread basket. "At least you realized your mistake and got out quick. You know, I just kept hanging on, hoping it would work. For thirteen years."

I look down at my glass, at the snowflakes of light that the decorative cuts along the bottom cast onto the table.

"I never wanted to end up without you."

I really wish he would stop talking. All this talking has been enough. But here it comes—no drumroll, no clearing of the throat, no pounding on the table. He is looking down at his empty drink. "When your mother and I split up, everything got very messy. I didn't tell you what I should have. I didn't know how to tell you."

A little squirrel of panic scurries through me.

"Or how to ask you."

More scurrying. Lots more scurrying.

"Like . . . how things were going with your mother." Dad looks at me, as if I'm supposed to say something. But I'm managing the squirrel. The squirrel is going to go into a small dark cage with a big fat lock on it, because I need to hear what my father is saying next, because what he is saying is "Leifer, your mother and I didn't break up over Abbie. I'm not that kind of guy. Your mother and I—"

"Right," I say, affecting my best completely over it, worldly voice. "You didn't have a good marriage."

"No. Your mom and I had a horrible marriage."

I'm sitting at a table, a table with a tablecloth, for God's sake, which, in the bush, is pretty much a pink polyester miracle. And I'm watching my dad talk. And I'm watching his mouth move, talking about all the times they separated, separations I have no memory of. And I'm also sliding down a wide black hole that tunnels through time and space and memory and leaves me dumped in the living room of our old house.

The Dukes of Hazzard is on TV. I'm in the family room, watching. I'm six years oldish. I'm hungry. I smell french fries. The kitchen is actually part of the family room separated by a high table with stools that Mom calls "the breakfast nook" even though we eat dinner and lunch there, too. In the kitchen, somebody has left a frying pan on the stove. Flames are roaring up from the pan. I run to the living room, but stop just at the edge of the carpet.

Mom is sitting in one of the Queen Anne wing chairs. Dad is in the other. They're drinking martinis in the glasses that always spill. They're talking, their mouths moving quiet and scary and mean. Mom laughs a sneery laugh and grabs the cigar out of Dad's hand and takes a puff.

"Guys," I say. "The kitchen is on fire."

Mom hisses something to Dad; Dad yells something to her. I hear how loud they talk but, for some reason, I can't understand their words.

"Guys?" I say. "The kitchen is on fire?"

Dad yells something to Mom, then Mom to Dad.

I'm so sick of them. They never listen. I stomp back to the family room and sit down in front of the TV. I watch and watch. From the sofa, I can see the breakfast nook and the stove behind it. But I keep my eyes on the TV. It's their fault if the fire just keeps burning.

Then, all of a sudden, Dad is in the kitchen screaming, "Jesus Christ!" Mom runs through the family room. I follow her. Now the whole kitchen is on fire—the ceiling, the walls, the stove, the pan of french fries. Mom tries to throw a pot of water. "No!" says Dad. "Not on grease! Get blankets!"

Mom runs for our coats. Dad runs upstairs. Mom throws on her parka and Dad's parka and my snowsuit with the mittens clipped to the wrists. I stand there, watching, as Mom comes back with her monogrammed hand towels from the downstairs bathroom. She throws those on the fire. But they just catch and get eaten by flames. The fire is moving and huge, a fast and blue wall.

Dad comes tearing in, a mass of blankets in his arms. He doesn't have any off my bed, though. He has the ones off his and Mom's bed—including the new bedspread that Mom calls a duvet. It's a cream-and-blue Colonial print of peacocks and floral vines that she had custom-made in the Lower Forty-Eight. It matches the drapes and pillows and bedroom chairs, all of which came up on the cargo barge just last week.

Dad runs to throw it on the fire, but Mom throws herself in front of him. "Not the duvet! Jim! Please!"

He pushes her out of the way—hard. He starts beating the flames out with the duvet. Almost immediately, it catches on fire. Mom starts sobbing in the corner. Black greasy smoke is curling all over. "Leigh," he says. "Towels!"

I stand there—a big fat jerky smile on my face. I can feel the smile. I know the smile is wrong. But I can't do anything about it. I'm just smiling and smiling. Dad strides over—boom—and slaps me on the face. I reel around. But still, I don't move. He goes on beating the fire and beating the fire. Mom goes on crying. Until the fire is finally out—our winter coats and dish towels and the duvet and the afghan off the sofa and the sleeping bags and other blankets that Dad must have gotten while I did nothing, all of them smoking and gray, heaped all over the kitchen.

An engine wails in the distance. Firemen storm into the room. One of them picks me up. I'm in my nightgown. I have no shoes on. "Don't worry," I say. "My dad put out the fire." I hide my head on his shoulder. I'm smiling still, and I don't want my dad or mom to see it.

There it all is, in that one incident—everything that played out over the next twenty-six years, everything that led up to me and Dad at this table.

Meanwhile, Dad is wrapping up his own story about the past.

"The point was, you looked up at me; you were five or so, my Leifer. And you said, 'Daddy, I don't like separations.' So I moved back in. And it was awful. Your mom and I—"

"It's okay, Dad."

"Let me finish. When you're in a marriage like that, it's not livable. It's not about your can-do or your won't-do. The loneliness gets to be so that . . . well . . . you'll do anything to end that feeling after a while. Even things you're not proud of."

After all these years, this is a feeling I can understand. Not that I can tell him. He is looking at me with such sadness in his eyes, the whole lecture inside his mind marching across his expression like subtitles: what he could have done different, better, kinder, earlier, louder, softer. It's too much to stand. Or maybe it's just that I don't want to stand it anymore, that whole greased trap of what we should have done—not just him, but all of us, me, Mom, him, Abbie— which is a trap not unlike the old bear traps we used to use at the cabin, the ones that snapped shut if you so much as cackled with glee over a winning hand of blackjack.

I'm in my own marital mess. I need help with me. And Lawrence. And me and Lawrence. I need help with: How do you know when it *is* working? How do you know that you're not just pretending to make it work so that you'll be different from your parents?

Lawrence and I fight over how far in advance to leave for the airport (me three hours; him twenty minutes), who is going to walk the dog, who swims faster or dances better or can ride the last, shaky, bucking car of the Cyclone roller coaster the most consecutive times without throwing up. He's so competitive and stubborn and afraid of commitment. Then he jokes drily about it, as if laughing will fix it. Which it doesn't, because even if I'm laughing, I'm also competitive and stubborn and—apparently!—immeasurably more afraid of commitment. I have no idea how we've lasted this long, except that we are so similar. And aren't opposites supposed to be the ones to attract?

Dad makes some kind of bring-food motion at the waitress, and I take a quick breath. "I can't hurt Lawrence anymore, that's for sure."

"In or out, I'm behind you either way. But you need to make up your mind."

"I will. I mean—"

"Worse comes to worst, you can always move back up here. We'll get you a condo. You can have the sofa bed in the upstairs den. We'll move it over with the truck—and so on. We'll figure out the rest."

A slow, warm wave rolls through me. I don't know what the wave is, but the feeling is a little like swimming in a puddle of syrup, the exquisite, not-quite-maple kind that my mother used to heat up in a pot of hot water on her rare Saturdays off work. I want to cry but I'm not that evolved; I can't undo the engrained idea that if I cry I might ruin everything; but I also know that a condo and a sofa bed are the answer I've been looking for. Because this is what it feels like, having somebody say they'll take care of you, having somebody say hey, you don't have to do this all by yourself.

Of course, I just sit there, nothing inside me making it onto my face.

Dad goes on, "You can write stuff about . . . well, about fish and . . . nature, that kind of thing. For the newspaper."

For a few, long, velvety moments, I see myself writing for the *Anchorage Daily News,* getting a Super Cub and living on the lake, down the street from Dad. Then, one day, meeting a bush pilot or an English teacher, and growing old together in my old hometown.

"Or stay in New York," he says. "I know a guy I can fix you up with! I went fishing with him in Wyoming. He loves books. And fancy musicals. And all that stuff. It'll be great!" Then he collapses, all the desperate enthusiasm flattened out of him.

"Thank you," I say, trying to get everything into my voice—all that huge and clumsy gratitude. I want to come back, I've always wanted to come back, it's just that I've gone so far away, I don't know if I can.

Dad studies the salt shaker, then the tablecloth.

I study the tablecloth too. By some unseen hand of God, it has been starched as well as ironed. "I don't want anybody else."

"We're okay," Dad says. "You're okay."

"I'm not sure about that."

"Well. I wasn't going to mention it, but you do have risotto all over your shirt."

I look down. Nothing.

He grabs my nose, pings it with his finger. "I can still get you!" he says, laughing. Because, of course, it's true.

Three months later, Lawrence and I are canoeing uselessly in up-state New York. Except only one of us is canoeing. Long Lake was Lawrence's idea. Long Lake is supposed to be our last trip together. This whole summer, it's been just like the old days of endlessly dating. We've gone boogie boarding, pond swimming, art-gallery-hopping. We've dined in the limited range of restaurants that take dogs and camped in the limited range of creepy so-called wilderness parks that also take dogs. In short, we've kept moving, not really confronting September, when the divorce is supposed to happen.

For other people out there in the world, this might have been more difficult. But the whole experience reminds me of the summer I spent with Dad, smoking salmon jerky, hauling railroad ties, not really registering that our lives together in Alaska were over. But only later—much later—does it remind me of this.

Three days prior to our divorce, I'm more concerned about getting to the food bag with the granola bars. It's ridiculously sunny, the sky a shot of straight watercolor. Leonard stands in the front of our boat, his chest puffed forward like the canine version of the buxom ladies curving up the prows of ships.

Nevertheless, Long Lake is a very long lake, and an astonishingly strong, fair-weather wind is blowing directly in our faces. As we paddle forward, we do not actually move forward more than a few inches. In the bow, Lawrence—perhaps suspicious—suddenly swings around in his seat to check on me. I paddle madly for a few strokes. He turns back to navigate. I drop my paddle. Very quickly, this turns into a game: Him swinging around. Me paddling madly. Him turning back to navigate. Me dropping my paddle.

Worse, having reached the food bag, I'm now eating all the granola bars, one after another. I can't help it. The sun is shining; the birds are chirping; and, for God's sake, should we not make it across Long Lake, we can take emergency shelter at one of the eighty-five cabins on the shoreline, perhaps fitting in a joyride on a stolen cigarette boat.

My wrappers crackle. Leonard bounds back to investigate the possibility of dropped raisins and chocolate chips. Lawrence ignores all this, just as he ignores it when I stop even pretending to paddle and settle for making splashing noises. His back is straight and sure up there in the front seat, the wind ripping through his flannel shirt. "You're not a good paddler," he says. "Why did you not tell me this before we got married?"

"Because I'm not very good at getting married," I say.

"Actually," says Lawrence, in his non-bantering voice, a straightforward and openly hurt voice. "You're awful at it."

Do the birds actually stop chirping? Does everything go huge and looming and still, or does it just feel like it? Luckily, Lawrence is still facing forward, paddling. I'm talking to his back, a back that is lean and muscular, but only by virtue of genetics, not gyms; it's a back that I have held on to each night without getting up to pack a jar of mayo and an extension cord into a bath towel, a back that is turned to me now out of love and consideration, because Lawrence understands what will happen if he swivels around to look me in the eye—the kitchen-on-fire smile, the wild, flailing inability to react the way the rest of the world reacts when it comes to really crucial, vulnerable moments.

Most of my life requires explaining. But only to others. Never to Lawrence. And the same goes for him. I know why he can't buy himself new shoes (fear of being old and poor). I know why he gets teary at highway historical markers (love for Mom). You can't just undo that kind of knowing, even if you try.

We pass a tiny island, clumped with bushes. We pass a catamaran lashed to a dock. The place where I grew up and how I grew up means I'll never be able to get into a boat without evaluating how far I am from shore, not to mention how I'll make it across the lake, should the canoe tip or the paddle break or my partner in front keel over due to a heart attack. It's a gift, this self-reliance. I know I can swim and swim and swim until I get to land. It'll just be miserable and cold and, like the last year of my life, dependent on my will not to go under, not anything else.

Life, however, may just hide in that anything else. Life may be other people, especially the ones who will not give up and go away. I'm pretty sure you can survive without them, but surviving isn't living, and once you've brushed up against the two conditions, you can't pretend it's not a choice either way.

A mosquito buzzes onto Lawrence's shoulder. He slaps it. I brush the granola bits off my lap and say, "Couldn't we just stay married?"

It's a very long lake. It gets even longer while Lawrence thinks about this, saying nothing. Because, of course, this is how life goes; he has no doubt found somebody else, somebody he's got squirreled away in his mind but has decided not to approach until we're finally done, somebody younger and hotter and infinitely more mature who loves over-frosted doughnuts and listening to the Trinidadian cricket scores on the BBC while falling asleep in bed. Which is why it's so crucial that I keep going, say something better, more revealing.

"I know you don't miss me. But I miss you . . . a lot, almost all the time."

We pass islands. We pass trees. We pass little cabins and docks. I pick up my paddle. I start to paddle. I sing the Native song Dad and I used to sing while canoeing; the song does what it's supposed to do—fill up the agonizing silence while Lawrence decides; *dip-dip and swing again, flashing like silver, fast as the wild goose flies, dip-dip and swing.*

"Okay," he says, finally, and turns around. His face is serious. He knows what he's agreeing to—us.

"What took you so long?"

"I was waiting for you to start paddling." Then he smiles.

So two years to the day after our wedding, Lawrence and I decide to give good old-fashioned living-together, staying-together marriage a try. This decision doesn't come after one enlightening canoe ride across a lake. We work at it, visiting each other for weekends, then long weekends. Thanks to *Bride-to-Be,* we even go on an all-expenses-paid, second-honeymoon cruise through Tahiti. It's wonderful. We bike up a volcano and race across peaceful blue lagoons on huge, crass, loud, shamefully exhilarating Jet-Skis.

But New York is not Tahiti. For one thing, we won't be living in a hut on stilts, with a personal valet to deliver fresh papaya with lime in a rowboat each morning. New York is real life: dog hair, freezer defrostings, deadbolts, chain locks, and window locks. When the time comes to move back in, I trudge up the steps with my two trusty duffels and nudge open the door.

My homey apartment looks as if I've never left it. Leonard is farting on the bed pillows. The overhead light sparks when I flip the switch. The same deep bass, bongo-heavy Dominican song is thumping through the floorboards as it has thumped through the floorboards for the past eight years.

"I took the left-side closet," says Lawrence from behind *The New York Times.* "You can take the other."

"Good planning," I say. Do I sound nervous? So what if I'm a little nervous . . . and suspicious. Lawrence was the youngest of three full-time siblings. He can't help but measure our ice creams with his forefinger to see who got the larger scoop. He has, I have no doubt, taken the roomier closet.

I throw open his door. An avalanche of paper—never-read issues of the *Smithsonian* and the *Economic and Social Review: The Obscure Irish Issue,* ripped clippings from *The Observer,* a ten-year-old real-estate newsletter, menus from a closed Mexican takeout, hotel matchbooks, ATM receipts, a hefty stack of light bills, a movie stub for *The Matrix,* coupon circulars, a scrap reading "Remember Wooden Beam!" and more and more and more sluices out all over my feet and the floor. I muscle the whole disaster back in and shut the closet door.

Then open the door and let it all slide back out. This is Lawrence's apartment now, too. A mature, loving, married thought that I handle well, I hope. At least on the outside. "You know what I think?" I say. "We should move."

Lawrence keeps his head in the paper: flip, rustle, rustle.

"I mean, we need more room. We need more space. We need to go someplace—"

Flip, rustle, rustle.

"Like Montreal! We could rent a house. With a garden. I could speak French. You could speak English. We could ski. And eat those fries with cheese curds and gravy. *Poutine.* And—"

Down goes the paper. Lawrence looks me over—his blue eyes moving briskly, scalping me into silence. "I'm a New Yorker, Leigh. I live in New York. I love New York."

I look down at the avalanche, now a drift of ragged paper at my feet. Hither and thither among the yellowing scraps wink other items—each a glittering little ruby of romance past. A seashell from the toxic-smelling beach in Queens behind JFK where Lawrence took me once to swim. A tiny swatch from his tattered, too-small khaki pants that I made him throw away in a Delhi hotel room. A single ski glove, circa 1985, kept with the all-too-understandable hope that one day the match (lost with me on a ski lift in Utah) might resurface. A dirty, gnawed, faded yet perfectly folded AAA map of Buffalo, evidently saved from the childhood Single Mom Mobile. All of which serves as a window into the mind of the beautiful man in the truly hideous golf shirt now lounging with my dog on my bed. "I'm a New Yorker, too," I say.

"No, you're not."

"Yes, I am."

"Name the order of the bridges," he says. "East River, starting with the Queensboro."

"One of them is the Brooklyn Bridge. And the other one is . . . the Verrazano?"

"What's the big street in Brooklyn? With all the Arab grocery stores?"

"I've got this one . . ."

"Atlantic Avenue. You've never even been to Brooklyn, have you? Except that one time I took you, and you ate an entire tub of hummus."

I pause. I have nothing. I growl at him, and Leonard jumps off the bed.

"You're not a New Yorker," trumpets Lawrence. "But—you get to live in New York."

"You mean I get to live with you."

"That is correct."

"Well," I say. "I can live with that. As long as we find a storage facility."

So this is our first legal, signed-on-paper home together, Room 3610 at City Mini Storage. It's a cozy, studio-sized cement room—a place made for people who can't let go of a taxi receipt from 1991 or a camera they found on the sidewalk; people who hang tenaciously on to matchbooks, canceled checks, and—let's not forget—a certain confused, difficult, overly independent, yet completely fearful wife.

Luckily, Room 3610 is also made for people who can easily let go of all these things, who can joyfully shove them all into boxes and shove the boxes inside, fitting them up to the ceiling (as if the cement room were the cramped back of a Cessna 185, where every millimeter of available space must be filled with possible survival gear), then whip that combination lock shut before a certain husband throws his coffee all over the wall, demanding his childhood coin collection back . . . or just his recent clippings (note the plural) regarding Niagara Falls.

The couple who lives in this charming, windowless, heat-free room has a lot of work do. They are not what one might consider emotional connoisseurs. He knows how to give the silent treatment. She knows how to yell. He likes to storm out. So does she. They will bump into each other storming out, then storm back in.

"Can't lives on won't street, Leigh!"

"It all happened so fast? You spent seven hours at the grocery store and came back with Grape-Nuts and a bottle of cumin! What the hell is cumin? I'm *definitely* on won't street! I am on *will not* street! I *will not* go out there and buy us food for the week when it's *your* turn."

Off he goes behind the latest issue of *Charge! The Civil War Newsletter.* Off I go to jump on the bed and annoy him, until he agrees to order Indian takeout for dinner. Because in this little family of two, we don't give up, most especially not on the really dumb issues. We overeat and underlisten. We ignore the obvious and daydream the improbable. We dare and double-dare and solve multiple problems with a stare-down, in which the first to blink has to do the laundry. When in doubt or fear, we repeat the wisdom of our elders: "Point that shotgun at the ground! The other ground, the one with dirt!"

But if you're looking for somebody to tell you that she adores you by dragging you up off the ice after a long, terrifying fall halfway down a slide-for-life couloir in Montana, only to confirm that adoration by ordering you to plant those poles and turn those skis and make it down the mountain, then I'm your woman. If you're looking for somebody to tell you that he adores you by absolutely forbidding you to go to Nairobi while eight months pregnant, then promising that after the baby is born, he will take you and the newborn to see the naïve gorillas of Gabon, all of which is a lie (a total lie!) just to shut you up, then Lawrence is your man.

Because talking is not always what is being said. Sometimes, there's a story underneath the words of husbands and wives—and fathers and mothers and grandmothers and dogs and children—and, in my small, inglorious experience, regardless of how it ends, regardless of every indication that seems so emphatically to contradict it, that story is almost always a love story.

Epilogue

Thirty years ago, I dreamed my mouth and my throat were full of water. It was cold water. It was dark and salty and thick. I opened my eyes, spit, thrashed. Water *was* in my mouth. Water was all around me . . . and around my father, still asleep in the tent beside me. And more water was rushing in, over our clothes and duffel bags.

I screamed.

Dad grabbed for the gun, then dropped it. "We're flooding! Out! Run! Now!"

The Kvichak River, where we were camped was—evidently—so near the ocean it was tidal. The river swept up the beach, carrying off our coffeepot and cooler and most of our tent. We sloshed toward higher ground, shivering in our underwear, just as our plane drifted past us on the river, turning in circles, headed toward the open sea; the force of the tide had pulled the tie-downs off the tree branches.

"Jesus Christ," said Dad running, leaping, diving into the current. He popped up on the surface in a panicked crawl. The plane was drifting fast. Dad swam even faster. He'll catch it, I chanted to myself. He'll catch it. And just then he grabbed the painter and heaved himself onto the float, screaming, "Save the goddamn gear!"

I wanted to see if Dad could get the plane turned around; we had no way home without it, no radio and no food and nobody to know we were out here alone. But . . . the gear. I fished out a sleeping bag, then dragged the heavy sodden mass up to higher ground. Next a tackle box, lures flashing up from the underwater mud and ooze.

Behind me, finally—a chuff of propeller. The engine roared on.

Dad forced the plane upriver, and retied it to a tree this time, a tree deeply rooted into the ground. "Well," he said, trudging up the beach, "I guess we learned something about the reliability of a half hitch." He laughed.

I laughed, too. I was nine. I laughed when Dad laughed. Besides, we were always learning something in the wilderness. Usually it involved being cold and wet.

We laid out what was left of the gear to dry, then cobbled together our rods and started fishing. The sun ricocheted across the river in little crackling bits. The air smelled of salt and ocean and bait. A few seagulls swooped in, cawing frantically overhead.

I cast over to a still patch behind a boulder. "Dad?"

"Yep." His reel clicked and set.

"What do I do if you get sick in the bush, or die or drown?"

"There's an SOS beacon in the back of the plane. You flip it on."

"But what if the plane floats away?"

"You settle in and figure out what to do about food."

"I could fish."

"Yep."

"But what if the rods floated off?"

"You'd make one. Or trap one of these stupid seagulls."

"But what if the seagulls don't come?"

"Well, if there aren't any seagulls and there aren't any fish . . ."

"And there aren't any lemmings or caribou or berries that I know I can eat?"

"Well, then, I guess you'll have to eat me."

"Dad . . ."

"Do you want to live?"

"I'm not going to eat you."

"It's not me. It's protein, plus some fat. You just look at me like a seagull. You make a nice long incision up the back, butcher out the shoulder, then the legs and arms. Avoid the abdomen, though, too many gut issues. Remind me: We really need to show you how to field dress."

"But you're my dad."

"Correct. And your dad would want you to live. And you would want you to live. And sometimes you just have to do things that you don't want to do to live."

"Okay." I looked over my shoulder at the alder bushes, as if someone were hiding there, waiting to watch me feel scared or disgusted. But all I felt was relieved. I had a plan of action now—one that went along with my plan of action for what to do if we crashed into the ocean (leap out of the spiraling, falling plane at fifty feet above the water), or what to do if we got hit by an avalanche (ride out the tidal wave of snow with my ski pole stuck up so that rescuers can spot it later, poking out of a drift). I knew what I needed to know to not be scared; I was safe.

Thirty years later, my plans of action are so different I sometimes wonder who the hell I am. I live in a New York universe full of speeding cabdrivers, terrorist alerts, and—once—a tornado. I have a plan of action against my beautiful but strong-willed eleven-month-old baby slipping in the bathtub and hitting his head on the faucet (a nonskid mat in the shape of a crocodile). I have a plan of action against my three-year-old preschooler choking on a hot dog (cutting the meat lengthwise into tiny pieces). I have a plan against either of them growing up in two distant geographically incompatible homes or even more than one home (a house that we can't afford to leave, a loving, calm husband who has taught me—God help me—how to trust even if, quite honestly, it doesn't seem like a particularly intelligent idea). Considering the dirty-handed, seismic vicissitudes of life, these plans are as unreliable and cockamamie as any other—but still as comforting in the middle of the night.

Day to day, I run after my whole family with toothbrushes and permission slips and nutless cupcakes slathered in a bonanza of sprinkles, all too often mistaking my desire to make their world orderly and stable with my desire for them to not end up alone on

Christmas Eve in Madrid, mugged at knifepoint by a transvestite (long story, another book). I have little to no idea how to teach them what I really want to teach them, which is that though this planet is vast and rambling, though people are flawed and sometimes leave you, the choice is never between two worlds or three worlds or not picking a world and drifting, drifting until you end up on camelback at the border of Libya (long story, another book).

The choice, in fact, is deciding between the world of your making and the ever-distant, ever-glittering, open-all-night never-never land of the supposedly wiser, happier rest of the world.

My mother tried to teach me this. Every morning as she dropped me off at school, she yelled hopefully out the car window, "To thine own self be true!"

I wasn't a good listener, even to the wisdom of Shakespeare. I suspect my boys aren't, either. None of us are. We learn by watching and trying and going splat—most especially, I believe, when the thing we're trying to master is love.

Which is why I find myself one morning at dawn in a bleak gray estuary in Maine. Everything about the last twenty-four hours has gone wrong. It's pouring. It's freezing. The night prior, we forgot to put a pull-up on Henry, our three-year-old son. We were sleeping on an inflatable mattress, which, due to our combined weight, had sunk into a deep trough at the center. At 4 A.M., when Henry released his bladder—with the complete and utter freedom of the dreaming—the trough filled up, and I woke up screaming, "Flood! Everybody out! Run!"

That is, until I realized this time we were drowning in pee.

As we trudge through the black, boot-sucking mud, I picture gold-flecked margaritas, a bungalow on an obscure Caribbean island called St. Way Out of Your Budget. Lawrence slumps under his poncho where the baby, Al (as in: Almanzo, the hardscrabble hero of Laura Ingalls Wilder's *Farmer Boy*), dangles in the organic fabric carrier around his chest, either asleep or silenced due to exhaustion. He was, after all, up all night screaming about the wet cold tent and wet cold sleeping bags and the whole ill-conceived plan that we go on a family camping trip four weeks after his birth.

Meanwhile, Henry continues to weep, as we slog on, hand in hand, looking for the stream that feeds into the swamp we have been circling for forty-five minutes.

"I want to carry Noodle Poop," he says, between wails.

Noodle Poop is Scooby-Doo, whose image is festooned all over the child-friendly fishing rod that Lawrence and I bought him for this camping trip. Like most kids, Henry has his own language: *Juicy* is cozy. *High road* is highway. *Brocamole* is guacamole. I love that language. And yet when I hear myself saying, "You can't carry Noodle Poop, Henry. The tip is too fragile," I have to imagine how the other people at the campground must perceive us, listening from within their dry, warm RVs as we speak like lunatics—or foreigners, conversing in our intimate familial tongue.

Is this what happens after a while—your family becomes not just your world, but your country? If so, I'm okay with that. I may just have been staggering around for most my life, waiting to be the middle-aged mom of two young citizens who like to play "baby cheetahs who lay eggs and live in a house made of couch pillows."

It's only some of the national customs I question—such as this afternoon's "adventure." It's hypothermically cold. I'm leaking breast milk. Lawrence's face is a gray color and the baby might be suffocating under his poncho, not that we would ever know.

And yet, Henry wants to catch a fish. I'm from Alaska—and I'm not going to give up until we have at least some kind of biggish minnow in hand. We're going to find that stream, we're going to fish it, and we're going to have fun—right this second!

On we trudge, slumping through the oozy black mud. "I want to play fishing," Henry says. "You promised."

"You're going to," I say, grimly.

His boot falls off, his sock gets wet, he has to pee, and there's still no sign of the stream.

"I want to play fishing," Henry says.

A gnat buzzes around my face and directly into my eye. I can't help it. I unleash a torrent of curses so visceral that all the chirping seabirds flutter up from the bushes in terror. I'm officially my own Great Alaskan Dad, down to the H. in Jesus H. Christ and my aching desire for a machete with which to chop down all the surrounding saw grass. Henry—clearly of Lawrence's stock—remains disturbingly undisturbed.

"I want to play fishing."

"You want to play fishing?" I say and, ding-dong, suddenly *hear* him. As does Lawrence, who takes Noodle Poop from my hands. Right there, on the semi-dry ground, he casts as far as he can into the bushes for Henry to run, run, run after the mitten we have attached to the line as a lure. And when Henry tugs on the line, notifying his father that he's "caught," the open, golden delight on his face as he gets reeled in—no fears about falling in the river or tripping into the propeller, no anger about facing down the mosquitoes or the cold or the always hovering, undiscussed past—there is so much joy in this.

And there is loss, too, for all of us. Where I grew up, there is no play fishing, and there are no play fish. There are only real fish, the kind that show even a three-year-old boy what it means to fight something alive, to watch it bleed real blood and void real bowels and flip toward the sky. It's as ancient as breathing, the desire to be free. And when you maneuver such a fish away from the rapids and haul it up the beach, only to see it flopping still, fighting still—and realize all of a sudden that you have already killed too many fish today, that you are long past the legal limit, that even if you're eight years old and very bewildered and unable to understand that you're grieving the end of your family by killing everything you can get your hands on, you can also understand that something big and ugly is happening, because of what you are doing.

And that you can stop. You can put the fish back in the water. And when it flops and floats to the surface, even after the hook has been removed and it's free to swim off—convinced, the way humans can also be, that it's dead, that everything is over—then you must do what my dad taught me how to do: Stand that fish upright in the running water and massage it back and forth, back and forth, until its gills take over, until it pauses and shudders and suddenly with a muscular gasp darts off, remembering, all at once, how to live.

Acknowledgments

Thank you to the friends and family who kept me writing over the years, for their kindness, love, and support: Lawrence, Anne, Patrick, Jon, William, Wilder, Sarah, Elisabeth, Anna, and everyone else who urged me after seventeen-plus so-called final drafts.

Thank you to my oldest friends in the wilderness who never let me forget who I am: Lesil and Jason.

Thank you to the generous and talented people who worked with me, listened to me, and always told me the truth: the amazing Jennifer Smith, Hannah Elnan, Karen Fink, Susan Kamil, Richard Pine, Mamie Healey, Lisa Kogan, Emilie Stewart, Fiona Maazel, Elizabeth Koch, Amy Brill, Allison Amend, Lisa Selin Davis, Robb Spillman, Michelle Wildgen, Hannah Tinti, Karen Russell, Danielle Claro, Heather Greer, Maeghan Kearney at the Alaska State Library, and Daniel Jones at The New York Times's "Modern Love" column.

Thank you to the institutions that provided me the holy writer's trinity, a desk, quiet, and time: The Corporation of Yaddo, Plymouth Church of the Pilgrims, and the L. E. Eichorn Foundation for Non-Income-Producing Writers.

About the Author

LEIGH NEWMAN's fiction and essays have appeared in *One Story, Tin House,* and *The New York Times*'s Modern Love and City sections. She is deputy editor and head of books coverage at Oprah.com.

About the Type

This book was set in Sabon, a typeface designed by the well-known German typographer Jan Tschichold (1902–74). Sabon's design is based upon the original letter forms of Claude Garamond and was created specifically to be used for three sources: foundry type for hand composition, Linotype, and Monotype. Tschichold named his typeface for the famous Frankfurt typefounder Jacques Sabon, who died in 1580.